Happy Christmas.
1979.
from Stephen + Rachel

THE WORLD OF RUGBY

THE WORLD OF RUGBY

A history of Rugby Union Football
by John Reason and Carwyn James

British Broadcasting Corporation

This book accompanies the BBC Television series
The World of Rugby, first shown on BBC 1 in February
and March 1979 and to be repeated on BBC 1 on Saturdays,
starting on 13 October 1979

Series produced by Dewi Griffiths

Published to accompany a series of programmes in consultation
with the BBC Continuing Education Advisory Council

This book is set in 11 on 12 point Monophoto Baskerville
Printed in Great Britain by Jolly & Barber Ltd, Rugby, Warwickshire
and bound by MacKay and Co Ltd, Chatham, Kent

Contents

Acknowledgment is due to the following for permission to reproduce illustrations

ASSOCIATED PRESS Peter Jackson, page 132, Chris Laidlaw, page 147; AUCKLAND STAR Johan Claasen in action, page 123; COLORSPORT Ken Catchpole, page 144, Phil Hawthorne, page 145, Sid Going, page 161, Gareth Edwards, pages 166 and 167, Tommy Bedford, page 176, Sioni Mafi, page 178, Mervyn Davies, page 179, Ray McLoughlin, page 186, Gerald Davies, pages 154 and 189, John Dawes and J. P. R. Williams, page 193, Barry John, page 199, Barbarians v New Zealand, pages 202 and 203, David Duckham, page 204, Peter Whiting, page 205, David charges Batty, page 206, Batty attacks David, page 207, Akira Yokoi, page 213, 1974 Lions pack, page 223, Australians pretending to hide ball, page 232, Hugo Porta, page 242, Phil Bennett, page 244; MIKE COX Mike Halliday, page 264; EVENING STAR, DUNEDIN Don Clarke, page 126; PAOLO GIOLO Dirk Naude, page 269; DON NELSON PUBLISHER 1891 international, page 45, Jaapie Krige, page 59, Paul Roos, page 60, first match of 1906 tour, page 60, first match at Swansea 1906, page 61, Springboks v Wales, page 61, Phil Mostert and team, Durban test, page 76, Bennie Osler, page 78, Midland Counties v Springboks, page 80, Danie Craven, page 81, Harry Martin and Aubrey Hodgson (Staar Terug – photo G. Gerber), page 86, big five of Springbok Rugby, page 87, King and Craven leading teams, page 87, Danie Craven dive pass, page 89, Danie Craven, page 90, Okey Geffin, page 103, Hennie Muller, page 111, Jack van der Schuff's dejection, page 116, Salty du Rand gripping Bryn Meredith, page 117, Tom van Vollenhoven scoring, page 119, Jaap Bekker's bruised face (Die Vaderland, Johannesburg), page 124, Frik du Preez, page 143, 'Tiny' Naude, page 151, (from SPRINGBOK SAGA); NEW ZEALAND RUGBY MUSEUM referee sending off player, page 68; RUGBY SCHOOL (photos Geoffrey Creighton Studio) Dr Arnold, page 10, football rules, page 12 and 13, sketches of Rugby activities, pages 15 and 16, start of game, page 19, 1851 game, page 21, Rupert Brooke's cap, page 26; RUGPIX plaque, page 7, Rugby school, page 8, Alan Thomas with ball, page 24, Sandy Thorburn showing cap, page 25, examining cap embroidery, page 26, Norman Mair, page 34, Bill McLaren, page 36, Tony O'Reilly, page 37, Bleddyn Williams, page 106, post sockets at Cardiff Arms Park, page 173, Mike Gibson, page 194, England on Kon-tiki raft, page 215, watching snake charmer, page 216, John Stewart, page 226, Raoul Barriere directing training, page 250, Béziers players, page 252, message on T-shirt, page 254, Ray Williams, page 258, Don Rutherford, page 258, Dickie Jeeps, page 261, Mickey Steele-Bodger, page 272, Wilf Wooller, page 275, Air Vice Marshal 'Larry' Lamb, page 281; SPORT AND GENERAL Peter Robbins, page 52, England v France 1922, page 71, Wakefield, Crawford and Llewellyn, page 74, Wavell Wakefield makes opening, page 75, Carl Aarvold scoring, page 77, Gerry Brand, page 78, Prince Alexander Obolensky, page 84, Wilson Shaw, page 91, 'Tiny' White storming line-out, page 108, Cliff Morgan passes to Ken Jones, page 115, Jeff Butterfield, page 119, Peter Jackson, page 133.

In the beginning, long before 1823...

The story about William Webb Ellis has never sounded very convincing. It is hard to believe that hundreds of boys at Rugby School suddenly cried *Eureka*, and stopped what they had been doing for years, and did something else, simply because one unexceptional and somewhat reluctant young footballer broke the rules of the game as it was played at the school in 1823.

If you believe the story, and accept this version of the manufacture of instant Rugby football, you will believe, without question, the inscription on the stone tablet which is built into the wall between Rugby School and what is still one of its playing fields. The inscription reads:

This stone commemorates the exploit of William Webb Ellis, who with a fine disregard for the rules of football as played in his time, first took the ball in his arms and ran with it, thus originating the distinctive feature of the Rugby Game.

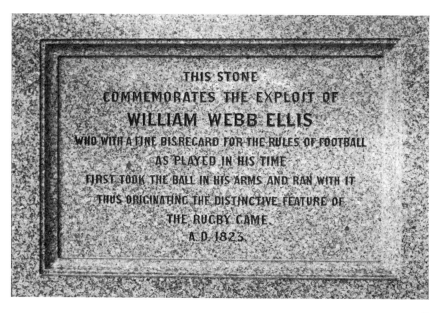

However, at a time when George IV was still early in his reign, and a man could still be hung for sheep-stealing, it is pushing credibility to suggest that any disregard of rules could ever be looked upon as 'fine' by the society of the time. It is also quite untrue to say that picking the ball up and running with it was a 'distinctive feature of the Rugby game', because it had been a feature of football since time immemorial.

Even the suggestion that William Webb Ellis was the first to do it at Rugby School takes some swallowing, because the only historical evidence to support this assertion is contained in a letter written to a magazine more than 50 years after the alleged event, and the letter was no more than hearsay. What is more, it was immediately refuted by a schoolboy contemporary of Ellis, who wrote: 'I remember William Webb Ellis perfectly. He was an admirable cricketer, but was generally regarded as inclined to take unfair advantages at football. I should not quote him in any way as an authority.'

This hardly sounds the stuff of which trail-blazers are made, and although it may be thoroughly disrespectful and even sacrilegious to say so, it is difficult to escape the conclusion that when William Webb Ellis picked up the ball it was already part of the game at the school, because it certainly was not an innovation. It may even be true, as has been suggested, that he was running away from the opposition rather than at them, though we would not go as far as those cheerful disparagers who dismiss young Master Ellis as both a coward and a cheat!

Rugby, the school which gave its name to a game of football. This is the view that boys have had of the school for generations as they have played football on Bigside. The wall in front of the school has a stone tablet let into it on the right, commemorating the exploit of William Webb Ellis.

Whatever the truth of the matter, it is a good story. All legends are, and no doubt it will be faithfully recounted in some suitable pamphlet to be read by endless American tourists when Rugby School takes its place on the summer circuit leading to Stratford-upon-Avon just up the road.

This process is already well under way. So many tourists call at Rugby School that Malcolm Lee, who, in 1978, was the master in charge of Rugby football there, said that some form of formal organisation of the tourism was inevitable in the near future. The school should be on to a good thing, because they can flatter their guests by pointing out that America are the current Olympic champions of Rugby football, having won the title when the sport was last included in the Olympic Games in 1924! The American visitors may also be delighted to learn that on at least two occasions, the International Rugby Football Board has decreed that American football is 'a form of Rugby'. How's that for putting the colonies in their place!

Not that the school is under any illusions about the William Webb Ellis legend. When the filming for *The World of Rugby* television series was taking place, Malcolm Lee acknowledged the doubts of the sceptics.

'There is very little evidence to support the popular belief that William Webb Ellis created a new form of football,' he said. 'The point is that the rules of the game as it was played at the school at that time were made by the boys themselves and those rules were constantly revised. If you look at the notes of the Big Side Levees – notes made by the boys themselves – you will see that the rules were discussed almost every time the boys went out to play and that adjustments were frequently made.'

Perhaps we should point out that despite its overtones of Mississippi *franglais*, a Big Side Levee was not a riverside embankment on the estate of the local Al Capone, but simply a meeting of interested parties on the field at the side of the Big School where most of the teaching was done and where Doctor Arnold and Tom Brown went their various ways.

The notes of these meetings were written by the boys and the books in which they were written were not even seen by the masters until one book had been filled and the next one was in the process of compilation. These books are still preserved at the school, and in the careful handwriting of the students of the time, various delightful playing conditions were recorded. One reads: 'At a Big Side Levee held on Tuesday, September 12, 1848, it was agreed that . . . for this year, the Sixth Match to last for Five Days or for Seven Days if a goal be kicked, instead of Three and Five respectively as heretofore . . .'

This constant revision of the rules was common to most of the public schools at that time. They all played their own forms of football and as often as not it involved most of the boys in the school. Sketches of games played in the early nineteenth century reveal that the two teams were hardly ever equal in number and anything up to a hundred a side. Boys of all ages and consequently vastly different physiques took part, and most

The august figure of Dr Thomas Arnold, the headmaster of Rugby School, watching a game of football on the Close on the occasion of a visit to the School by Queen Adelaide, the Queen Dowager, in 1839. Watching the game with the Queen Dowager and Dr Arnold is his son Matthew, the poet. The drawing is by Dr Arnold's daughter, Jane, a gifted artist with an eye for sartorial detail, but clearly, at that stage, not very good at drawing feet.

of them seemed to have been there just for the age-old pleasure of competing for possession of a ball and achieving a goal, with the added satisfaction of being expressly permitted to kick each other in the process!

Certainly, Rugby football was not evolved in the space of a wet weekend, as the game of lawn tennis was by the celebrated Major Wingfield, or as the game of badminton was by two bored guests at the Duke of Badminton's estate in the West country.

The evolution of the different codes of football was much slower. The people living in Victorian Britain were the most energetic and inventive since the Romans, but football was too deeply rooted in history to be susceptible to the sort of dramatic change suggested by that stone tablet at Rugby School. If you watch children playing a game of their own invention, or adaptation, you will see that it is inconceivable that Rugby football should have been produced like a great blinding light suddenly shining forth. When children play a game, perhaps the most noticeable feature is that they invariably make it up as they go along, partly by experiment, partly by argument and partly by invention. It is a slow process and the essential point about the different games of football played at the public schools at that time was that they all *were* games developed by the boys themselves.

There was nothing new about football, of course. That had been played for at least 2,000 years. There was nothing new about picking up the ball and running with it, either. That had been the essence of the game throughout its history. Indeed, if you study the history of football you will see that the one truly remarkable thing about Rugby football is *not* that it is a new game but that it is precisely the opposite, because it is the football which most closely resembles that played from before the time of the Romans and right through the Middle Ages. The real innovators were those footballers at schools like Eton, who wanted just to kick the ball, rather than pick it up and run with it, because they disapproved of the sweatily violent exercises such as hacking and mauling, though no doubt even they would have shut their eyes in horror if they had seen the lack of physical challenge and hurly burly in the game of Association football as it is played now. The boys at Rugby School simply defended the faith, probably unconsciously, and stuck broadly to the game played by their forefathers.

The similarities between the football played in the British Isles for the last 2,000 years and that played at Rugby School are remarkable. The Romans played *harpastum*, which involved two sides contesting possession of a large ball which had to be thrown into the opposing goal. The game was started by throwing the ball into the air between the two teams, who then tried to carry it forward to lines marked at each end of the field of play. To do this, they had to maul for possession of the ball, they had to support each other to drive it forward, which is the essence of the scrummage, and they had to pass it.

The first set of rules of football drawn up at Rugby School. They read:

At a levee held on August 28th, 1845, it was enacted

That the Puntabouts be six in number.

That the Bath key be confined to the School House, and the three houses which next to the School House have the largest number of Sixth, Twenty and Fifth. The following football rules became the Law of the School by securing the assent of the Sixth.

1 Fair Catch is a catch direct from the foot.

2 Off Side. A player is off his side, if the ball has touched one of his own side behind him, until the other side touch it.

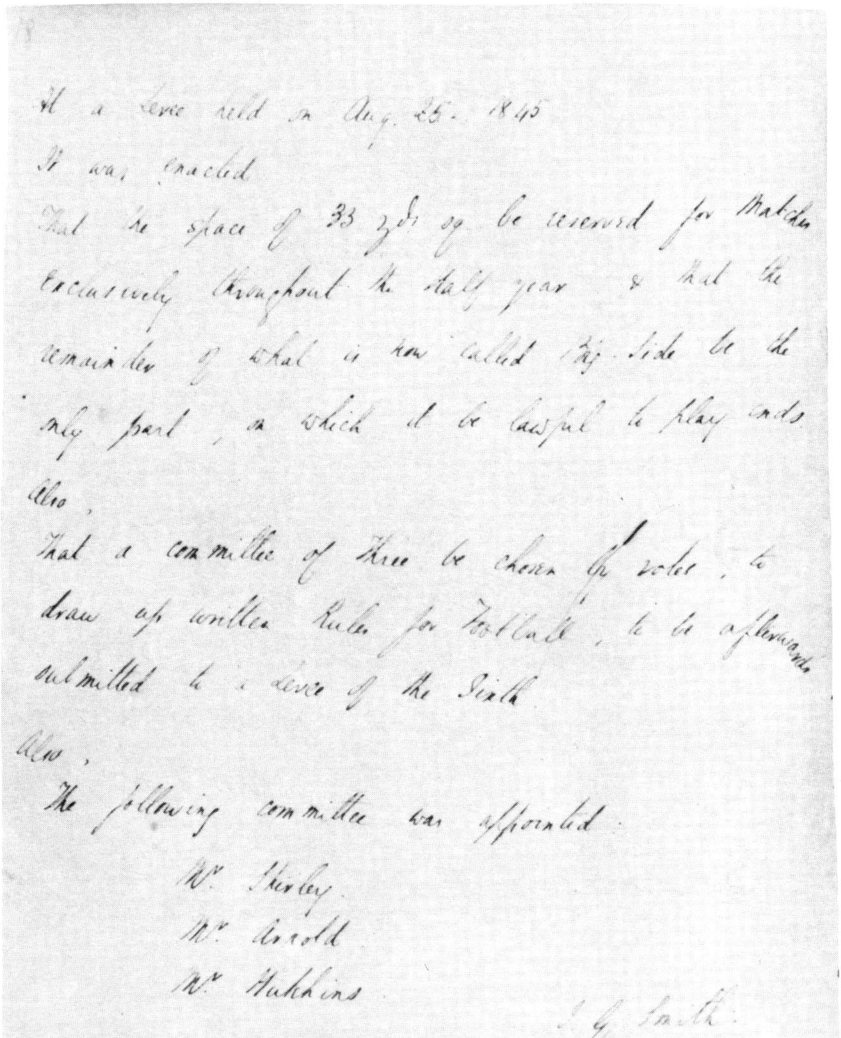
At a Levee held on Aug. 25. 1845
It was enacted
That the space of 33 yds sq. be reserved for Matches
exclusively throughout the half year & that the
remainder of what is now called Big Side be the
only part, in which it be lawful to play ends.
Also,
That a committee of three be chosen by vote, to
draw up written Rules for Football, to be afterwards
submitted to a Levee of the Sixth
Also,
The following committee was appointed:
Mr. Shirley
Mr. Arnold
Mr. Hutchins
J. G. Smith

3 First of his Side is the player nearest the ball on his side.

4 A knock on, as distinguished from a throw on, consists of striking the ball on with the arm or hand.

5 Try at Goal. A ball touched between the Goal Posts may be brought up to either of them, but not between. The ball, when punted, must be within, when caught, without the line of Goal; the ball must be place kicked and not dropped, even when it touch two hands; and it must go over the bar and between the Posts without having touched the dress [?] of any player or the person. No goal may be kicked from Touch.

Whether the game of hurling at goals derived from *harpastum*, or whether it was the other way round, no one can be sure. The games may even have developed independently. At any rate, the similarity between hurling and *harpastum*, and the ancient games of camp-ball and cad, in Ireland, is there for all to see.

Edward II, Edward III, Richard II, Henry VIII and Elizabeth I all took a poor view of football, and either made laws against it, because it deflected too many young men from the more useful sport of archery, or made disapproving noises. In 1531, Sir Thomas Elyot said that football was 'nothing but beastely fury and extreme violence, whereof proceedeth hurte and consequently, rancour and malice do remayne with them that be wounded, wherefore it is to be put in perpetual silence'. James II forbade the heir-apparent to play football, because it was too rough, but the Irish took exactly the opposite view. In 1527 the statutes of Galway forbade every sport except archery and 'the great footballe'. No wonder the traders hurriedly shuttered up their shops to protect them from damage when the apprentices played mob football in the narrow streets of London.

In 1583, Stubbes referred to football as a 'devilish pastime, and hereof groweth envy, rancour and malice, and sometimes brawling, murther' (perhaps he had some Irish relatives), 'homicide and great effusion of blood, as experience daily teacheth'. A Shakespeare character also commented, 'I shall not believe thee dead until I can play football with thy head'.

For some reason, Shrove Tuesday was the day upon which some of the oldest established football matches were played, as often as not between the male inhabitants of entire villages. Two of the oldest of these games were played at Derby and Chester, and another extremely vigorous contest was held annually on the same day at the Cross of Scone in Scotland. The men drew themselves up on opposite sides, a ball was thrown up, and they played from two o'clock until sunset.

Sir Frederick Morton Eden wrote: 'The game was this. He who at any time got the ball in his hands, ran with it till he was overtaken by a player of the opposite party, and then, if he could shake himself loose from those who were holding him, he ran on; if not, he threw the ball from him, unless it was wrested from him by one of the other party, but no person was allowed to kick it. If neither side won, the ball was cut into equal parts at sunset.'

Apart from cutting the ball in two, what is the difference between the broad principles of that game and 'the distinctive feature of the Rugby game'?

Similar games were played at Corfe Castle, at Alnwick Castle, at Bromfield in Cumberland and, of course, in Derbyshire. A history of Derbyshire written in 1829 describes the game which gave rise to the modern expression 'local Derby'.

A series of pen and ink drawings made by C H Chambers, who was a boy at Rugby School at the time the first rules of the game were drawn up. He made these sketches at the time.

The Kick off, with the three trees in the background.

Ball worked out of a scrummage. Only those allowed to 'follow up' and dressed like present day cricketers, are allowed on the field of play. The others are packed behind the posts in goal.

Touched in Goal, and punting out of goal. Only the immediate participants in this part of the play are keyed up for action. Some of the others have a relaxed approach, to say the least! Some of the players are identified in these drawings, and W W S in this sketch, is W W Shirley, a member of the committee of three at the time the first rules of the game were drawn up.

The ball being thrown in from touch. An excellent illustration of the ancestor of the modern lineout, with the opposing sides, Whites and Stripes, lined up against each other.

'The players are young men from 18 to 30 or upwards, married as well as single, and many veterans who retain a relish for the sport are occasionally seen in the very heat of the conflict. About noon, a large ball is tossed up in the midst of them. This is seized upon by some of the strongest and most active men in each party. The rest of the players close in upon them, and a solid mass is formed. It then becomes the object of each party to impel the course of the crowd towards their particular goal. The struggle to obtain the ball, which is carried in the arms of those who have possessed themselves of it, is then violent, and the motion of the human tide heaving to and fro without the least regard to consequences is tremendous.

'Broken shins, broken heads, torn coats and lost hats are among the minor accidents of this fearful contest, and it frequently happens that persons fall, owing to the intensity of the pressure, fainting and bleeding beneath the feet of the surrounding mob. But it would be difficult to give an adequate idea of this ruthless sport. A Frenchman passing through Derby remarked that if Englishmen called this playing, it would be impossible to say what they would call fighting. Still, the crowd is encouraged by respectable persons attached to each party, who take a surprising interest in the day's sport, urging on the players with shouts and even handing oranges and other refreshment to those who are exhausted.'

If that is not a fair account of a match between Gloucester and Pontypool in the last quarter of the twentieth century, we do not know what is! The match starts with a lineout, of which even Ray Prosser would approve because of the opportunities afforded of making one's presence felt; it then turns into a scrum to warm the hearts of Messrs M. A. Burton, R. W. Windsor and G. Price; that scrum breaks up into a maul which Terry Cobner and John Watkins would thoroughly enjoy; and even the best of referees would find himself tested by the vigour of the contest! There is even a reference to 'Charlie' Faulkner at the beginning, speaking so kindly, as it does, of those 'many veterans who retain a relish for the sport', and who 'are occasionally seen in the very heat of the conflict'.

Hurling, camp-ball and cad had similar derivatives, and in the very year when William Webb Ellis was supposed to have originated 'the distinctive feature of the Rugby game', a writer was describing the old game of camp-ball thus:

'Each party has two goals. The parties stand in a line, facing each other, about 10 yards distance, midway between their goals and that of their adversaries. A neutral throws up a ball about the size of a cricket ball between the two parties, and makes his escape. The rush is to catch the falling ball. He who can first catch it or seize it speeds home, making his way through his opponents and aided by his own sidesmen. If caught and held, or rather in danger of being held – for if caught with the ball in his possession he loses a snotch [shades of Michael Bentine] – he throws the ball (he must in no case give it) to some less beleaguered friend more free and more in breath than himself who, if it be not arrested in its course or jostled away by the eager and watchful adversaries, catches it. He in like manner hastens homeward, in like manner pursued, annoyed and aided, and winning the notch or snotch if he contrive to carry or throw it within the goals. When the game is decided by snotches, seven or nine are the game.'

Clearly, camp-ball was as full of 'the distinctive feature of the Rugby game' as hurling or *harpastum* or any of the local forms of football played throughout the Middle Ages. It contained the essence of the lineout, the scrummage, the maul, the tackle and passing. It even contained the essence of offside, because in some of the games it was expressly forbidden 'to deal a fore-balle' or, in other words, to throw a forward pass. In addition, the field was marked out and there were goals at each end. There is no doubt, either, that another of the attractions of this game and the others like it was that these games were so robust and vigorous as to be positively dangerous. Those who played football in the Middle Ages did not expect it to resemble a game of bowls. They expected to kick and be kicked, they expected to get a few elbows in the ear and to give a few punches in the nose, they expected to jostle and heave and wrestle, to tear their clothes and to get both injured and dirty, and they thoroughly relished the prospect. A television camera taking close-ups of a scrimmage playing mob football in the streets in the Middle Ages would no doubt reveal a state of affairs that would appal the viewers. Much heart-searching and wringing of hands is done about violence in Rugby football, but perhaps it is worth remembering that the violence and vigour have always been there, and they have always been one of its attractions. For centuries, of course, it has been a question of what the eye does not see, the heart does not grieve over. Even as late as 1956, when the All Blacks played South Africa in New Zealand, there must have been some truly titanic battles between Kevin Skinner and the Springbok front row, but in those days, as it had always been in the past, only the players really knew what had gone on. There were no television cameras with lenses and operators and directors good enough to reveal their secrets, but those who throw up their hands in horror at what they, in cold blood, see to be brutality in Rugby football today, would do well to remember the game's history, and they would do well to remember that marvellous television shot in the tunnel at Murrayfield after the match between Scotland and France in 1978. Gerard Cholley, the French loose head, and Norman Pender, the Scottish tight head, had clearly been dealing with each other in the most peremptory fashion of which they were capable, and Cholley, remember, was one of the best amateur heavyweights in France. They came face to face in the tunnel. For a moment, there was the wariness in their faces of men who had fought each other hard. Then, as if someone had pressed a button, the wariness dissolved into rueful grins and they clasped hands like gladiators. The grins and the clasp of hands said it all. Cholley and Pender knew. They understood. They bore no malice. Indeed, they had enjoyed themselves, though it was an enjoyment which would be impossible to justify from the comfort of an armchair in front of a television set. And remember the philosophical remark made by Graham Price, the Welsh prop, on his return from the tour of Australia where he had his jaw broken by a punch from Steve Finnane. 'You give a little,' said Price, 'and you take a little'.

Rugby football has always had its critics on the question of violence, even in the middle of the nineteenth century when it was in the process of acquiring a more precisely defined set of rules than it had had for two thousand years. A lively correspondence in the magazine *The Field* in 1863 provoked an energetic defence of the game from J. A. Babington, writing from Oxford University under the pen-name 'Trebla'. He wrote:

'One of your correspondents, a year or two ago, decried Rugby football as "an absurd medley" and confessed that he did not see on what principles it could be defended.

'I wish, sir, I could transport any of your readers who condemn Rugby football to Rugby during the football season. I wish I could let them hear the cheers that peal again and again down our old cloisters when the

A photograph of players about to start a game at Rugby School. The photograph was taken in either 1860 or 1861 and it is the oldest that the School has. Both the numbers of players involved and their dress pay tribute to the accuracy of the sketches made by C H Chambers when he was a boy at the School twenty years earlier.

motion that football do come in is proposed in our Rugby parliament. I wish I could introduce them into my house and let them hear (as I have heard) night after night of nothing but football, football, football, in every study, in every passage, from tea-time at five till bed-time at ten. I wish he could have been in our hall that morning, years ago, when the champion of our house (who had sent his cap to be re-tassled) entered with the trophy in his hand, and shouted out in a stentorian voice, "Three cheers for football!" and the whole house rose as one man to pay their tribute of adoration to our beloved deity. If our game be indeed an absurdity, is it not strange that it should possess for us so inexplicable a fascination? If it be indeed no football, is it not possible that it may justly lay claim to be esteemed as something better still! In the first place, sir, I think our exemption from all numerical rules is a great advantage. All our best matches on Big Side are played regardless of numbers. This enables us to admit any old Rugbeian who chooses to play; it enables us to continue the same matches year after year, without regard to disparity of numbers; it enables us to promote to Big Side at any time any one who is deserving of the honour; it inspires everyone with the feeling that honour is never out of his reach: it acts as a universal stimulant, because no one need ever despair of playing in our best matches from the knowledge that there are a fixed number who play better than himself. As a natural consequent on this, you see in our game what I do not think you see so strikingly anywhere else, the victory of skill over sheer weight and numbers. In our game alone (if I am not mistaken), can you see a side of 15 or 20 beat a side of 50 or 60. In our game alone can you see the remarkable difference which the presence or absence of a single player will make. I remember a match some time ago between the best house in the school and another, in which the match was drawn for the inferior house solely through the play of their captain. He left the school at Michaelmas, and his house sank down to fourth; and this, you must remember, was in a match of 20 a side.

'Again, our game has been abused because it permits running with the ball. In our opinion, it forms one of the most striking as well as one of the most attractive features of our game.

'But our game is barbarous! This is the sweeping charge brought against it even by those who attack it on no other grounds. What then, is this charge worth? We are told, for one thing, that our game is barbarous because it is impossible to exhibit any skill in playing it. I wish gentlemen who decry it on this ground would try to run in at the old Rugbeian. I wish they would try to drop a goal at the sixth match. I wish they could hear some of the discussions that precede an important house match; how two half-backs are to do nothing but look after Jones; how the best back is to mind nobody but that terrible fellow Smith; how Williams is always to tackle the inveterate runner-in, Brown. Why sir, I have known the question whether a distinguished player was to be placed five or fifteen yards behind the scrimmages occupy some of the wisest intellects of Rugby for a whole fortnight. Nay, more I have known a hard-fought match irrecoverably lost by a single mistake.

'It is said our game is barbarous because it permits brute force to form so important an ingredient. Is it not because of brute force that no nation in the world can face us at the bayonet? And does not brute force form a large element of boating? What overpowering reason then is there for excluding it from football? This brings me to the last and most important charge, the charge of hacking, or shinning. Our game is barbarous because it permits hacking! For my own part, sir, this is the point above all others concerning which I am most confident that we are in the right. I do uphold hacking, because it develops that quality of which every Englishman ought to be most proud – his pluck. I know sir, it is objected that he ought to learn pluck by the use of his fists. I admit the correctness of this objection in theory, but I deny its possibility in practice. We are too phlegmatic a nation to use our fists for nothing, to fly into a passion without any cause. This cause is supplied in football. If your readers had seen players appearing on Big Side day after day, either in house matches or in school matches, carrying the ball gallantly through scrimmage after scrimmage, till they could hardly stand, perhaps they would be inclined

A painting of a game being played at Rugby School at about the time of the 1851 Exhibition, though it is clear from Messrs Gilbert's products that the type of ball they were manufacturing at the time was much less rounded than that depicted by the artist.

to admire hacking more than they do at present. In all this, I am not speaking of purely vicious hacking: I am not even speaking of hacking such as our house displayed in a memorable scrimmage some years ago, after we had sustained an unexpected reverse, when, for five minutes, both sides ignored the existence of anything but their own hostility and the two best forwards of our house severally hewed their way four times through the enemy's ranks, kicking (I need hardly add) something else than the ball. Yet even this last-named instance is not wholly indefensible. Surely it is better if one does lose one's temper to show it in this way than to show it in any other, and I will venture to say that we were all the better friends, and fought all the more stoutly together at the Two House match for that very encounter.

'Our game requires much practice thoroughly to know and appreciate it. But I venture to say that those who have learnt to know and to appreciate it will be amply rewarded for having conquered their first repugnance. Let unbelievers inquire of those who ought to be the true judges of this – who have worshipped a tarnished cap, and a bit of ribbon, and a certain stoutly built pair of boots – who have hundreds of times, in exhortation or triumph, rang out the cheery cry of "Follow up Stripes!" "Follow up Whites!" – who have struggled on through a long winter's afternoon till the shades of evening closed around their hard won victory – who have known, in the words of our great poet, "to scorn delights and live laborious days." They, and they only, can tell what Rugby football is, what it has been to them. They better than all others can tell, as far as Rugby is concerned, with what justice our greatest general declared that the field of Waterloo was won on the playgrounds of England.' (New College, December, 1863. Trebla.)

Magazines such as *The Field*, in which protracted correspondence was printed, in microscopic type, are of great value in understanding the issues and the arguments which dominated the evolution of the various codes of football in the nineteenth century. Rugby School has a fine selection of extracts from these magazines in its archives, and the correspondence is interesting as much for the information it gives about the evolution and eventual breakaway of Association football as for the details of the preservation of the more traditional forms of the game.

However, the fact remains that the best description of the football played at Rugby School in the 1830s is that contained in the immortal schoolboy's book, *Tom Brown's Schooldays*. A surprising number of worldly and intelligent men connected with the production of *The World of Rugby* confessed, rather shamefacedly, that until they began work on the programmes, they had never actually read *Tom Brown's Schooldays*, but every single one said how much they had enjoyed the book as soon as it became required reading!

The book, by Thomas Hughes, is an account of his own life at Rugby School in the early 1830s. The solid and worthy Tom Hughes was perhaps not such a good football player as his fictional schoolboy hero, Tom Brown, but the book is obviously based on his own experiences at the school and the experiences of his brother. He describes his introduction to football on his first day at the school. He is befriended by a boy called East (it would be interesting to discover if there was a boy called West at the school at the same time as Hughes), who takes him round the school and shows him the field. 'Tom . . . followed East across the level ground till they came to a sort of gigantic gallows of two poles eighteen feet high, fixed upright in the ground some fourteen feet apart, with a cross bar running from one to the other at the height of ten feet or thereabouts.'

'This is one of the goals,' said East, 'and you see the other, across there, right opposite, under the Doctor's wall. Well, the match is for the best of three goals; whichever side kicks two goals wins; and it won't do, you see, just to kick the ball through these posts, it must go over the cross bar; any height'll do, so long as it's between the posts. You'll have to stay in goal to touch the ball when it rolls behind the posts, because if the other side touch it they have a try at goal. Then we fellows in quarters, we play just about in front of goal here, and have to turn the ball and kick it back, before the big fellows on the other side can follow it up. And in front of us, all the big fellows play, and that is where the scrummages are mostly.'

East then explains the bounds of the field to Tom, and tells him that when the ball goes beyond those bounds, it's in touch, and it has to be knocked back in between two lines of opposing players, with a space between them (*not*, we are happy to say, anything as ridiculous as 500 millimetres). While he is explaining this, some boys bring out some practice balls, called punt-abouts, and they practise kicking. By the time three o'clock arrives, and the match is due to start, one hundred and fifty boys are practising hard.

The boys then split up into their two sides, with fifty or sixty on one side and nearly twice as many on the other. The author writes 'You don't mean to say that those fifty or sixty boys in white trousers, many of them quite small, are going to play that huge mass opposite?' 'Indeed I do, gentlemen; they're going to try, at any rate, and won't make such a bad fight of it either, mark my word: for hasn't old Brooke won the toss, with his lucky halfpenny, and got choice of goals and kick-off?' (Shades of Don White, in his days of captaining Northampton against Coventry!)

Significantly, the book continues, 'The new ball you may see lie there quite by itself, in the middle, pointing towards the school or island goal.'

In other words, the ball is not round, but oval, and noticeably so, otherwise it could not have pointed anywhere. It would be surprising, to say the least, if manufactured leather balls, of the type then in use, had not been a feature of the football at the school for at least fifty years, and probably for very much longer. Indeed, the firm of Gilbert's, who made leather goods for the school, still have the ball they produced for the 1851

London Exhibition, and they have the showcase in which it was displayed. The ball is a thoroughly sophisticated production, differing only in that it is more rounded at the ends than the ball of today.

The ball was made of four pieces of cowhide stitched together, and turned inside out. A pig's bladder was then put inside and blown up by nothing more than lung power. The neck of the bladder was tied to keep in the air and the opening to the ball laced. Manufactured rubber bladders were introduced later in the nineteenth century, and a pump was adapted for use in blowing up balls, but the principles of the manufacture of the ball were exactly the same as those used by Messrs Gilberts (still using the same premises, incidentally) in their shop today.

Balls such as these were used by Tom Hughes (or Tom Brown) in his first match at Rugby School, and had clearly been in use long before William Webb Ellis attended the school. Similarly, the description of the match between the School and School House in *Tom Brown's Schooldays* is so detailed and it so closely resembles the ancient and traditional game of football played in the British Isles and France that it is unthinkable that it could have been changed significantly by one action of one boy only ten years before Thomas Hughes had his first day at the school.

Mr Alan Thomas, a director of Gilbert's, the ball manufacturers, showing the ball that his firm made for the Exhibition in 1851. Behind him is the case in which the ball was displayed at the Exhibition. Gilbert's premises are still just across the street from the school.

Indeed, in the paragraph of *Tom Brown's Schooldays* preceding the description of the goals, Tom asks East if he will be allowed to play in the match, saying, 'I love football so, and I've played all my life'.

East replies that Tom will not be allowed to play, saying, 'Why, you don't know the rules – you'll be a month learning them. And then it's no joke playing up in a match, I can tell you. Quite another thing from your private school games. Why, there's been two collar-bones broken this half, and a dozen fellows lamed. And last year a fellow had his leg broken.'

Even the risks attached to football at Rugby School were the same as those inherent in playing the traditional game. The only question is: Why was the ancient game of football preserved so faithfully at Rugby School, and codified there, rather than anywhere else?

Possibly the shrewdest explanation was advanced by Sir Montague Shearman late in the nineteenth century when he produced various works on the origins of football. His view was that the different types of football played at the different public schools were conditioned simply by the playgrounds available, 'and that as these were infinitely various in character, so were the games'.

Sandy Thorburn, the Scottish Rugby historian, showing one of the caps awarded to Scottish footballers, and one of the small round leather balls, slightly larger than a cricket ball, for which footballers in Scotland contested possession for hundreds of years.

The World of Rugby

Above: The football cap of Rupert Brooke, the poet. Rugby School started the practice of giving a cap for eminence at games, and the players had the insides of the caps embroidered with dates and details of the major matches in which they played. Brooke, who left the School in 1906, was such a good footballer that his number one cap was filled up with embroidery. This is his number two cap. How appropriate that it should have been Brooke who wrote those lovely lines, 'If I should die, think only this of me; that there's some corner of a foreign field that is for ever England'.

Below: Malcolm Lee, master-in-charge of football at Rugby School in 1979, with Jennifer Macrory of the library staff examining the embroidery on the inside of the caps first awarded to footballers at the school more than a hundred years ago.

Shearman wrote that the ancient game of football 'was risky to limb even when played on a grass plot, but when played in a walled-in space such as the cloisters at Charterhouse or on a small and confined playground with a flagged pavement, [it] would probably have been dangerous to life. One school alone seemed to have owned, almost from its foundation, a wide open grass playground of ample proportions, and that school was Rugby; hence it happens, as we should have expected, that at Rugby School alone do we find the original game survived almost in its primitive form. As far as we can discover, no school but Rugby played the old style of game where every player was allowed to pick up the ball and run with it, and every adversary could stop him by collaring, hacking over and charging or any other means he pleased.' In fact, Rugby School only had a field to play on from about 1750, but it was inevitable that the game they played from that date should be the traditional game.

This verdict was not well received by old Rugbeians at the time, who naturally wanted to accord their school some, if not most, of the credit for 'inventing' the game, but a hundred years on, nothing looks less convincing than their rejection of Shearman's eminently sensible explanation. As Shearman concluded, after studying the account of the match between School House and the School in *Tom Brown's Schooldays*, . . . 'somewhere about 1835, the original game of football was having a hearty and healthy existence at Rugby School. At no other public school, however, as far as we are aware, was the running and collaring game kept up.'

The more you study the history of football, the more unlikely becomes the assertion that William Webb Ellis was 'the man who started it all'.

There is no doubt, however, that having preserved, quite unconsciously, the original game of football, Rugby School and its pupils did provide the game with a set of rules and a system of scoring. They also placed the emphasis on kicking goals, and there is not much doubt that they evolved the idea of touching the ball down over the opposing line to give them the 'try at goal' which gave us the try of today. They also started a practice which seems to have been completely original and which has spread to almost every other sport. They gave a cap to those good enough to take part in the play, to distinguish them from those who were only allowed to stand behind the posts in goal. The cap entitled the wearer to follow up after the ball, rather than act as one of a battalion of goalkeepers. The cap was awarded, therefore, to 'follow up' and not to play for Rugby School. It still is.

2 The big bang

As organised leisure activities began to take a much more prominent place in society in the middle of the nineteenth century, there was a games-playing explosion throughout Britain. The football played at Rugby was familiar enough to the entire population and so there was no difficulty in playing it to the rules evolved at the school. The amendments to the old game were readily accepted and they were spread with passionate enthusiasm by the former pupils and even by the masters of the school. Old Rugbeians went up to the universities of Oxford and Cambridge and played the game there; masters who had taught at the school were appointed to other schools and taught Rugby football with an almost missionary fervour; clubs were formed in different parts of the country, often by a nucleus of old Rugbeians; young men with experience of playing the game joined the armed forces and played the game in ports and barracks all over the world; businessmen from England, beavering away in the far-flung outposts of Queen Victoria's magnificent Empire, introduced the game to the natives, and even did it in marginally more civilised places like France. (Remember, Napoleon was still a recent memory, but the wines of Bordeaux did suggest that perhaps it might be better to let bygones be bygones!)

Within the space of 30 years after 1840, many football-playing clubs were formed. There were still wide differences in the way these different clubs played, so there had to be discussions about the rules before almost every match. Strangely, the universities of Oxford and Cambridge did not form clubs until nearly thirty years after the game was first played there. This was odd, considering the influence those universities had on the development and the spread of the game. A club of sorts was formed at Cambridge in 1839 and was probably the first football club in the world, but there were so many arguments about the rules that the Cambridge University Rugby Club was not formed officially until 1872, three years after a club had been formed at Oxford.

Inevitably, bureaucracy began to rear its head in the shape of the formation of governing bodies. The English Union, or the Rugby Football Union, as it called itself, was formed in 1871, a few weeks after the challenge had been issued which was to lead to the first international

Rugby match. The Scottish Football Union was formed in 1873. The Irish Football Union was formed in 1874 and the Irish Rugby Union was formed in 1879. (Ireland celebrated their centenary in 1974, which gave rise to the speculation that they may celebrate it again in 1979!) The Welsh Rugby Union was formed in 1880. In England, there were some distinctly dubious manoeuvres as counties sought to persuade the new Union that they had enough clubs to qualify for representation.

Rugby football had already been played in Australia and South Africa for twenty years, and in New Zealand for ten years. A couple of old Rugbeians even took time to invent the Rules game for Australia, because they thought that the grounds in that country were too hard for Rugby football. The Civil played the Military in the first game of Rugby in South Africa, but for a long time that colony persevered with Gog's football, a version of the Winchester game practised and preached by the celebrated Canon Ogilvie, who was known as Gog. A boy called Monro returned to his home from School in England and started the game at Nelson, at the top of the South Island of New Zealand. It has been frequently suggested that Monro went to school at Sherborne, but no boy of that name was at Sherborne at that time and it is believed he went to Christ's College.

By then, too, Rugby footballers had already encountered a little local difficulty with old Etonians on the subject of hacking, the practice whereby players were allowed to kick each other's legs. The footballers who had learned their own game at Eton thought that hacking was barbarous. They also disapproved of running with the ball, and prolonged scrummaging and mauling. At this distance, it is hard to see how the two groups ever had anything in common, but the fact remains that it took them nearly twenty years to go their separate ways.

As we have already seen from the correspondence in the sporting magazines of the time, the passions that were aroused by hacking were considerable. Old Etonians at Cambridge also howled at Old Rugbeians when they picked up the ball. A meeting at Cambridge produced a set of rules called the Cambridge Rules in 1848 but as these eventually formed the basis of what became the Football Association's rules, there was no possibility that they would satisfy those who wanted to play the more traditional form of football.

The arguments about the rules went on for nearly 20 years. Some clubs were as vehemently in favour of hacking as A. G. Guillemard (who incidentally played for England in the first Rugby international against Scotland in 1871). Others disapproved of it. Still more accepted it conditionally. To add to the confusion, there were disagreements about scrummaging and mauling and picking up the ball. Some clubs agreed that it was permissible to pick up a bouncing ball but that it was illegal to pick up a rolling ball. However, it is clear that all those involved in the argument were concerned only with what football should be. Public schools such as Uppingham, Winchester and Charterhouse naturally went on playing their own forms of football and they all thought that their own way of playing it was the best. None of them had any idea that they were in the process of evolving two entirely different games which would require footballs of a different shape.

It seems probable, too, that the development of the different codes of football was influenced still further by the pressure of the Industrial Revolution. Mob football had always been played on high days and holidays but the various Acts of Parliament, which had the effect of forcing the population away from the country and into the towns and cities, meant that for a period of sixty or seventy years there was little opportunity for ordinary people to play football, and therefore to affect its development. Only the comparatively well-to-do, whose sons went to public schools, were able to indulge in the sport regularly and therefore to influence its evolution.

The clubs met in 1863 to try to agree a set of rules, and the first draft expressly permitted both handling the ball and running with it, and it also permitted charging, tripping and hacking. It was then argued that such a game was all very well for schoolboys, but business men, who had their livings to earn, could not possibly expose themselves to the physical risks of playing it.

The tide began to flow towards a dribbling game. Blackheath's delegate derided this. He said that hacking was a part of the true football game and no one had any right to ban it. Men who wanted to ban it ought to be in their armchairs with their pipes and slippers. If hacking was banned, he declaimed, he would bring over a gaggle of Frenchmen who would beat the lot of them after a week's practice. This was obviously intended as the supreme insult.

Despite Blackheath's oratory, the majority eventually agreed on a set of rules which abolished hacking, handling and running with the ball. The number of players in each team was also reduced to eleven and the clubs agreeing to abide by these rules called themselves the Football Association. Blackheath and the other clubs who supported the handling code withdrew, but even then it did not seem to occur to either side that what they had done was to create two different games of football.

This state of affairs continued for seven years, when it became apparent that there were far more clubs who wanted just to kick the ball than there were clubs who wanted to pick the ball up and run with it. This was the greatest irony of all, far stranger than the preservation of the traditional game of football at Rugby School, because when the long gestation period eventually ended and a choice of games became available, by far the greater popular support was given, not to the traditional workingman's game, but to the breakaway dribbling code of football produced by the elegant and slightly effete old boys of what was then the most exclusive school in the world. Guy de Maupassant would have relished a story which began within the walls of Eton College and led, among other places, to the docks of Millwall and the terraces of the Stretford End of Old Trafford, Manchester. Rugby football became something of a snob game and Association football became the game for the masses. When that happened, the history and the traditions of football were stood on their heads.

Not that Rugby football was short of popular support. It took root firmly in the North of England, and Wales, and it is significant that when it was taken overseas to Britain's colonies it proved far more popular in places like South Africa, New Zealand and Australia than Association football. This lends support to the theory that agricultural communities, with ready access to grassy fields, most enjoyed what Sir Montague Shearman called 'the old style of game where every player was allowed to pick up the ball and run with it, and every adversary could stop him by collaring, hacking over and charging, or any other means he pleased'.

Within the cobbled streets of towns and cities, it simply was not possible to play this game, just as it had been impossible to play it, as Sir Montague suggested, at those schools which only had stone courtyards or quadrangles as playgrounds. For the same reason, therefore – and this situation prevailed until the second world war – it was only practicable for boys to kick a ball in those streets. It followed that the ball they kicked had to be round and the game they had to play was Association football.

The football codified at Rugby School soon produced other ironies. The practice of hacking opponent's shins, which had done so much to precipitate the evolution and breakaway of Association football, and which had been defended so vehemently as the reason why no nation could face the British at the bayonet, was abandoned by some of the clubs who had fought so hard to retain it. It was even abolished at Rugby School. The headmaster who abolished hacking at the school was Frederick Temple. He eventually became Archbishop of Canterbury, but even as a headmaster, he retained sufficient of the boyish imp of mischief to slip out under cover of darkness for the pleasure of climbing trees!

While all this was happening, it still did not seem to occur to Britain's footballers that what had happened in 1863 was a fundamental parting of the ways. This was made clear in 1870, when the Football Association arranged a match on the Surrey cricket ground at Kennington Oval which they advertised as being between England and Scotland.

The qualifications of some of the Scottish players were open to doubt. One was known to have crossed the Border to shoot grouse. Another confessed to a liking for Scotch whisky, which was all rather reminiscent of a forward who played Rugby for Scotland ninety years later and opined, rather vaguely, that he thought that one of his grandparents may have visited Scotland once. The game caused such interest that another match was arranged for the autumn of the same year, again at Kennington Oval. On that occasion, efforts were made to gather a more representative Scottish team, but England still won by a goal to nil.

It was suggested that a third match should take place the following February in Scotland, but the Scots pointed out the weaknesses of the previous selections and said that they thought that there were not enough good Association footballers in Scotland to give England a game. Still, the Scots were urged to take up the challenge by, it is thought, H. H. Almond, who became headmaster of Loretto. He said 'no one need be under any misapprehension of their [the Scots] ability to play under the Association rules. These are only a modification of the great parent code, with the more violent features expunged and there is probably no better training for them than Rugby play.'

Within a matter of weeks, this challenge and counter-challenge led to the arrangement of a match played in Edinburgh between Scotland and England under the rules of 'the great parent code'. That became the first Rugby international played between two countries anywhere in the world, but it is apparent that to many of the Scots, at any rate, they were just playing football, and they were quite prepared to regard that third match between England and Scotland as part of a sequence.

It was the result of a challenge, published in *The Scotsman* and in *Bell's Life* on December 8, 1870. The challenge read:

Sir, There is a pretty general feeling among Scotch football players that the football power of the old country was not properly represented in the late so-called International Football Match. Not that we think that the play of the gentlemen who represented Scotland otherwise than very good – for that it was so is amply proved by the stout resistance they offered to their opponents and by the fact that they were beaten by only one goal – but that we consider the Association rules in accordance with which the late game was played, not such as to bring together the best team that Scotland could turn out. Almost all the leading clubs play the Rugby code, and have no opportunity of practising the Association game even if willing to do so. We therefore feel that a match played in accordance with any rules other than those in general use in Scotland, as was the case in the last match, is not one that would meet with support generally from her players. For our satisfaction, therefore, and with a view of really testing what Scotland could do against an English team we, as representing the football interests of Scotland, hereby challenge any team selected from the whole of England, to play us a match, twenty-a-side – Rugby rules, either in Edinburgh or Glasgow on any day during the present season that might be found suitable to the English players. Let this count as the return to the match played in London on the 19th November, or, if preferred, let it be a separate match. If it be entered into, we can promise England a hearty welcome and a first-rate match. Any communications addressed to any one of us will be attended to.

We are, etc.,
A. H. Robertson	West of Scotland F.C.
F. Moncreiff	Edinburgh Academicals F.C.
B. Hall Blyth	Merchistonian F.C.
J. W. Arthur	Glasgow Academical F.C.
J. H. Oatts	St Salvator F.C., St Andrews

Apart from the challenge itself, perhaps the most interesting point was the assertion that the rules of Association football were not such as to bring together the best team that Scotland could turn out. The history of football in Scotland went back almost as far as it did in England and the game they played was almost identical. Apart from the town and village games, Scottish schools were playing each other at football in the early nineteenth century. None of them had even heard of William Webb Ellis, but the game they played came to be known as Rugby football.

'Sandy' Thorburn, who has done a great deal of research into the history of Scottish Rugby, shares Sir Montague Shearman's view of the development of the game. 'What Rugby School did was produce the first set of printed rules,' says Mr Thorburn, 'and they must be given credit for that. But the game that they played had been part of the fabric of the British Isles and Western Europe for centuries. It certainly was not invented at Rugby School by William Webb Ellis or by anybody else.'

The Scottish footballers who made their challenge to England, therefore, represented a country which had centuries of experience of playing the game. The game they had played, of course, was not Association football, or anything like it, and so the challenge that was issued was not taken up by C. W. Alcock, who had helped to organise the first two games. The suggested rules were unacceptable to him, and so was the number of players. He had already made it clear that 'more than eleven we do not care to play as with greater numbers it is in our opinion that the game becomes less scientific and more a trial of charging and brute force.'

However, the Rugby playing clubs in the London area accepted the challenge. They had little time to form a representative team, and some of their best players were not available, but they agreed to play the match in Edinburgh on Monday, March 27, 1871, and asked the Edinburgh Academical Cricket Club if they could play the match on their ground at Raeburn Place. Apparently, not all the members of the cricket club were in favour of this, because a vote had to be taken to establish that the majority were prepared to allow the ground to be used for the match.

The Scots held two trials before the game and were urged by their supporters to keep the game among the forwards. The English, when they arrived after a tiring journey overnight, thought that there would be no choice in the matter, because the pitch was only 55 yards wide and that did not suit them at all. They had hoped for a wider pitch to use their backs. A strong body of opinion in Scotland still held that passing the ball out from the forwards was akin to cowardice.

The game was played for 50 minutes each way, with two umpires, and Scotland won by a goal and a try to a try. The try from which Scotland scored their winning goal was hotly disputed by the England players and 20 years later the Scottish umpire admitted that he was probably wrong to give it. Mr Almond wrote: 'Here let me make a personal confession. I was umpire and I do not know to this day whether the decision which gave Scotland the try from which the winning goal was kicked was correct in fact. . . . I must say, however, that when an umpire is in doubt, I think he is justified in deciding against the side which makes most noise. They are probably in the wrong.'

Scotland relied on eleven of the same players for the return match at the Oval the following year, but England were able to choose a much more representative team and won by two goals and two tries to a goal. The field was 15 yards wider than the one at Raeburn Place.

Even then, it would have been apparent to those sufficiently far-sighted that senior Scottish Rugby was much too closely tied to its schools for its own ultimate good. Norman Mair who hooked for Scotland and whose delightful Rugby writing in *The Scotsman* blessedly keeps alive the classic tradition of the essayist, says, 'The first ten times Scotland played Wales, Scotland won eight and drew one. The first 15 times Scotland played Ireland, Scotland won 14, but the legacy of those great years has been eroded. France achieved parity in results against Scotland in 1978 for the first time since the countries started playing each other, and Scotland are behind both England and Wales. We are still ahead of Ireland, but when we played Wales in those early years, nobody said that Welshmen were born intrinsically better Rugby players than we were. We had this tremendous start, and since then it has gone.

'Now why has it gone? Well, I think that the big difference was the way the game developed in the respective countries. In Scotland, it evolved round the school system mainly, except in the Borders, where they had

Norman Mair

the Border League, and that's why I think the Borders have always punched their weight as far as Scottish Rugby is concerned. They have made a tremendous contribution.

'The school system around which the rest of Scottish Rugby evolved was good in many ways, and provided a lot of fun, but it did mean that we had no chance of producing great town and city sides like Cardiff and Newport. If Scottish Rugby had evolved round two city sides like Edinburgh and Glasgow, it would have been a tremendous advantage.

'A large proportion of the players in the first teams to represent Scotland were from the public schools, by which I mean the great boarding schools. As I say, the evolution of the game can be traced from these schools. My old school was Merchiston, for example, and you can read some very interesting things in the register.

'On one occasion, we played Fettes under protest because they were heeling the ball out of the scrum deliberately, instead of letting it come out by accident! They were deliberately heeling it back! We thought that was frightfully bad form, and indeed played the match under protest (I'm happy to say we won it comfortably).

'Then we played Loretto in another match where there was a certain amount of ill feeling. They'd started passing the ball out before they were held, and there was a very scornful reference in the register to the fact that this was no longer football, this was handball. But there is no doubt that this was where our game evolved. There is an account of a Merchiston match against the Edinburgh Garrison. The formation of the teams consisted of goalkeepers, half-backs, quarter-backs and what they called bull-dogs. These obviously became the forwards, but then they were called bull-dogs. Merchiston also had a pair of quarter-backs called Fasson and Neilson who divided their duties so that one was obviously working the scrum and the other was feeding the ball to the half-backs. So there you see the first sign of a scrum-half and a stand-off.

'But of course, the clubs formed by the former pupils of these great school sides were closed clubs and therefore there was a limit as to how good they could get because they were dependent for their recruitment of new players entirely on one school. If you had taken Barry John and Gareth Edwards and told them that they had to stay with their old boys' sides, their development would have been inhibited because great players learn from each other. Also, the talent available is diluted by that process. That is what happened to Scottish Rugby.'

This limiting factor in Scottish Rugby did not really become apparent until after the second world war, when the home countries first began to make a serious effort to match the skills, techniques, team organisation and physical presence of teams from South Africa and New Zealand. As soon as that happened, Scotland's lack of depth at club level sent them sliding down the tables of international success when measured against the other countries.

This process might have happened much earlier but for the breakaway of the clubs in the North of England to form the Rugby League. At that point, in 1892, England were already four ahead in the international series against Scotland, and were climbing steadily away, but when they lost their Northern clubs, they lost the next four matches against Scotland in succession, and by 1910, Scotland were five matches ahead in the series for the first and only time in their history.

By then, England and Scotland had already been playing each other for the Calcutta Cup for 31 years. This trophy was presented by the Calcutta Football Club in 1878 and it was made by Indian workmen from silver rupees melted down when the club closed its account at the bank. The club had lasted only six years, and had been hard hit by the rapid spread of the popularity of polo, which was rightly considered a far more suitable sport for the climate of India than Rugby football. However, the Calcutta Football Club had £60 in the bank, which was a lot of money in those days, and they decided to offer the new Rugby Football Union a trophy rather than spend the money on a drinking spree. The Rugby Union accepted the offer with a grace and a readiness which they might have found difficult sixty years later when competitions of any sort were frowned upon. A. G. Guillemard, then President of the Rugby Union, said that the trophy would be used as 'an international challenge

Bill McLaren

cup to be played for annually by England and Scotland – the cup remaining the property of the Rugby Football Union'.

The cup is a beautiful piece of Indian workmanship, with three snake handles, and an elephant on the lid, and unlike the exquisite antique clock given to the International Rugby Football Board by the Irish Rugby Union, no one has stolen it yet.

Five years after the Calcutta Cup was presented to the Rugby Football Union, a different sort of competition was started in the Scottish Border country. This competition had far more mundane origins than the Orient but it quickly became woven into the fabric of the game. This was seven-a-side Rugby.

Bill McLaren, the BBC television Rugby commentator, is a Border man himself, and he says, 'In 1883, the Melrose club had fallen on hard times financially and a local butcher called Ned Haigh had the idea of organising a seven-a-side competition to raise money. The rules were very much the same as for the fifteen man game, except that the teams had three forwards instead of eight or nine or even ten. The great beauty of the game was that the ball moved around. That was why the game caught on so spectacularly. In those days, much of the play in the fifteen-a-side game was confined to the forwards, and it must have been pretty dull by today's standards, but the seven-a-side game suddenly produced fluent,

Tony O'Reilly

exciting handling, and in a sense, required different skills, because the forwards had to run and handle and pass just like the backs. But probably the most important thing for the Scottish Border clubs was that it was a success financially, and even today, they would find it hard to keep their heads above water if it was not for their sevens tournaments.'

Tony O'Reilly, one of Ireland's most colourful Rugby sons, insists that Irish Rugby began in a pub and that William Webb Ellis was an Irishman anyway.

'Contrary to British propaganda, [says O'Reilly] Rugby football was started by an Irishman, William Webb Ellis. All these good things are stolen from us. First our country, and then the fact that we started the game. William Webb Ellis was the man who first picked up a ball and ran with it, thereby originating the distinctive feature of the Rugby game, and he came from Tipperary. I am a bit bothered by the fact that he became a man of the church, because when I am asked where Rugby football fits into Irish society, I have to admit that it is mainly in the pub. Mind you, the pub is the hub of pretty nearly every activity in Ireland, and Rugby football is no exception. Other countries see the playing field as the focal point of their Rugby activities and why not? They can do it their way. We'll do it ours – like the seasoned campaigner who was sitting in the corner of the dressing room having a quiet smoke before the match. In the middle of the dressing room, a young fellow was touching his toes and swinging his arms about and counting up to ten in a loud voice, and this young fellow suggested that it might be a good idea if the veteran did the same thing. "Listen, son," he said, "you warm up your way, I'll warm up mine".'

O'Reilly treats with a proper disdain the facts that although William Webb Ellis may have been conceived in Ireland, he was born in England, and that he did not invent the game anyway.

'The remarkable thing about Irish Rugby is that it developed as it did considering the rather narrow social strata that play the game in Ireland. It was never really a working class game here, as it was in all the other countries. It was played in the public schools and the universities, and it was played mostly by men who had attended those institutions. The schism in Irish life, particularly of Irish nationalism, was reflected in the early development of the game. Schools that had a national character, a Gaelic character, were precluded from playing Rugby football by what was known as the foreign games ban. Even in my youth, you could not play both Rugby football and Gaelic football. This cut Irish Rugby off from an enormous source of possible playing talent.'

This explains why Ireland has always found success so difficult to achieve in international Rugby. England played their first match against Ireland at Kennington Oval in 1875, and won ten and drew one of their first 11 games. This gave England a lead in the series which they have never lost.

The same is not true of England's matches against Wales. The first match, at Blackheath in 1881, was won by England by such a huge margin that the fixture was not played in 1882. England won the first five games played, but after the Northern clubs had broken away to form the Rugby League, England suffered a succession of defeats which was not broken until the Rugby Union built and opened its new ground at Twickenham in 1910.

Interestingly enough, the BBC have a recording of an interview with R. H. B. Summers, who played threequarter for Wales against England in the first Rugby international played between the two countries.

He was asked if the game was very different in mid-Victorian days. His reply was, 'In essentials, it was the same, but the disposition of forces was different. At Cheltenham College, where I learned the game, we made up our fifteen with nine forwards, two half-backs, two threequarters and two full-backs. I believe this formation was almost universal, and was the one used by Wales in the first match against England. Generally speaking, the forwards scrummaged and dribbled, and the two threequarters were expected to do most of the scoring, usually from a scrum, or squash, as we called it. The halves stood near the squash, one on either side, each supported by one of the two threequarters. The half-back nearest the ball as it came out would throw out a pass to his supporting threequarter, who ran for the line, trying to evade his opposite number and the two full-backs who converged upon him from either side of the field. There was less passing than today, but in my opinion, the game was more spectacular, and gave more scope for individual brilliance by the threequarters.

'We played in ordinary light walking boots, with a bar of leather nailed obliquely across the sole to help us in swerving; jerseys which fitted closely high up round the neck, so that no fellow could get his fingers in, and dark blue serge knickerbockers fastened below the knee with four or five buttons.

'There were no wing-forwards as such in those days, but there were work-shy forwards, and we called them skirmishers. Scotland claim the honour of having first introduced a third threequarter, against Ireland in 1881, but I remember at Cheltenham several years earlier, we had a forward who was something of a skirmisher, but able to handle the ball well.

'Occasionally, at a signal from the captain, he would leave the scrum, take a pass from the half-back and throw out a long pass to one of the threequarters, who meantime had moved out towards the touchline, and so was able to run round the threequarter who opposed him. There, surely, was the genesis of the idea of the third threequarter. I did not see the introduction of the fourth threequarter, because I left for India soon after the international match in 1880, and did not return until 1893, when I first saw the formation used by Wales against Ireland at Llanelly, but I understand that it was first introduced by Cardiff, under the captaincy of F. E. Hancock, in 1885.'

According to Summers, it was hardly surprising that Wales were beaten as badly as they were in their first game against England. 'I had just left Cheltenham when I received my invitation to play for Wales. The game was played at the Rectory Field, Blackheath, and we changed at a small, old-fashioned inn nearby. When we got to our changing room, we discovered that we were two men short, their invitations apparently having gone astray. However, we picked up two 'Varsity men with Welsh qualifications, and they agreed to fill the vacancies on condition that they were allowed to play threequarter!

'The game was played before a small crowd of Rugby enthusiasts, ranged perhaps three deep round the ground. There were no huge stands or terraced banks in those days. I am not sure that the playing pitch was even roped off. The match was a runaway victory for England by eight goals and six tries to nil, and Lennie Stokes, the England captain, had most to do with our downfall. He had a most baffling, swerving run, and his left-footed kicking, which broke our forwards' hearts, astounded us all, for we had never seen a player who was able to kick with his left foot before. The Blackheath crowd called Stokes the "something" snipe. The adjective was spelt with a *b*, but was not quite BBC. In spite of the odds, we never gave up trying and at the dinner that night we were much encouraged when Stokes said, "I have seen enough to know that you Welshmen will be hard to beat in a few years' time, when you get together".'

Prophetic words.

3 The International Board, the breakaway of the northern clubs and the 1905 All Blacks

Three years after the first match between England and Wales, another playing dispute between England and Scotland led to a temporary suspension of matches between the two countries and, eventually, to the formation of the International Rugby Football Board. The argument arose over the goal which England scored to win the match. The ball was knocked back by one of the Scottish players and an Englishman followed up to score a try. The Scots said that knocking back was illegal. England did not agree and said that in any case, a team should not be allowed to benefit from its own offence. England added that the Irish referee, a player himself, had allowed the score and that he was the sole judge of fact. Scotland wanted to put the matter to arbitration but England would have none of it.

Two years later, at a meeting in Dublin, Scotland agreed to concede the match if England would join an International Rugby Football Board on equal terms with the other unions but, as much the biggest union, England would have none of that, either. Eventually, England offered to put the matter to arbitration, and to accept the findings of the arbitrators. The other unions agreed.

The arbitrators were Lord Kingsburgh, the Lord Justice Clerk, and Major F. A. Marindin, the president of the Football Association, and their award was so crushingly in favour of England that it established the climate and the conditions by which England were able to dominate the world of Rugby until after the second world war. Because of the vast number of clubs within their union, England were given six seats on the new International Board, as opposed to two each for Scotland, Ireland and Wales, so England could never be outvoted. For more than 50 years, New Zealand, Australia and South Africa had direct representation on the Rugby Union as such, and were not represented on the International Board. England gave up two of its six seats in 1911, but the overseas unions did not become members of the International Board until 1948, when England gave up two more seats. Even then, Australia, New Zealand and South Africa had only one seat each. This number was increased to two each in 1958, and then, in 1978, France was admitted as the eighth member of the International Board.

For many years, the advancement of the game was hindered by the bye-law of the Board which requires a threequarter majority for any changes in the laws. In the first place, when there were only four member countries and England had half the votes, the system was less obstructive than it became when England conceded first two and then four of their six votes. The admission of France in 1978 brought about a highly significant change in the voting, because now three countries have to vote against a motion to defeat it.

Ironically, while England were establishing their domination of the International Board, their domestic Rugby was undergoing such a profound upheaval over the question of broken time payments and professionalism that they were never able to achieve the position of unchallenged world-wide playing dominance that ought to have followed inevitably from their overwhelming advantages of playing resources. Just as the early arguments about the rules led to the formation of the Football Association and the creation of a new game, so the arguments about professionalism in the last decade of the nineteenth century led to a massive breakaway by the powerful Northern clubs and the formation of the professional Rugby League. In 1893, before the breakaway occurred the Rugby Union had 481 clubs as members. Overnight, they lost 22 of the most powerful clubs in the country, in three years they lost nearly 100, and seven years after that, there were only 244. The effect on England's international Rugby was catastrophic, and it is fair to say that, for all their successes since, England have never realised the potential that was theirs when the International Board was established in 1890 and the game was ready to stride into the future.

Among the clubs to secede were Batley, Bradford, Halifax, Hunslet, Hull, Huddersfield, Leeds, Leigh, Oldham, Rochdale Hornets, St Helens, Wakefield Trinity, Warrington, Wigan and Widnes. By themselves, they would still be enough to fuel successful international teams for almost any of the countries in membership of the International Board.

The popularity of Rugby football in Lancashire and Yorkshire was the cause of the split. Clubs began to take a lot of gate money, as they always have in Wales, and they sought to strengthen their teams by offering financial inducements to good players from other clubs. English, Scottish and Irish players have always believed that this has always happened in Wales, and that it still does, and they are now equally certain that it happens in France. However, believing is one thing; proving is something else. The difference in England at the end of the nineteenth century was that the Northern clubs did not deny that they were paying players for time lost at work and, of course, the rules of the game had not been framed with the idea of making amateurism an issue.

The idea of paying star Welsh half-backs to play for Northern clubs had already been established, and Broughton Rangers had recruited the Welsh international half-backs from Swansea, David and Evan James.

(Incidentally, the facial resemblance between Evan James and David Watkins, the Welsh international and British Lions fly-half who left Newport in the late 1960s to pursue a most successful career in the Rugby League, is absolutely uncanny.)

The path first trodden by the James brothers has since become something of a motorway, but it is interesting to note that although, in 1893, the Rugby Union professionalised Evan and David James, they took no action against their club, Broughton Rangers.

Within six months of that decision, though, a general meeting of the Rugby Union was held in London to vote on the question of broken time payments. A member of the Rugby Union establishment, as they have done so often since, scurried around collecting 120 proxy votes before the meeting and these proved decisive, especially as the Northern clubs alleged that all the individual colleges at Oxford and Cambridge voted, instead of the Universities having one vote each, as they should have done. The meeting defeated the proposition to allow broken time payments by 282 votes to 136. Considering that there were only 480 clubs then in membership of the Rugby Union all over the world, and taking into account the enormous difficulties of travel, the vote was rather reminiscent of the returns in present-day political elections in the Soviet Union.

The cost of the victory, if victory it was, was the virtual destruction of Rugby Union football in Yorkshire, the most powerful county in England, and its enfeeblement in Lancashire, the second most powerful county. That in turn led to a period of twenty years when, internationally, England could do little more than lick her wounds.

Wales took this opportunity to establish a real international presence for the first time. Graduates coming down from the Universities of Oxford and Cambridge had taken the game of Rugby football to Lampeter College, Llandovery and Christ's College, Brecon, three of the great centres of Welsh education, and the game quickly spread to other schools. The boys leaving these schools first formed old boys' clubs and then established the powerful clubs of the towns and cities like Cardiff, Newport, Swansea, Neath and Llanelli. The rapidly developing industries in South Wales also brought about a huge increase in population. In the last twenty years of the nineteenth century, 200,000 people moved into Glamorgan alone. As the coal-mining towns flourished, so did Rugby football, because it enabled neighbouring communities to preserve the rivalries established in the age-old game of *knappan*, another derivative of the basic football game. This rivalry was given immediate expression by the organisation of the South Wales Challenge Cup in 1887.

The poetry and the grace of the physical movements in feinting and swerving and dodging touched some primeval artistic chord in the Welsh. Not that half-back and threequarter play as we know it today existed then, but the Cardiff club developed the modern concept of using four

43

threequarters and the whole of South Wales found a relief from the grim working-class life style of the Industrial Revolution by developing and cherishing its footballing heroes. The day of the darting little man with magic in his hands and hips and feet had arrived. This elusiveness is so beautifully expressed in Welsh that even the English can understand it. *Dig-dag-doe*. The changes of direction, the unexpectedness, the *insouciance*, they are all there.

Wales won the Triple Crown for the first time in 1893. They used the new formation of eight forwards and four threequarters developed at Cardiff. This development was an accident because it happened after F. E. Hancock had become available again after injury, and rather than leave out the man who had substituted, Cardiff put them both in. Before that, the orthodox formation was of nine forwards and three threequarters. Hancock came from Somerset but eventually played for Wales. His brother played for England. Neither players nor Unions were particularly fussy about birth qualifications in those days and indeed various countries went on selecting players who had no real qualifications to play for them until long after the second world war.

Two players in that 1893 team who were unmistakably Welsh, however, were W. J. Bancroft and Arthur Gould. They were among the first of the Welsh Rugby folk heroes and Gould's admirers even went so far as to give him a house. It is alleged that the same thing has happened in Wales even in comparatively recent times, but in Victorian Britain the frankness with which it was done swiftly earned the disapproval of the English, and a tightening of the rules relating to professionalism.

In the last quarter of the nineteenth century, the game spread quickly beyond its first offshoots in Cambridge, Oxford, London, Edinburgh, Liverpool and Manchester. In 1872, the same year as Cambridge University established a club officially, a club was formed in Le Havre. It has been shrewdly pointed out that Rugby football in France has never really flourished north of the line where the vine stops growing, but the fact remains that it gained its first foothold in Le Havre. Perhaps it would be more accurate to say that it was in Le Havre that the game was re-established in France, because the French game of *soule*, which was certainly played at the time of the Vikings, long before the Norman Conquest of England, was obviously basically the same game of football as that played in ancient Britain. It was just as violent, too.

Rugby football was welcomed more enthusiastically in France along the banks of the Gironde leading to Bordeaux, and the English were only too happy to take it there because it meant that they could combine business with pleasure, or perhaps, pleasure with pleasure, by developing the very considerable wine trade between the two countries. Rugby football at least gave them an excuse to enjoy themselves on Sunday, Monday, Tuesday, Wednesday, Thursday and Friday. The French took this strange sporting ritual straight to their hearts.

Henri Garcia, in his excellent history of French Rugby, says that the game became more firmly established in the poorest areas south of the river Loire, where the life was much rougher than in the rich industrial plains of the North but where the inhabitants had a warmer temperament and a love of the romantic. This acceptance of the game by the working classes of agricultural France was the reverse of what was happening in England but in essence it was the same kind of development as that occurring in the wide open spaces of Britain's colonies.

The great difference was that the French relied upon the missionary British to instruct them in the finer arts of the game in those early years, whereas the New Zealanders, Australians and South Africans, while welcoming the latest knowledge and the skills of all the new immigrants, quickly developed the resource and the initiative to experiment with playing formations and tactics themselves and to take great pride in developing their own skills.

The earliest development of Rugby football in the Southern hemisphere was in Australia, and particularly, in New South Wales. There is a record of a game being played there in 1829, and by the end of the nineteenth century, Rugby was firmly established. A club was formed at Sydney University in 1864, and a governing body called the Southern Rugby Union was formed in 1874. It was re-named the N.S.W. Rugby

The first time that international Rugby football was played at Newlands under the shadow of Table Mountain, Cape Town. South Africa versus the British Isles in 1891. South Africa lost the match and the series.

Union in 1892, but four years before that, the first team from what British colonials always called 'the home country' had toured Australia and New Zealand. It was an English team, managed by A. E. Stoddart and captained by R. L. Seddon, and although it was nothing like a fully representative selection, it lost only two matches out of the 27 played. An augury of the future was the fact that both the defeats were in New Zealand. Seddon, the captain of the side, was drowned in an accident while sculling on the Maitland river in Australia, and so Stoddart then combined the duties of captain and manager.

Teams from Australia and New Zealand had already been playing each other for six years, but until their two defeats in New Zealand in 1888, English Rugby had no idea of the enthusiasm with which the game had been taken up in that country. Any suggestion that those results were a fluke was soon dispelled. Within the space of little more than ten years after the formation of the New Zealand Rugby Union in 1892, the techniques, tactics and skills of the game and the organisation of team-work in New Zealand were taken so far ahead of the understanding of the game in Britain that the All Blacks were able to send their first touring team to the home country and overcome what ought to have been a crippling disadvantage in playing resources.

The game in New Zealand was taken up by ordinary working folk in a way that it never was in England, Scotland and Ireland. Wilson Whineray, captain of one of New Zealand's finest teams, and subsequently a headmaster, says, 'In the early times, Rugby football must have been an enormous help to lonely rural folk living in a widely scattered community. The game obviously exploded quite sharply in the 1880s, and it's always interesting to hear one of the old Australians, especially in country areas, stand up and say, "Well, in 1910 we used to jump on the dray and the family would come and we'd have the afternoon. We'd play the local opposition and we'd have a drink afterwards and a bit of a meal, and the wives would have a cup of tea. We worked hard in those days. We had little company, no telephones, no wireless. The Saturday get-together was a very important thing for us." It could have been any sport, but it just happened to be Rugby in those early years. I think the exploits of the 1905 side and the 1924 side did help to bring some sort of national pride to a very young, emerging country.

'I think, too, that there is nothing else that finds such a natural affinity of *pakehas* [strangers, or white men] and Polynesians in this country, and that's good. I think too that our Maori people have always enjoyed a great and deserved sense of pride from their exploits at the game.'

The Maoris, indeed, toured the world long before any other Rugby team from New Zealand. They played the incredible total of 74 matches on tour in 1888 and 1889, and naturally, were a nine-day wonder wherever they went. When they played Oxford University on February 21, 1889, the local undergraduate wags printed the names of the Maori players upside down in the match programme, because, of course, everyone who lived in the Antipodes lived their lives upside down!

Despite having to play three or four times a week to pay for their tour, the Maoris won 49 of their matches but even this feat was eclipsed by the extraordinary success of the 1905 All Blacks. Fortunately, we can easily understand why the 1905 All Blacks achieved the triumphs they enjoyed, because their captain, Dave Gallaher, and his vice-captain, Billy Stead, between them wrote one of the best books ever produced about Rugby football. Borrowing perhaps from Izaak Walton, it was called *The Complete Rugby Footballer* and on page after page is material which is as relevant today as it was when it was written seventy-three years ago. It is a work of startling maturity, brimful of common sense and real footballing shrewdness.

Some years ago, Jeff Butterfield, the England and British Lions centre and an artist of a Rugby player himself, expressed his surprise at the continuing relevance of *The Complete Rugby Footballer*.

'No wonder it took us seventy years to catch up with New Zealand,' he said.

No other book written in the first hundred years of the game first codified at Rugby School brushed away the dry dust of history and illuminated the actual playing of the game in the way that Gallaher and Stead did, and consequently, it could lay fair claim to being as significant a contribution to the literature of the game as *Tom Brown's Schooldays*.

The book was a fascinating mixture of the elementary and the technical. It skipped from one to the other and back again as if it was the most natural thing in the world to be mixing differential calculus with the sum of one plus one. The authors made it clear from the beginning that the essence of the game is possession, followed by quick, controlled and accurate passing supported by close backing up, with the object of creating a situation where two attacking players are running against one defender.

They stated that the mere act of passing the ball was the most important science in the game and they left no doubt that in their view, team organisation, planned movements and careful choice of lines of run are much the best ways of breaking an opposing defence. It took British Rugby sixty-two more years to come to the same conclusion.

The 1905 All Blacks had a wide selection of planned moves, even to the extent of splitting lineouts and throwing the ball into the gap for the blindside wing to take in full stride. They broke clean through the defence with this move in the international against Ireland, and only failed to score because the New Zealand winger put a foot over the dead ball line in trying to run round behind the posts.

Gallaher and Stead were firmly of the opinion that in 1905, the art of planned deception was in its infancy, but they took pride in the fact that they had enough tricks up their sleeves to confuse most of the opposition

Dave Gallaher and Billy Stead, captain and vice-captain of the 1905 All Blacks.

throughout the British Isles. 'Each side, and each player on the side, must have their recognised ruses . . . A ruse can seldom be tried more than once in a game, but every ruse has, as it were, a double edge. When you have cut with it one way, you can turn round and cut with it the other. You gain by the mystery you create and nothing has such a demoralising effect on a side as being beaten by these feints.' They insisted that players had to be equipped with all the skills. They derided a player who could only pass off one hand or kick off one foot as being only half a player, and they said unequivocally that if a back was not really quick then he should either give up the game or play somewhere else.

The 1905 All Blacks developed their own distinctive playing formation and it influenced New Zealand Rugby so strongly that the echoes are still being heard. They used the hooker to throw in at the lineout, and not the scrum-half, as was then common practice, or the blindside wing. Again, it took European Rugby another sixty years to come to the same conclusion, although it is interesting to see that the wheel has come full circle in that Béziers, the French club champions, and the most successful club in the world throughout the middle and late 'seventies, again used the scrum-half to throw in.

The forwards of the 1905 All Blacks packed two-three-two in a seven-man scrum, and most of the forwards were specialists. They did this partly because they wanted a quick heel and therefore needed the scrum-half ready at the back of the scrum waiting to pick up the ball after the eighth forward, called the wing forward, had put the ball into the scrum. The wing forward was used to spoil the opposition possession if they hooked the ball from the New Zealand put-in. The 1905 All Blacks' use of specialisation in some of the forward positions was also an innovation and they worked out the mechanics of angle packing – mechanics which certainly were not understood in Europe for the better part of fifty years – and they used this knowledge to hold or beat nearly all the eight-man scrums they played against.

Behind the scrum, they were already using the formation of a scrum-half working in front of two link players who always played next to each other, and so were called a first five-eighth and a second five-eighth, rather than the British system of a fly-half and two centres. The 1905 All Blacks used code words as signals for planned moves, too, and they established a fundamental difference in approach to the loose scrum which they called the ruck. This difference did more than anything to characterise the New Zealand game as distinct from that in Britain.

'Our backs never go down and lie on the ball as they do in Britain – permitted to do so by the referees. In New Zealand, a back is allowed to stop a rush by throwing himself on the ball, but nothing more than that. If he does not get up immediately, he is penalised. We find that lying on the ball, as practised in Britain, slows the game a great deal, particularly when the referee merely gives a scrum. Besides, this method of procedure is a fruitful cause of accidents.' Almost every confrontation between British and New Zealand teams in the years since has been either influenced or dominated by that one issue.

It is also surprising to discover that the 1905 All Blacks almost certainly originated the hip-swing pass which became a fundamental of the British, and particularly the English, game. Before the 1905 tour, British backs passed the ball with a completely different technique, which was more of a flick. Describing the New Zealand technique, Gallaher and Stead said, 'The point to be emphasised is that it is a swing pure and simple, and a body swing, not a throw or a jerk. The body movement gives the ball all the necessary propulsion. The hands merely balance and guide it as it leaves them.'

The ruck was not the only area in which there was a significant and lasting divergence between New Zealand and British Rugby. Another difference was the attitude of the forwards to running. The 1905 All Blacks established the principles of blanket support running by *all* the forwards, and this gave them an inestimable advantage over European teams for more than half a century. 'Our forwards always seem to be more eager, to follow up better, and to do a far greater amount of work – back work, as it might be called – than the majority of those we encountered on our British tour. In England, it seems to be considered unorthodox for a forward to take part in a passing movement, or to initiate an attack from a lineout, but we believe in our forwards being as quick as the back division in taking the ball.'

Gallaher's All Blacks were also the first to use the lineout as a platform from which to launch attacks. The fact that they scored 33 tries on tour direct from lineouts proved that they were not only thoroughly well organised but also that they kept statistics to establish the percentage of profit from different phases of the game. They were astonished to find that British teams ignored the possibilities of attack from the lineout. In those days, it was possible to choose a scrum instead of a lineout, as indeed it was until comparatively recently, and British teams invariably opted for the scrum. As a result, they were confounded by the flexibility of the New Zealanders, who sought to attack from lineouts in all parts of the field except their 25, when they kicked for position. The only other time they kicked was when the ball was wet, and then they played a close game, foot-rushing the ball in the same way as the British.

Of all their incredibly fertile pioneer work, though, the ruck must stand as the supreme contribution made to the game of Rugby football by Dave Gallaher's 1905 All Blacks. It stemmed from their understanding of the value of committal play. 'What we call a loose ruck . . . represents the disordered state occurring, for example, when an opponent has slipped in trying to block a forward rush. In such a case, it has been our policy to enter this ruck with the particular object of heeling out the ball. Our backs are all ready to strike if we can do so, and when the ball is duly heeled out, the scrum-half sets them going, not the least important consideration being that we are a man to the good numerically.'

New Zealand's thinking about the ruck has not changed materially since. In 1978, on his farm in Te Kuiti, Colin Meads said, 'The ruck is born of a desire to get the ball for the backs. One of the greatest facets of New Zealand Rugby in the past has always been where you could have eight men charging to hit the ruck and produce a good ball for the backs to use. Invariably, we would aim to have one of the opposition backs tied up with us, and that would always give us a basic overlap without us ever having to bring in an extra man or anything.'

Gallaher's All Blacks kept a record of the way they scored their tries, and the way tries were scored against them. This is still a part of the game which is nothing like as developed as it might be. Chance happenings which produce tries, or oddities of formation which do the same thing, can be studied and possibly reproduced deliberately. Gallaher and his players did that. They were always seeking new moves, too. 'One must always be searching for some new construction, the very ingenuity of which will flabbergast the enemy, and the side which has most of these will be the strongest. At the same time, one must take account of past experience. If any wise footballer at the beginning of his first-class career were to make a practice of committing to paper after every match a record of some kind of the best and most successful movements that were introduced into it, with explanatory diagrams, and kept this up until his football days were no more, this reference book by that time would be the most valuable thing that any club could be possessed of, that is, if the said club were intelligent enough to place it to proper account.'

That advice was pure gold in 1905. It is the same now. Gallaher continued, 'Study the tactics of the old masters, and then adapt them to modern conditions. It is wonderful what a trifling change will do in the way of furnishing a most complete alternative to an existing system of play. In many cases, the missing out of one man in the passing movement will throw the whole of the defensive machinery of the opposition out of gear.'

This proves that the 1905 All Blacks used what are now called miss moves – long passes missing out an intervening attacker – and yet most of the players of today believe that organised miss moves were a tactic unheard of before the mid-'sixties.

Gallaher and Stead had strong views about the skills required for forward play, views which were obviously at variance with what was then common acceptance in Britain. 'We have noticed shocking neglect in the choice and cultivation of the men of the front rank. The prevailing idea [in Britain] seems to be that anything is good enough for a forward, and that you put in this department all those men who are not thoroughly capable for any other task. Our principle is that every forward should be a potential back, and in the team that toured through Britain there was not a man in the pack who could not have fulfilled the duties of a back if emergency had demanded.'

Peter Robbins, one of the most creative forwards England have ever produced, did come out of the pack when Phil Horrocks-Taylor was injured, and played well in the centre when England beat Australia in Peter Jackson's match in 1958, but apart from Robbins, very few British

Peter Robbins, one of the most creative forwards England has produced.

forwards who played before 1970 would have been able to meet Dave Gallaher's requirements.

These requirements included the fitness, the speed and the mental resolution necessary for effective backing up and support play – an aspect of the game which again, is assumed mistakenly to be a modern development. It was the rule of the 1905 All Blacks that 'every man engaged on an important movement to which the least degree of risk attaches, shall be backed up by a colleague. We never played a match in which our players were not thus guarded, and our gain from the precaution must have been something too enormous for calculation.'

Similarly, any notion that the attacking full-back is a product of the touch-kicking restriction introduced in 1970 is firmly dispelled by Gallaher and Stead. They insisted that the full-back was the best man to give an attack its final impetus. 'Either on the outside or the inside of the wing, he is invaluable as a last man to take the ball. . . .'

British teams made little use of the reverse pass. If they used it at all, they only did so from the open side wing. Gallaher's team used the reverse pass all the way along the threequarter line – indeed, wherever they had a man backing up on the inside to take the ball and create an overlap.

It is apparent, too, that those New Zealanders understood the technique of either taking the ball early, or drifting along a pass either to get inside or outside an opponent, and the chapters devoted to combined attack on the open side and the blind side show that they were exploring the possibilities offered by subtle adjustments in lines of running. Always, though, the emphasis was on combination, and not individualism.

Gallaher's All Blacks developed scissors plays, and they actively tried to score from opposition kick-offs. Reading the precise requirements of the positional placing necessary to achieve this brought recollections of Geoff Mold, the coach of the refreshingly inventive Australian schoolboys team in Britain in 1978. It was his belief that scoring a try from an opposition kick-off was always a possibility. The key, like a false move on the chess board, was the positioning of the open side flanker. Dave Gallaher and Billy Stead would have approved – and made a note!

As if all this fertility was not enough, the 1905 All Blacks used dummy runs without the ball, pulled spare men out of the scrum in defence, made dramatic advances with the attacking kick and cross-kick, and even went to the lengths of having lighter-soled boots made, with tapering studs, or buttons, as they called them, rather than the heavy boots and standard studs then in use in Britain. They even varied the length of their studs, according to the conditions. No wonder they swept through the country, overwhelming all their opponents by remarkable scores until, stale and tired near the end of an historic tour, they lost by the only try of the match against Wales.

Gallaher and Stead said that by then, their team was exhausted and suffering badly from injuries, and was much too conscious of preserving an unbeaten record which no-one, least of all the tourists themselves, expected at the beginning of their tour. Scotland, indeed, thought so little of the appeal of the All Blacks that they would not guarantee them the £200 fee they asked for each match, and instead, conceded the All Blacks any profit that might be made after expenses had been paid. The match, which the All Blacks won, made £1,000. The Scottish Rugby Union groaned in anguish for years and they were still so peeved about the episode that they declined to play the All Blacks when they toured Britain unbeaten in 1924–25. Once again, though, the Scots were the losers, because that year was the greatest in their history. It was the only year in which they beat all the other three home countries and France and so would have had a fine chance of becoming the only team to beat the 1924–25 All Blacks.

Arguments have raged about the 1905 match between Wales and New Zealand ever since. The All Blacks had a try disallowed which was decisive, but the captain and vice-captain of the team made no reference to it. They simply said that their team did not do itself justice; that they were stale and overplayed; that with one exception, their formidable backs were right off colour; and that on the day, New Zealand could have no complaint at losing.

The success of the side staggered the British Rugby public. It accused them of professionalism, of being sustained by magic Maori potions, of cheating in the scrums, and in the case of Dave Gallaher himself, of adopting illegal and unsporting tactics by his development of the wing-forward game. It was even suggested that the All Blacks' shirts, which were reinforced at the neck with canvas and chamois leather, were made of eel-skin to stop tacklers gaining a fair hold!

Gallaher's play undoubtedly was illegal. He was offside in front of the ball when it was heeled to his scrum-half and he obstructed opponents trying to tackle his scrum-half, but that was a comparatively trivial part of the whole touring exercise. The 1905 All Blacks toured Britain with an attention to detail, both on and off the field, which would be a credit to any modern professional sport. The All Blacks even had a recipe for the embrocation they used. Six parts of eucalyptus oil to three parts of whisky and one part of hartshorn! 'Our whole bodies were rubbed down with this training oil before and after every match, and we can confidently recommend all other players to use the same system.' They were equally confident in all their other systems, too, and they burst upon European Rugby much as Emil Zatopek burst on middle distance running after the Second World War, achieving standards of fitness and athleticism which no-one had thought even possible before.

The play of the 1905 All Blacks literally took Rugby football into the twentieth century. Their play was obviously representative of the development of Rugby in New Zealand and it is equally obvious that it amounted to no less than a revolution in the techniques and the tactics of the game, a revolution which was almost certainly the most profound in the history of the game.

At the same time, Dave Gallaher's All Blacks revealed the shattering effect which the breakaway of the Northern Union and the formation of the Rugby League had had on the game in England. The giant of world Rugby had been brought to its knees by the loss of so many of the great clubs that had formed its life-blood. Playing standards had been painfully devalued. Popular support had switched to the new game of Association football, and Welsh Rugby was able to take full advantage of England's decline.

In modern times, it has been evident for at least twenty years that but for the constant drain of its best players to Rugby League, Australian Rugby Union would be of a higher standard than either New Zealand or South Africa, but it is worth remembering that England's Rugby Union football has suffered even more acutely for nearly a hundred years. For all their successes against the other countries in the 'twenties, 'thirties and 'fifties, English Rugby has always been a shadow of its real self and it will never realise its true potential until all its players in the North become available for selection again. Perhaps this will come about because of changed attitudes to professionalism. Perhaps the game of Rugby League itself will die, as it has to a great extent in France, where it is socially and financially much more attractive to play Rugby Union. For the moment, it is just sad to see so many fine Rugby players in the North of England playing a game which has discarded nearly all the classic elements of the true football game and which, in the last 15 years in particular, has become quite pathetic.

The 1905 All Blacks were even more saddened by the depths to which English Rugby had sunk. They won their international against England by five tries to nil, but Gallaher and Stead said firmly, 'One cannot help thinking that England might have picked a stronger side. By this time, we had had considerable experience of the class of player to be found in the towns and shires and we certainly did not think that the fifteen who were put up against us at the Crystal Palace were fully representative of the best to be found in the country.'

'Twas ever thus, apparently. The quality of England selection has rarely been high.

The 1905 All Blacks finished their tour in Wales with an itinerary that would bring screams of protest from any modern touring team. After a tour which in terms of travel and playing commitment was infinitely more arduous than anything contemplated today, they ended with matches against Wales, Glamorgan, Newport, Cardiff and Swansea. Despite that, and despite the fact that Wales were in the middle of one of the most successful periods in their history, they lost only the international, and that by one try scored in circumstances which are argued about to this day.

Dave Gallaher and Billy Stead were no more impressed by the team organisation of Welsh Rugby than they were of that in England, Scotland and Ireland, but they were impressed by the individual skills of several of the leading Welsh players, and they said so. This contest between individual skill and team organisation developed into a massacre of a victory for team play in the first seventy years of the twentieth century, but on the rare occasions when individual skills triumphed, as they did when Wales beat New Zealand 3–0 in 1905, they passed into folklore as glories of the national heritage. 'Now is the time to speak of famous men . . .' New Zealand and South Africa preferred to speak of famous teams, and they did much better as a result.

Rhys Gabe partnered Gwyn Nicholls in the centre for Wales against the 1905 All Blacks, and he played for Wales almost throughout their golden years at the beginning of the twentieth century. The BBC archives have a recording of his reminiscences about the play and the players of his time.

'W. J. Bancroft played the last of his 33 games for Wales when I played my first, against Ireland in 1901. Bancroft had marvellous speed and dodging powers, which he used to tire out the forwards before finding touch. He was a master of the arts of place-kicking, drop-kicking and punting, and he could kick the ball tremendous distances with either foot.

'Two other great Swansea players were Dicky Owen, a tireless, fearless scrum-half, as full of tricks as a monkey, and W. J. Trew, the best all-round player I ever saw. He was capped for Wales as a wing, centre and stand-off half.

'Then there were my colleagues in the Cardiff team, Gwyn Nicholls and Percy Bush. Nicholls was the perfect centre. Only a partner who had played alongside him for years, as I did, could appreciate the all-round strength of his play.

'Percy Bush was capable of the most amazing feats of individual brilliance. I once saw him score a try directly from a kick-off. The outstanding wings of my time were Teddy Morgan and Willie Llewellyn. Both were very fast, and capable of scoring whenever there was the semblance of a chance.

'In some respects, the most remarkable game against England in which I played was the match at Swansea in 1903, when Wales won by three goals and two tries to a goal. Tommy Pearson, the Newport wing-threequarter had come out of retirement to captain Wales. I was his centre. H. T. Gamlin was the English full-back. He was a great gorilla of a man with a most devastating tackle.

'Pearson scored one try early in the game, and soon afterwards he went racing up to Gamlin again. That time, Gamlin caught him, and Pearson retired with two broken ribs. Jehoida Hodges, the burly Newport forward, came out of the pack to play on my wing, and three times I ran up to Gamlin and sent Hodges galloping away out of reach to score three tries, an astonishing feat for a forward, and one which I believe has no parallel in international Rugby.'

Wales won seven Triple Crowns in the years before the first world war, and it was not until the Rugby Union bought and developed a ground at Twickenham, and made the place their headquarters, that England began to reassert the playing authority they had enjoyed before the breakaway of the Northern clubs.

4 The era of Stoop and Wakefield

The tour of the 1905 All Blacks was so successful financially that by the time they left for America on their way home, after outclassing a French team in Paris early in January, 1906, arrangements had been made already for a representative team from South Africa to tour the United Kingdom later the same year. Approaches were also made to the organisers of Rugby football in New South Wales, suggesting that a national team from Australia should tour Britain as soon as possible after the South Africans.

The 1906 South Africans were almost as successful as the All Blacks had been the year before. They beat Ireland and Wales and drew with England and lost only to Scotland and to Cardiff in the last match of the tour. Technically, they were not as advanced as the All Blacks, but they confirmed the high opinions formed of their individual ability by the British team that had toured South Africa in 1903. They had a centre called Jaapie Krige, then nearing the end of his career, who is regarded as the best ever to represent his country. Apart from Krige, whose footwork was mesmerising, their backs were fast and direct, just as Springbok backs have always been since, and their forwards gave notice that sheer physique, developed by a good diet and back-breaking manual work in the open air, would soon make them one of the dominant forces of the world.

Australia's first visit to the United Kingdom, in 1908, was nothing like as auspicious because the game in that country had just suffered its own version of the 1892 breakaway which led to the formation of the Rugby League in England. Ironically, the man who had most to do with the inauguration of Rugby League in Australia was the legendary cricketer, Victor Trumper. Again, the division occurred because of a dispute about broken time payments, but the success of the new professional code was largely assured because Trumper and his associates managed to persuade Australia's most famous Rugby player to turn professional.

The player in question was Dally Messenger, and he was such a gifted player that he was the best in Australia at either Rugby or soccer. He was so good that he was paid £150 a match to play against the newly formed New Zealand Rugby League team on its way to tour Britain, and when

Jaapie Krige, one of the 1906 Springboks, said to be one of the finest South African centres of all time.

the three-match series was over, the New Zealanders promptly invited Messenger to tour Britain with them. He accepted and so impressed the football public in Britain that Tottenhan Hotspur offered him an enormous sum to stay on in London and make a career in professional soccer. He refused and went back to his native Australia, where the sporting public so revered him that he was called 'The Master' long before anyone thought of applying that supreme title to anyone else.

Dally Messenger's skill as a footballer was not the only aspect of him that caused confusion. In an Italian history of Rugby football, it is solemnly recorded that a journalist from *The Daily Messenger* who had reported the tour of the New Zealand Rugby League side in England, had returned to Sydney to applaud the merits of Rugby League !

Playing contacts between South Africa and Britain, of course, were much easier than between Britain and New Zealand, because of the much shorter boat passage, and the Springboks returned to the United Kingdom in 1912. That time, they left no one in any doubt of their ability. They beat Scotland 16–0, they smashed Ireland 38–0, they beat Wales 3–0 in rain and mud that has always seemed to bedevil encounters between the two countries in Britain, and they held off an inspired opening attack by England to win 9–3 on the new ground at Twickenham. The England try was scored after a brilliant run by Ronnie Poulton, believed by many to be the greatest threequarter ever to play the game. Poulton (later to inherit a fortune on condition that he changed his name

Left, above: Paul Roos, the captain of the Springboks in Great Britain in 1906, leads some of his players out to practice. *Left, below:* East Midlands play the Springboks at Northampton in 1906 – the first match of the Springbok tour of the British Isles and the first time a South African national team had ever played abroad. Paul Roos, the moustached Springbok captain, turns at the front of the lineout to see his jumper win the ball with so little opposition that it was an indication of the shape of things to come. The two East Midlands forwards at the front of the lineout seem to be wearing bathing hats!

Right, above: Wales have never beaten South Africa, and although one of their backs is quickly through on to the ball in the first match at Swansea in 1906 he cannot stop Joubert picking up and clearing. *Right, middle:* The Springbok half-backs work the ball away from a scrum against Wales in 1906.

Right, below: South Africa kick the winning goal against Wales at Cardiff Arms Park in 1912.

to Poulton-Palmer) nearly scored another breathtaking try in that opening assault which the Springboks confessed they were lucky to survive. Tragically, Poulton-Palmer was among the many gifted Rugby players to be killed in the Great War.

The first match played at the Rugby Union's new ground at Twickenham was in October, 1909 and, early in the New Year of 1910, England beat Wales there before going on to win the championship for the first time since the Northern clubs had broken away to form the Rugby League 18 years before. The match also made a profit of £2,000, a highly satisfactory initial return on the investment first made in 1907, when the Rugby Union took the advice of a man named Billy Williams to buy $10\frac{1}{2}$ acres of market garden at Twickenham for £5,572 12s 6d. Williams was well known as both a player and a referee – as a referee, in fact, he did as much as anyone to draw attention to the illegalities of Dave Gallaher's play at wing-forward with the 1905 All Blacks by giving no fewer than 12 penalty kicks against him for offside and obstruction in the first half of the tourists' match against Surrey.

Before the development of the Rugby Union's ground at Twickenham, England had played their matches at the Kennington Oval, the Crystal Palace, Blackheath, Richmond and various provincial grounds. Twickenham turned out to be an inspired purchase in every way, because Greater London grew at such a rate that early criticisms of the ground's inaccessibility quickly became invalid, and the Rugby Union were able to acquire enough additional land to give them their present 30 acre site. Their only regret must be that they did not buy another 28 acres on the East side of the ground when it became available. The Rugby Union had an overdraft at the time, and it is very difficult to take a long view in those circumstances. It may also have been difficult to persuade their bankers to share that vision.

Anyway, the opening of the ground at Twickenham coincided with a revival of England's fortunes, and nowadays, in a period of almost unbroken Welsh domination, England can be grateful that Wales did not win their first match at Twickenham until 1933.

Since then, Twickenham has become the capital of the world of Rugby. When it was built, New Zealand, South Africa and Australia were represented directly on the Rugby Football Union, and although they have all since gone their separate ways, the list of the Rugby Union's affiliated clubs and unions still reads like a lexicon of Queen Victoria's Empire. Any new country wanting to take up the game, or even a single enthusiast in some remote part of the globe, invariably writes to the Rugby Union at Twickenham for guidance and assistance.

The world of Rugby was long ago split into spheres of influence in which New Zealand was supposed to be the overlord of the Pacific countries; South Africa was supposed to look after the rest of the Southern hemisphere; France was supposed to look after Europe; and the four home countries were supposed to look after the rest of the world. It made no difference. Nearly everyone went on writing to Twickenham, and from Fiji to Finland, they made no bones about why they do it; Twickenham has always been consistently the most helpful.

Air Cdre Bob Weighill, secretary of the Rugby Union in 1978, said, 'There is no doubt that we do act as a father confessor to many clubs and unions throughout the world. A large number of the old Commonwealth countries are associate members of the Rugby Union, and other countries like Japan and Uruguay come to us and ask to be put on our mailing list, so that they can be in receipt of all the publications and films that we produce. We are delighted when a new country comes into the fold, as it were, and we are always ready to accept them.'

Twickenham is now an institution, like Lord's and Wimbledon. Jean Denis, who writes for the influential French newspaper, *Sud-Ouest*, describes it lovingly as 'the cathedral of Rugby football'. Perhaps it has never echoed to the anthems which might have been sung in it if it had not been for the breakaway of the Northern clubs, but there is no doubt that it does have an almost ecclesiastical presence, with those gaunt stands towering above that vivid splash of green in the centre. Millions of visitors to Britain look down on it every year as their aircraft approach the final stages of their run in to London Airport. In its way, it is almost as much of a monument as Nelson's Column.

In January, 1910, England beat Wales in the first international match played at Twickenham by 11 points to 6. Kenneth Rankin, who saw the game, told a BBC interviewer, 'When Wales came up for the first international at Twickenham, England hadn't won for eleven years and some people were beginning to feel as though we never should. But Adrian Stoop, England's captain and fly-half, had other ideas, and decided on immediate audacity.

'When Gronow kicked off for Wales towards the South end, Stoop caught the ball and ran slightly to the right. Just as everyone was waiting for the usual return to touch, he suddenly slewed off to the left and ran upfield as hard as he could. When the Welsh defence began to get across and back, he made a short punt. England followed up, out came the ball, there were a couple of quick passes and F. E. Chapman, England's right wing, was over. It all happened so quickly that hardly anyone understood it. Lots of people, still getting to their seats, didn't properly see it, but from an English point of view, it was a rare experience to have got in the first blow, and to watch the puzzled faces and muttering mouths of the Welsh team as they gathered behind their goal-line.'

The events of that game, of course, are still within living memory, and they were followed with a passionate interest by a twelve-year-old boy who was just about to leave his preparatory school to go to his senior school at Sedbergh. That boy was William Wavell Wakefield, and he went on to become probably the greatest forward ever to play for his country and to exercise an even more profound influence on the tactical development of the actual playing of the game than Stoop himself.

Stoop, by any standards, was a remarkable man, and it cannot have been a coincidence that when he and Wakefield were at the height of their influence on the game, England enjoyed one of the most successful periods in her Rugby history. Both men were members of the Harlequin club and they did more than anyone to wrest the crown of being England's premier club away from Blackheath.

Stoop's great contribution to the playing of the game was his development of half-back and midfield play. Wakefield, with a tactical brain to match his superb physique and athleticism, developed the whole modern concept of loose forward play. Gallaher's 1905 All Blacks undoubtedly explored some of the possibilities in both these areas of team play; Stoop and Wakefield took them to conclusions that became the basis of the modern game.

Lord Wakefield, as he is now, said 'Adrian Stoop had a profound influence on half-back play. I know that all sorts of people tried all sorts of new ideas in midfield play almost throughout the nineteenth century, but the fact remains that when Adrian Stoop started playing first-class Rugby, the half-backs still took it in turn to play what we would now call scrum-half and stand-off half. He decided that it was important that

Below, left: The only known action photograph of R W Poulton-Palmer, one of England's greatest players before the First World War. This was England's match against France in 1914. *Below, right.* A portrait photograph of the player. He was killed by a sniper's bullet in 1915.

there should be specialisation in these two positions. Gallaher's All Blacks undoubtedly made a great impression on him, because English football at that time was very much down in the dumps. The split between the North of England and the Union on the question of broken time payments meant that English Rugby lost a vast number of players, including nearly all their best forwards. This meant that England had to devise something else and when the New Zealanders drove home the point in 1905, Adrian Stoop was encouraged to develop his ideas in a whole variety of ways. Before his time, backs were mostly noted either for their speed or elusiveness – what they used to call dodging. I think Adrian Stoop was the first to see the value of different lines of running and to see how quite subtle adjustments in the angles of run in midfield could produce really dramatic differences in opportunity for runners further out in the centre or on the wing. Adrian Stoop always used to watch matches from behind the North End goal at Twickenham when he finished playing. He wanted to see if the Harlequins' midfield backs were running straight. Very few things in Rugby football are new of course – for instance, I believe Stoop was the first man in Britain to introduce code numbers for different moves. The emphasis seems to be put on different aspects of the game as part of a great historical cycle. Still, it seems to me as if we are now coming back to the point where we shall have to emphasise, once again, Adrian Stoop's teachings about straight running in midfield.'

In the same way that Adrian Stoop consolidated the idea of specialisation at half-back, Wavell Wakefield concentrated on developing specialists in the pack, both in set play in the scrummage and the lineout, and in attack and defence in the loose.

He admits himself, 'In those days, that wasn't too easy because the advantage of putting the ball into the scrummage was not fully appreciated. However, in the mid-'twenties, the International Board decided that the non-offending side should have the right of putting the ball into the scrummage and they also decreed that there should be only three players in the front row.

'Before that, though, there was a continual struggle, first of all to get hold of the ball so that you could have the advantage of putting it in, and then to pack in an extra forward on the left so that you had the advantage of the loose head. Sometimes the scrum consisted of two rows of eight forwards walking sideways across the field, clearly an impossible situation.

'Also, when I started playing, the scrum-half was the player who threw the ball in from touch. I thought that was a mistake for two reasons. It seemed to me that it was better for the wing threequarters to throw the ball in from touch because the scrum-half could then position himself behind his forwards and form an extra line of defence if the opposition broke through. By standing there, the scrum-half was also able to read the game better and clear the ball faster if it came quickly from his forwards. This seemed to me to make sense, and it soon became general practice.

The World of Rugby

'I also tried to define the different functions of all the forwards in the lineout. We did not develop this to the point it is today, or anything like, but we did start the essence of jumping and support play and even more to the point, we worked out precisely what the functions of the back row forwards were in both attack and defence.'

Wakefield, of course, was a phenomenon of a forward. He was a really big man, and yet he was as quick as any back. He was a star sprinter at

W J A Davies (left), the most successful fly-half England have ever had, and C A Kershaw, an exceptionally powerful scrum-half, who partnered Davies at half-back both for the Royal Navy and England in the first four seasons after the First World War. Kershaw was also an Olympic fencer.

school and he was the R.A.F. quarter-mile champion. He it was who first developed corner-flagging by a number eight in defence and showed that it was possible for a back row forward to provide a third line of defence to support his winger and full-back on the open-side wing.

His loose forward tactics in attack were different. He made his backs pass the ball as fast as they could to the open side wing, where it was their task to draw the defence before cross-kicking back into the middle where Wakefield used his speed and strength and uncanny skill as a dribbler to pick up any number of tries. Even if the opposition caught the ball, they were under pressure. It sounds very obvious now, but it was revolutionary stuff in 1920.

Before Wakefield's time, forwards did not do much defending. It was mostly lone combat between the backs. By threatening the opposition scrum-half with his blind-side wing forward and by putting himself and his open side wing-forward behind his fly-half, he created the concept of cover defence. As he says, 'This nullified most of the brilliant threequarter tactics developed first by the Welsh and then by Adrian Stoop'.

Wakefield was undoubtedly fortunate in that both he and England had an exceptional fly-half to take control of the midfield tactical direction. W. J. A. Davies first played for England in 1913 and he went on playing international Rugby for six more seasons after the Great War. When he retired in 1924, he looked back on an international career spanning eleven years in which he won 22 caps and in which England never lost an international championship match in which he played.

It was England's forthright tactics, under the captaincy of Wakefield, that led to the rumpus among the forwards in the match against New Zealand at Twickenham in 1924 which in turn led to Cyril Brownlie, the All Black forward, being sent off the field. Lord Wakefield attributes this directly to New Zealand's 2–3–2 scrummage formation and to the struggle for the loose head. 'Instead of packing in the centre of our three-man front row which naturally would have always given us the loose head, they kept trying to work the loose head for themselves, which meant that our far prop overlapped into thin air. Well, we weren't going to have that.

'Reg Edwards, the England prop, had already played for his club Newport against the tourists, and he had had a pretty tense struggle over this question of the loose head, so I think a few old scores were being paid off. But it is quite wrong to blame Reg Edwards for what happened at Twickenham. The prime cause of the trouble was the lack of law to define a front row, and then when things started to get out of hand, Albert Freethy, the referee, said that he would send off the next player he saw do anything wrong. Well, the next player happened to be Cyril Brownlie, and off he went. Brownlie was a Hawke's Bay player, and he made the mistake of taking the part of another All Black from the same province when there was a bit of trouble.

'It might seem strange to say so, but I have always felt that the sending-off of Brownlie lost us the game. It affected the England team far more than it did the All Blacks, who played above themselves. We had already scored one try from a long, controlled dribble by the forwards and were about to score another when Brownlie was sent off.

'Early in the tour, the All Blacks had played London Counties and we wheeled a scrum in midfield so that we could dribble the ball through. Mark Nicholls, the brilliant New Zealand five-eighth, came in and fell on the ball in an attempt to stop the rush, but we heeled the ball back quickly and scored because Mark was on the ground and so we had a man over. Years afterwards, Mark came up to me and said "You held me down on the ground, you so-and-so." I said, "Mark, how could you say such a thing?"

'Anyway, when we wheeled a scrum in the same situation in the international at Twickenham, the All Blacks decided not to be drawn in to fall on the ball. Instead, they went back and back and we went on and on and scored between the posts. We were doing exactly the same thing on the second occasion when Brownlie was sent off.'

Despite the support of his captain, Edwards was never chosen for England again. 'I thought that was unfair,' says Lord Wakefield. 'Edwards did the job I wanted him to do.' Perhaps a contributory factor to the treatment of Edwards was that the sending off of Brownlie became a national scandal as the match was watched by Edward, Prince of Wales.

The All Blacks won all 28 of their games in Britain on the 1924–25 tour.

Albert Freethy, the referee, sending Cyril Brownlie off the field in the match between England and New Zealand.

They did that even though their seven-man scrummage formation was such a self-imposed handicap that their forwards were beaten for possession in the tight in a way that no team would accept without much national heart-searching these days. The handicap was made even more crippling by the fact that the opposition could choose to take scrums instead of lineouts, which naturally they did. In addition, the All Blacks' roving wing-forward was so heavily penalised for offside and obstruction that he must have been an appalling liability, but such was the impact and the reputation of the 1905 All Blacks that their successors seemed to feel that it was their bounden duty to remain loyal to every article of the 1905 faith.

This was astonishingly impractical, for such a practical people, but New Zealand went on choosing a roving loose forward to play and obstruct as Dave Gallaher had until a British team toured New Zealand in 1930 and their manager, 'Bim' Baxter, stood up at a dinner and uncompromisingly called that loose forward 'a cheat'.

On the other hand, Rugby football in Britain did not accept the obvious lesson that if the All Blacks could win all 28 of their matches with about 30 per cent of the ball, then the New Zealanders' methods of using what possession they had must have been staggeringly superior to those of all their opponents.

Undoubtedly, the support play of their forwards in the loose was still as far ahead of the rest of the world as it had been in 1905 and this was

Bob Scott and George Nepia, two of New Zealand's greatest full-backs.

augmented by an individual performance from George Nepia, their young Maori full-back, which was of such breath-taking dimensions that it rivalled the impact made upon the game of cricket by the young Don Bradman when he first toured England with Australia in 1930. Nepia could do everything required in his position – catch, kick, tackle, run, turn, drop on the ball, retain possession, pass and position himself. He could do it all off both hands and both feet and he did it despite the fact that New Zealand's line kicking generally was poor because in their domestic Rugby they had been given a dispensation to abolish kicking direct to touch outside their 25. The stories of Nepia's kicking are told to this day and as if all that was not enough he was born with such a marvellous physique that he played in every match on tour. Fifty years later, John Tallent, chairman of the Four Home Unions tours committee, said, 'I saw George Nepia as a schoolboy, and I don't think I've ever seen a better full-back'.

The only team who might have beaten the All Blacks were Scotland. They were in the middle of the greatest period in their history and they had in Ian Smith one of the finest wings and one of the most remarkable

King George V, who proved to be a staunch ally both of Rugby football and the Royal Air Force, being introduced to the Cambridge team by Wavell Wakefield before the University match in 1922. Wakefield captained both Cambridge University and the RAF.

Right: R Crabos, of France, photographed before the match against England in 1922. M Crabos went on to become one of the most influential administrators French Rugby has ever had.

Below: Wavell Wakefield (left) the England captain, watches anxiously as one of his lineout forwards wins the ball against France in 1922, but France scored three tries to one in that match at Twickenham and by drawing 11–11, escaped defeat against England for the first time ever.

characters ever to play the game. He did not play Rugby at Winchester and only took it up at Oxford to win a bet and persuade a girl friend to change her allegiance from Cambridge. Within a year he had won his Blue (and his bet) and the following season was capped for Scotland. Among many extraordinary feats was the fact that he scored five tries against Wales in one match, and four tries against them the following year. The Scottish Rugby Union, however, was still groaning, like the drone of an expiring bagpipe, about the loss of all that lovely money in 1905, and so they declined to play New Zealand in 1924–25.

As Norman Mair says, 'Five of Scotland's eight Triple Crowns were won before the first world war when we had some tremendous forward play in this country, but I suppose most Scots would say that the golden era of Scottish Rugby was in the 1920s. The only time Scotland won the Grand Slam was in 1925 when we had Herbert Waddell and Alf Wilson at half-back, and the famous Oxford threequarter line of Ian Smith, Phil MacPherson, G. G. Aitken and A. C. Wallace. That team should have played the 1924–25 All Blacks.'

Had they done so, Scotland must have had the best chance of any team in Britain of defeating the team that became known as 'The Invincibles'. Even more to the point, Scotland would have made their attempt in front of what would have been a packed house.

Certainly, the Scots of that time would not have accepted that their

Tom Voyce (second from right), who played alongside Wavell Wakefield in England's back row throughout their golden years, prepares for emergency action as one of the British Lions defenders is unceremoniously tackled by Kruger at Newlands in the final test of the series between South Africa and Dr R Cove-Smith's British team.

Above: The New Zealand All Blacks score against England at Twickenham in 1925. This was the match in which Cyril Brownlie, the New Zealand forward, was sent off the field by Albert Freethy, the famous Welsh referee.

Below: Wavell Wakefield, captain of London, sitting alongside Cliff Porter, captain of the 1924–25 All Blacks, before the match between the two teams at Twickenham. George Nepia, the legendary Maori full-back, is sitting on the right of Wakefield.

Rugby football had anything to learn from New Zealand. As Norman Mair says, their forwards had always been masters of the foot-rush away from a wheeling scrum. 'It was a very good attacking manoeuvre. A defender had to fall to check the rush, and if the forwards then heeled from what they used to call a loose scrum, their backs automatically had a man over. The dribbling was brilliant. One of the great forwards of that time was a doctor named MacMyn. He used to go out practising dribbling and his dog tried to get the ball off him by nosing it away as dogs can. Dribbling is a lost art now, but MacMyn used to keep the ball very close to him by using the outside of his foot so that the ball spun back. He had terrific control. The game has always been aimed at trying to create a situation on the field where the attacking side had a man to spare and Scotland did it by making defenders fall on the ball in front of a foot-rush. The balls were rounder then, too, and easier to dribble than when they became more pointed.'

Still, the results of that All Blacks tour in 1924–25 left no doubt in the rest of the country that by then, Britain's colonies were rapidly becoming the masters of Rugby football, particularly in the matter of team organisation. This was proved when a team from Australia calling themselves the Waratahs toured Britain in 1927–28. They used an attacking formation

Wavell Wakefield, captain of England, photographed with Ernie Crawford, captain of Ireland, and the referee W J Llewellyn after the match in Dublin in 1926. Ireland won 19–15, beating England for the first time for 15 years.

behind the scrum which was much less orthodox than the traditional arrowhead alignment of British backs. Their backs ran criss-cross lines of the type now called scissors in an attempt to breach the opposing defence and create space for their wingers. Fifty years later, an Australian schools side of enviable talent toured Britain and re-adopted the principles of the Waratahs. If the originals were half as good as the boys who copied them, they must have made wonderful watching.

British Rugby was nothing like so well organised. Judge Rowe Harding, who played for Cambridge University in their brilliant years in the 1920s, and then for Wales, recalls, 'Even as late as 1928, it had not filtered into Welsh Rugby that there should be specialisation in forward play. I remember very well that the Welsh pack once scrummaged against six Cardiff city policemen and failed to get the ball once in six put-ins. That pack had gone into the scrum on the old principle of first up, first down. In other words, the first forward to arrive was the first into the scrum. As soon as Wales did start to introduce forward specialisation, we trampled on England at Swansea.'

The Judge recalls with a smile that at that time the Welsh selection committee was thirteen strong, 'and they were so confused that they thought that a five-eighth, which was what the Australians and New

---

Wavell Wakefield breaks from the back of a lineout to make a try for England against Scotland at Murrayfield in 1927, but Scotland won the match 21–13.

Zealanders called their fly-half, was a wing-forward, and to counter him, they picked an extra half-back. The whole thing was a nonsense.'

If any wishful thinking remained in Britain about the development of Rugby football in the colonies, it was firmly dispelled when New Zealand toured South Africa in 1928. On that tour, the all-conquering All Blacks had to fight for their lives, and although they shared the series 2–2, they lost five of their 22 games on tour, and in several others they were pushed all the way. In the early games, in particular, their forwards were rubbed into the dirt from the Cape to the reef and it says much for their resilience that they pulled themselves together so well, particularly in the matter of scrummaging, that by the end of the tour, they were able to meet and to hold the Springboks as equals in the tight. More than forty years were to pass before British packs succeeded in doing the same.

Early in that 1928 tour, though, the All Blacks were appalled at the problems they had been bequeathed by the New Zealand Rugby Union's outdated loyalty to the seven-man scrummage formation. Mark Nicholls, their brilliant five-eighth who, for some reason, was chosen to play in only one of the four tests, spoke of his fears as early as the second match of the tour, which the All Blacks lost 7–3 to Western Province Town at Newlands. 'The game emphatically demonstrated the inferiority of our scrum

The Springboks' answer, although it looks pretty tentative, to the All Blacks' haka. Phil Mostert (No 8), the captain of South Africa, leads his team in their own version of a war dance before the first test in Durban in 1928, but only one of the Springboks looks as if he has any real confidence in what he is doing!

formation. Possession is nine-tenths of the game, and the Town team were thus able to gain the initiative, giving the wily Osler the opportunity to take one man from his pack and place him in the threequarter line.

'Another feature of their play was their line-finding, at which they are adept. With us, touch-finding is a lost art. The special dispensation of the kick-into-touch rule applied to New Zealand and to New South Wales has had the effect of pleasing the spectators, but no one knows better than a tired forward, or a harassed back, the feeling of security and relief which a long and accurate touch-finder can give to his side. In this respect, we had no Nepia, and our kicking up to now had been terribly weak. After each kicking duel, we invariably found that we lost 30 or 40 yards.'

The 'wily Osler' referred to by Mark Nicholls was, of course, Bennie Osler, the Western Province fly-half who went on to captain South Africa. He had played his first game for his country against a weak Lions team in 1924, but the 1928 series against New Zealand established him as a world class tactical kicker. Perhaps accidentally, and perhaps unconsciously, Osler was to have a profound influence on the thinking about the game throughout the world, because it was he who first exploited the possibilities of playing what became known as ten-man Rugby; using the possession won by his forwards to kick for better and better positions and

---

Carl Aarvold, England's captain, runs in past the somewhat senior figure of Ian Smith to score a try for England in their 16–3 win over Scotland at Twickenham in 1932.

The World of Rugby

Right: Bennie Osler, the fly-half who started the conception of ten-man Rugby, walks out to inspect the pitch at Bristol on the Springbok tour of Britain in 1931–32.

Below: Gerry Brand, a supremely talented footballer and full-back, was an essential part of South Africa's domination of the world of Rugby in the 1930's. His left-footed place-kicking won many matches for his country. Young players looking at the lower photograph might not realise that until comparatively recently, the ball had to be held above the ground until the moment of the kick, when it was placed in position by the player lying on the ground.

so increasing the pressure on the opposition until they conceded either penalty kicks, which he accurately converted into goals, or the positions from which he was able to drop goals.

The iron strength and the technical ability of the Springbok forwards in the scrums all but overwhelmed the All Blacks in the early matches and Osler took advantage of that superiority to drop two goals, then worth four points each, and kick two penalty goals in the first test alone. South Africa won the match 17–0 and Osler's 14 points remained an individual record score in a test match until Okey Geffin kicked five penalty goals against New Zealand in 1949.

The All Blacks had no comparable line kicker because they had to tour without Nepia. In those days, teams touring South Africa accepted without question that country's laws and customs about racial segregation. It was not until 1967 that New Zealand said, 'If we cannot bring our Maoris, we won't come'.

In 1928, both New Zealand and Nepia accepted his exclusion without question and without malice, and nearly 50 years later, when the British Lions toured New Zealand in 1977, Nepia's attitude was exactly the same. His only concern, like that of nearly all the Maori elders in the various tribes in New Zealand, was to hold out the hand of friendship to South Africa so that the Maoris could tour that country as Rugby players in their own right. 'We know what racial discrimination is all about because we have experienced it in our own country,' they said. 'We are just glad to know that now we would be welcomed in South Africa.'

Even without Nepia, the 1928 All Blacks came back to win the second test 7–6, and Phil Mostert, the Springboks hooker and captain, was honest enough to admit afterwards, 'It was their forwards who carried the day'. It took all Osler's kicking skill to nurse South Africa to victory by 11 points to six in the third test, even though the Springbok pack had been reinforced by the introduction of Boy Louw, to win the first of many caps for his country. For the last test, New Zealand brought back Mark Nicholls at fly-half, and his performance as he scored ten points out of New Zealand's win by 13 points to five only confirmed the bewilderment of all those who could not understand why he had been left out of the first three tests.

That series established that the games between South Africa and New Zealand had superseded those involving the four home countries as being for the mythical title of world Rugby champions, and this was a state of affairs not seriously challenged until South Africa failed to win an international in Britain in 1969–70, and the British Lions beat both New Zealand and South Africa in 1971 and 1974.

The footballing supremacy of Britain's colonies was confirmed when the Springboks toured Britain again in 1931–32. South Africa were captained by Bennie Osler, who frankly admitted that he was past his best and playing the worst Rugby of his career. Nevertheless, that Springbok team won all four internationals against England, Scotland, Ireland and Wales and was beaten only once, by Midland Counties at Leicester.

The Springboks were criticised for playing the new style of ten-man Rugby almost throughout the tour, but Osler was unrepentant. He felt that the South African forwards were so good and that Gerry Brand had developed into such an outstanding full-back and goalkicker that the Springboks would have been foolish to play any other way, particularly as their midfield backs suffered so many injuries on tour.

'We played to our strength,' said Osler. 'We had a magnificent pack, and we had outstanding scrum-halves in Craven and de Villiers. We also had a match-winning full-back in Gerry Brand. Our best wing, Jock van Niekerk, was injured right at the beginning of the tour, and several of our other attacking threequarters were also injured. Our steadiest centre, J. C. van der Westhuizen, as well as the other senior players, were in general agreement with my tactics on the heavy grounds we invariably encountered in Britain.'

Boy Louw, a delightful rock of a man who had a hilarious stock of malapropisms in his attempts to master the English language, played in all the greatest Springbok scrummaging teams until the outbreak of the

---

The Midland Counties of England have a fine record against touring sides, despite the handicap of playing always as a scratch combination. Here they are in white shirts playing against the Springboks at Leicester in 1931–32. The youthful Danie Craven is pictured on the alert behind his forwards waiting to see the outcome of the lineout. The numbering of players was then in the reverse order of what it is today. The massive Ferdie Bergh is the Springbok forward in the white scrum-cap about to win the ball.

second world war, and he has said that the 1931–32 Springbok team in Britain was unquestionably the best pack he ever played in, better even than the legendary 1937 Springboks who won the series in New Zealand. Louw had with him in the front row his brother Fanie, and behind him they had Ferdie Bergh, 6 ft 4 in and 16 stone, who was an absolute giant of a lock by current European standards. The sheer strength and physique of that Springbok pack impressed everyone who saw them and who tried to play against them, and to those who were interested, it emphasised again what a good diet and unremitting hard work and an open air life could do to genetics. Bergh was not only a physical colossus in those days, but he was also extremely mobile, because he scored seven tries for his country and that stood as a Springbok record for more than twenty-five years.

Another significant innovation was introduced by a young scrum-half called D. H. Craven. He was only selected for the tour as a rank outsider and that was entirely due to the selectorial genius of a man called A. F. Markotter, whose ability to discern the footballing essentials served South Africa marvellously well at a time when travel within that vast and inaccessible country was almost impossible. Craven's selection for the tour was greeted with such ribald disdain by the newspaper in Bloemfontein, near his home in Orange Free State, that his father cancelled his subscription! Craven moved from his home town of Lindley to study at Stellenbosch University near Cape Town, and Markotter nursed him

Danie Craven, then only 22 years of age but already considered the best scrum-half in the world, scores the first try for South Africa at Newlands in the 1933 series against Australia.

through the junior sides with a judicious mixture of the whip and the carrot until he was selected for the tour of Britain.

On that tour, Craven developed a dive pass which added the impetus of his diving body to the strength of throw in his arms and so enabled him to give his fly-half a far quicker and longer pass than had been possible hitherto. He won his place in the international team and so began a career which was to make him one of the greatest men in the history of Rugby football, first as player, then as captain, and on through the positions of coach and manager to gain the experience which made him such a determined and formidable adversary as an international nego-tiator before he became president of the South African Rugby Board.

All that was a long way in the future when the 1931 Springboks left for Britain on the *Windsor Castle*, surely an infinitely more civilised way of getting to know one's team-mates and beginning a tour than sitting packed like cattle for 24 hours in an aircraft, short of sleep and short of privacy, unshaven, feet swelling, body smelling, revolted equally by what is laughingly called both the food and the conveniences on board. The 1931 Springboks had their problems on the *Windsor Castle*, too. They lost three new practice balls overboard and in trying to stop one hurtling over the side, Jock van Niekerk hurt a knee so badly that his tour was ruined and his career brought to an end.

When the Springboks arrived, they played so poorly that they had to rely on two dropped goals and two penalty goals to win their first match 14–3 but they improved by scoring four tries in the next match against Newport. They then beat Swansea 10–3 in one of the roughest matches ever seen in Wales and the crowd was so incensed that the players had to stay locked in their dressing rooms until things quietened down. There was more trouble against Abertillery and Cross Keys, and the team did not settle down until the game against London, when they scored six tries, all converted immaculately by Gerry Brand. The defensive pattern of the tour had already been established, and an exceptionally wet winter did not encourage the Springboks to expand their game. It could be argued that their results justified Osler's choice of a kicking game, but they disappointed the Rugby fraternity in their own country as much as they disappointed the Rugby public in Britain.

5 South Africa conquers the world

Despite these criticisms, the decade of Rugby before the second world war was dominated by South Africa. New Zealand Rugby was at its lowest point since the turn of the century and although they beat the British Lions 3–1 in 1930, the All Blacks found the road much harder when they toured Britain in 1935. They only lost three matches, to Swansea, Wales and England, but after the 1905 and the 1924 All Blacks, that was at least two defeats more than the New Zealand public regarded as acceptable.

New Zealand's greatest problem, as it had been for years, was their lack of scrummaging technique, particularly in the front row. Propping had become an art, and so had hooking, and the All Blacks were still suffering from the legacy of their adherence to the seven-man scrummage.

Despite that, the All Blacks lost only 13–12 to Wales, and that only in the last five minutes after coming back from 10–3 down to lead 10–12. Wales were served by the genius of Haydn Tanner, scarcely more than a schoolboy, and Cliff Jones at half-back, with the tall, long-striding Wilf Wooller in the centre alongside Claude Davey, a stocky, powerful man, who tackled as hard as anyone ever has. Wooller had already made one try with a thrilling kick and chase when in the closing minutes of the game, he did it again. What made the achievement even more remarkable was the fact that by then, Wales were playing a man short. A scrum had collapsed and one of the Welsh front row, Don Tarr, had broken his neck. Indeed, it was only the presence of mind of the referee, Cyril Gadney, that saved Tarr's life, because he refused to allow Tarr to be moved without medical supervision.

Replacements for injured players were not allowed in Britain then, but Wales somehow found enough strength to make one final thrust. Wooller broke through in the centre and kicked over the New Zealand full-back and was in despair when he was beaten by a wicked bounce of the ball. However, Rees Jones was following up from the wing and he caught the ball to score the winning try.

The All Blacks were soundly beaten in only one match, and that was by England. New Zealand could find no way to contain the speed of the England right wing, a Russian prince by the name of Alex Obolensky, and he scored two tries to give England a 13–0 victory. One of the tries Obolensky scored is ranked with the classics of the game. According to his contemporaries, Obolensky was not a great wing but he was a marvellous athlete, and such was his speed that on one occasion he was able to come all the way across field from the right touch-line to round the New Zealand defence and score to the left of the posts. It was one of the first tries to appear on the news reels of the rapidly developing film industry and so it is still possible to admire the easy grace of Obolensky's apparently effortless running.

The tight forward problems experienced by All Blacks in Britain in 1935–36 were made to look even more serious when New Zealand lost a series at home to South Africa in 1937. Fred Allen, the coach of the supremely successful 1967 All Blacks, says wryly that the 1937 Springboks were the best team ever to leave New Zealand, but neither Boy Louw nor Dr Danie Craven think that the 1937 team was as good as the one that had toured Britain six years earlier.

The only hiccough in this era of South African conquest occurred in 1933, when Australia's first full representative team startled their hosts

Prince Alexander Obolensky, who scored two tries for England when they beat New Zealand in 1936, playing for the Rest when they beat England 17–3 in the final trial in 1939. A few months after this photograph was taken, Obolensky was killed in a flying training accident.

even more than the rest of the world by winning two tests in a drearily protracted five-match series.

The first Wallabies earned a lot of respect from their opponents in South Africa, even when they were losing matches in the build-up to the first test. They developed a wide-ranging style of play, based on the ability of Bill Cerutti, Aub Hodgson and others in a mobile pack to get to the loose ball, and the capacity of Australia's talented backs to react to impromptu situations. This convinced South African thinkers, and particularly Bennie Osler, that the last thing the heavy Springbok pack could afford to do was take on the Australians at their own game. South Africa's rise to world domination had been based on the temporary advantages of sheer physique which a superior diet and open air life had given to their farmers, particularly those born of Afrikaaner stock. This gave their forwards a physical presence which literally overwhelmed their opponents, particularly in the scrummage and the lineout, but Osler knew that the South African pack would only continue to exercise that domination as long as the forward play remained fairly static, and therefore his kicking was essential. The trouble was that this kicking game was not spectacular, and consequently it was not popular. Inevitably, the pressure started to grow in South Africa for the Springboks to expand the range of their game.

Both the South African selectors and the Springbok team ignored this pressure in the first test. Osler kicked the leather off the ball, the South African forwards played the game as tight as they could, and the Springboks went grinding on to a convincing 17–3 win. This was not enough for the South African public, who much admired the Australians' dashing style of play. Bennie Osler, who had lost the captaincy to Phil Nel, formed the impression that it was not enough for his country's Rugby authorities either.

Accordingly, in the second test, Osler decided to run the ball. As he had been restored to the captaincy because of an injury to Nel, he was in a position to change the tactics as he pleased. The result was a disaster for South Africa. Their ponderous forwards simply could not cope with a running game and they were beaten 21–6, at that time the heaviest defeat in the Springboks' history. The Springboks won the third and fourth tests to take the series, but Australia showed their resilience yet again by winning the final test 15–4. No one took much pleasure from the game though, and it convinced the South African Rugby Union that five matches in a test series was one too many.

In that series, the Australians showed that in every generation, they were capable of producing some world-class players. Even then, their problem was to hang on to them in face of the money offered by Rugby League, a rapidly growing game in Australia. The Australians also showed that whatever else they lacked, they certainly were not short of spirit. The explosive zeal of forwards like Cerutti and Hodgson is remembered still, and when the British Lions went through Australia in 1971 on their way to New Zealand, they met Aub Hodgson and enjoyed him for the character he was and obviously always had been.

The Springboks had good cause to remember him, because when they went through Australia on their way to their victorious tour of New Zealand in 1937, Aub did his full share of looking after himself and any other of his team-mates who felt in need of care and protection. South Africa won both the test matches played, but after taking a 26 point half-time lead in the second test, the Springboks found themselves embroiled in such a rough-house of a second half that those who saw it and played in it still contend that it was the dirtiest test match ever played. With the Springbok scrum-half Pierre de Villiers stretched out unconscious, Hodgson and Harry Martin, one of the South African forwards, had a stand-up fight. The Springboks took a poor view of Hodgson's tactic of taking the ball and driving straight at de Villiers and then generously giving the ball to him. As soon as de Villiers took hold of the ball, Hodgson and the Australian forwards smashed him down and rucked over the top of him. Even with plate cameras, the local photographers in Sydney finished up

Warming up for New Zealand! Springbok Harry Martin looks a bit apprehensive about taking on a bantam cock as fiery as Aub Hodgson in the first of the two tests the Springboks played in Australia before going on to New Zealand in 1937. The cause of the argument is lying prostrate in the background.

Above: The big five of Springbok Rugby in New Zealand in 1937, from left to right: Danie Craven, Gerry Bland, Lucas Strachan, 'Boy' Louw and Phil Nel. South Africa won the series against New Zealand 2–1.
Below: Ron King and Danie Craven lead their teams on to the field for the first test between New Zealand and South Africa in 1937. The forward behind Craven is Ferdie Bergh, one of the anchor men of the mighty Springbok pack.

with more pictures of punches being thrown than in a 15 round heavy-weight championship fight. No wonder Aub Hodgson smiled a far-away smile in 1971 when someone waxed indignant about the appalling incidence of violence in modern Rugby!

Perhaps Aub Hodgson and that fiery Australian pack did the 1937 Springboks a good turn, because Australia scored 11 points without reply in that tumultuous second half. The Springboks never lost their cool again and were ready for anything when they arrived in New Zealand.

As it turned out, however, they were not too severely exercised, because as Danie Craven himself says, 'In a way, the 1937 Springboks were lucky. We struck New Zealand at a low ebb. They were so used to breaking quickly from the scrum and the lineout so that they could use their forwards in cover defence that in the early games, we often found their locks tackling our wings. We knew then that the answer was to pin them down in the scrum by pushing them and to hold the ball in the lineout to bring them in. Then we would let the ball out, and their backs were so used to having the assistance of their forwards in defence that when they had to defend by themselves, they couldn't do it. And we had brilliant backs. So that was the pattern. Our forwards pushed them enough to keep them on their heels, and we drove enough from the lineout to pull their forwards in, and then we used our backs.'

The 1937 Springboks won the series despite losing the first test 13–7, which they approached altogether too lightheartedly after smashing the provincial opposition in New Zealand. They were also short of some key players through injury and they compounded their problems by opting for a kicking game and choosing Danie Craven at fly-half. He disagreed with this decision strongly at the time, and his view was amply borne out by the result.

However, the Springboks chose the right team for the second test which they won despite a demoralising set-back early in the game when the All Blacks, defending for their lives, made an interception and Jack Sullivan streaked away to score the first of two tries. With their crushing scrummage superiority, the Springboks could afford to wait, because that sort of forward advantage always pays its richest dividends in the last twenty minutes of a match. In that time, the Springboks not only came back, but pulled away to win 13–6.

The victory was not achieved without some alarms. Apart from Sullivan's tries, the Springboks were disconcerted by another injury to their massive prop, Boy Louw, who had missed the first test. In the second test, he was so badly concussed that he scarcely knew what he was doing, and to make the whole thing even more unnerving, his concussion had the effect of giving him a never-ending fit of the giggles! This made it difficult for friend and foe to concentrate, and it must have lulled Dalton, one of the All Black props, into a false sense of security.

Dalton had been making life awkward for Craven at scrum-half, by breaking through on to him from the lineout. In the middle of his giggles, Boy Louw kept asking what was going on and what should he do, so in exasperation, Craven told him to stop Dalton coming through the lineout. At the next lineout, Louw stood simpering by Dalton and sailed into him with everything. The referee was following the ball, and did not see what turned out to be an almost thermo-nuclear hatchet job.

'Was that what you wanted, Danie?' giggled Louw delightedly.

'No, Boy,' said Craven, 'but it will have to do'.

Giggling or no, Louw and his brother Fanie, combined with hooker Jan Lotz, gave the Springboks a weight advantage of nearly five stones in the front row alone. Just before the final test, they received a famous telegram from South Africa urging them simply to 'Skrum, skrum, skrum', but by then, they did not need such a statement of the obvious to remind them what they had to do. They just went out and did it. The Springboks scored two tries in the first half and then wrapped the game up by scoring a third try from a decoy move.

Craven waved his half-back partner, Tony Harris, further and further away until Harris was standing in the middle of the field. The All Blacks had such a healthy respect for the power of Craven's dive pass that Trevathan, their first five-eighth, took the bait and moved right across to mark Harris. When the ball came out of the scrum, Craven slipped it to

The dive pass from scrum-half that Danie Craven introduced to the world of Rugby. The All Blacks did not know how to counter it in the 1937 series.

Turner running in from the blind side wing, and he carved through the huge gap straight up to the New Zealand full-back. Turner drew Taylor and a simple transfer by 'Flappie' Lochner in the centre gave Louis Babrow his second try. That finished the All Blacks, and although Gerry Brand kicked only one conversion (he felt that there was something wrong with the ball), South Africa scored five tries to two penalty goals and won 17–6.

South Africa sustained this brilliance the following year, when Craven replaced Philip Nel as captain and the Springboks beat the British Lions. Dr Craven regards South Africa's performance against the Lions in the first test as one of his country's greatest performances on the Rugby field. The Springboks won 26–12, despite some fantastic goalkicking by the Lions' full-back, Vivian Jenkins, and in doing so they repeated the move they had used against the All Blacks the year before to make so much room for Turner on the blind side wing.

This time, Jeff Reynolds, the Lions' fly-half, thought that it was an attempt to push the defence across field to make room for an attack on the blind side, but again Turner came in from the wing and again Lochner linked before putting Dai Williams in for a try on the right. The try was

Danie Craven preparing to kick after breaking from a scrum against the British Lions at Cape Town in 1938. The Springbok pack is already moving across to obstruct, in the most gentlemanly way, of course, and to support!

converted with a beautiful kick by Gerry Brand, and the Springboks led for the first time, 8–6, Vivian Jenkins having already kicked two magnificent penalty goals for the Lions.

Brand's goal kicking was as inspired as that of his opponent, and it was a goal he dropped from a penalty kick inside his own half that broke the Lions. Even Brand did not think that he could get the distance, but Craven asked him to try and the whipping power in his left boot sent the ball curving over the bar. It was Brand's last test, and he finished by pushing his way back into the crowd to make enough room to convert the final try from the touch-line. Craven had to clear burning cigarette stubs from the pitch before he could lie down to hold the ball off the ground for his kicker and the sight of Brand straining back in the arms of a well-built lady in the crowd prompted him to remark, 'Gerry, if you get this one over, I'll buy you a farm in Eloff Street'.

'Just you watch,' grinned Brand, and he catapulted forward in a drastically shortened run-up to kick his sixth goal of the match and equal his own record of scoring 14 points in a test. It was the perfect ending to Brand's remarkable international career. Injury prevented him from playing in the other two tests and then the war came to end all in-

Wilson Shaw, Scotland's fly-half, making an acrobatic kick against England at Twickenham in 1936. England won 9–8. Two years after this match, Shaw won the Triple Crown for his country with a brilliant display at fly-half which enabled Scotland to win 21–16 at Twickenham.

ternational Rugby for seven years, by which time Brand's own Rugby playing days were over. His first captain, Bennie Osler, thought that Brand was an even better winger than full-back, in which case it is possible that great as his career was, he had even more depths of versatility which were not fully exploited in international Rugby.

The 1938 Lions lost the second test at Durban, and with it the series, in tropical heat of such exhausting intensity that some of the forwards hardly knew that the score was 19–3 when the match ended. They had dehydrated to the point where they were near collapse.

Against all the odds, the Lions came back to win the last test at Newlands, and win it well, but in an age when travel was far more time-consuming than it is now, they knew that it simply was not possible to beat South Africa in a test series without the best available team. With New Zealand and South African players, the honour and prestige of playing for their country on a tour abroad took precedence over everything; in Britain it did not. Business commitments and other considerations always prevented the British Lions from touring with anything like their best team, and by then, New Zealand and South African Rugby was technically so far ahead of the game in Britain, that only the best of Britain's individual skills could have narrowed or closed the gap.

5 The banishment of France

Ironically, that pre-war decade, so glorious for South Africa, was full of ignominy for France. The Four Home Unions had been concerned for some time about the spread of professionalism in France and in the end lost patience to such an extent that in February, 1931, they announced that all fixtures with France, at both club and international level, would be abandoned after the end of the current season.

Trouble had been brewing for a long time. As early as 1913, only seven years after France had played international Rugby for the first time, against England, the International Board wrote to France to protest about the threatening behaviour of the crowd towards both the referee and the Scottish players in the recent match between France and Scotland in Paris. The Board warned the Union des Sociétés Françaises de Sport Athletique that 'unless they take adequate steps to prevent the recurrence of such treatment, international matches with France will have to cease'.

The French Union apologised for the behaviour of the Paris crowd, which was then even more ignorant of the laws of Rugby football than French crowds are today, and promised to do all they could to prevent a recurrence. England, Ireland and Wales then agreed to continue their matches against France, but the Scots were not so easily mollified. They refused to play France in 1914.

The appalling years of the Great War healed the breach, but France did not seem to be in the least abashed by what had happened. Indeed, they applied to join the International Board themselves, and repeated their request in 1920, but on both occasions their application was refused. However, in 1924 France was invited to attend a meeting of the International Board.

In view of what was already happening in France, it was as well that the Board did maintain a position of some reserve, because Rugby football spread so rapidly through France, and was received so enthusiastically, particularly in the South West, that French Rugby soon found itself facing precisely the same dilemma as that which had faced English Rugby when the Northern clubs broke away to form the Rugby League in 1892. The causes of the trouble were the same, too. The popular appeal of Rugby football was such that the clubs found themselves taking large sums of money at the gate, and a fair proportion of that money soon found its way into the pockets of the players, particularly the good ones.

The Four Home Unions could not have been all that well informed about the exact mechanics of the professionalism, because the heart-lands of French Rugby were far more remote than they are today, but the French were so carelessly imprudent, probably because it did not occur to them to be otherwise, that even Dr Watson would have found the detective job fairly elementary. Players moved from small clubs to the big ones for better money, and the star players were delighted to find themselves in much the same position as the modern soccer player. French Rugby footballers also thought nothing of switching from Rugby Union to Rugby League and back again.

The catalyst for all this player bargaining was the French club championship. Rugby football arrived comparatively late in France, but as soon as it did, the essentially practical French could see no point whatever in playing it unless there was a bit of competition involved. The Four Home Unions kept bleating about the essence of Rugby football being concerned with friendly games between clubs, but as far as the French were concerned, that was for the *oiseaux*. Friendly matches only served the purpose of getting the players fit for the real thing. Accordingly, the French inaugurated a club championship in 1906, only twenty-three years after the first recorded game of Rugby football between two French clubs. This championship is, as a result, the oldest national club championship in the Rugby world. It is true that the Border League in Scotland pre-dates it, but as its name implies, the Border League is not a national championship.

Before the first world war, French international Rugby was comfortably dismissed as second class, so it must have come as a nasty shock to the Scots when France beat them in 1911. This was France's first victory in international Rugby, and when they beat Scotland at Murrayfield in 1978, they achieved parity with Scotland for the first time in the international series between the two countries.

In 1920, the USFSA, which sounds like an American fencing society, disappeared from the scene in French Rugby and was replaced as the organising body by the Federation Française de Rugby. Shortly after that, twelve of the leading French clubs seceded to form the Union Française de Rugby Amateur, but when the Four Home Unions broke off all playing contact with France at the end of the 1930–31 season, these clubs rejoined the Federation.

Curiously enough, the minutes of the International Rugby Football Board contain no reference to the decision taken by the representatives of the Four Home Unions to abandon fixtures with France, but the wording of the resolution was:

After examination of the documentary evidence furnished by the French Federation and the dissentient clubs, we are compelled to state that owing to the unsatisfactory condition of the game of Rugby Football as managed and played in France, neither our Union nor the Clubs or Unions under its jurisdiction will be able to arrange or fulfil fixtures with France, or French Clubs, at home or away, after the end of this season, unless and until we are satisfied that the control and conduct of the game have been placed on a satisfactory basis in all essentials.

Throughout the 1930s, there were meetings between the Home Unions and the French Federation, but the French were not able to satisfy the British that they had made enough progress towards purging their game of professionalism, even though the rapidly worsening international situation with Hitler's Germany provided a climate in which there was an instinctive desire to put the whole sorry business behind them and re-forge the alliance that would be so obviously necessary in the war to come.

On March 17, 1939, the Four Home Unions approved the following letter to the French Federation.

Dear Sir,

The letters that I have received from you and M. Dedet were brought before the Representatives of the Four Home Unions at their meeting today.

I have been instructed to inform you on behalf of the Four Home Unions of Great Britain and Ireland that further consideration has recently been given to the unfortunate circumstances underlying the severance of relations between the Federation Française de Rugby and ourselves.

It is felt that the time has arrived to make it clear that progress cannot be made towards a rapprochement between the Rugby Football Unions of England, Scotland, Ireland and Wales, and your Federation, without a clear analysis of the situation which has existed since matches of every kind were banned because it was admitted that within the Federation Française de Rugby there had been:

a Payments to players.

b Non compliance with the spirit of the Laws laid down by the International Rugby Football Board of Great Britain and Ireland.

Your Federation was reluctantly informed that relations could not be resumed until such time as they had put their house in order.

It is right to say that such unofficial information as has reached us from time to time led us to believe that although much has been done, the conduct of affairs is still unsatisfactory.

In these circumstances, we feel that the Federation Française might appreciate it if we specified clearly certain fundamental conditions which must be fulfilled before it can be considered that the game under their control is administered and played as it is in the Four Home Countries. These conditions are as follows:

1 That no player who has been proved guilty of receiving payment, other than actual out-of-pocket travelling and hotel expenses, is ever allowed to

play Rugby Football again, or to act in any official capacity in connection with any Rugby Football Club.

2　That no official who has been concerned in, or has countenanced the payment of players, continues to serve as an official of any Club or federation of Clubs.

3　That no paid coach or trainer is employed by any football organisation.

4　That no player ordered off the field of play is allowed to take further part in that game, or play again until his case has been dealt with by the Federation or other governing body to which the necessary powers have been delegated.

5　That the game is played strictly in accordance with the Laws framed by the International Rugby Football Board.

The real foundation of the game as played in our countries is the friendly match between Clubs.

It is not for the Four Unions to lay down whether or not leagues or Club championships should be instituted and played for in other countries, but as the result of their lengthy experience and in the desire to be of assistance to the Federation Française de Rugby, they would tender the advice that the Federation would find that it would be more effective in the prevention of veiled professionalism and foul play if competitive football such as Club championships were barred.

The Home Unions are pleased to note from M. Dedet's letters that it is the proposal of the Federation Française de Rugby to adopt this principle. They hope that their expression of opinion will be of assistance to your Federation at their meeting in May.

It is clear from that letter that the gap between France and the Home Unions was still enormous, and it is equally clear that if its conditions had been met in full, there would have been no one left either to play the game or to administer it in France. Similarly, it is inconceivable that the French clubs would ever have agreed to abandon their club championship, yet France were so desperate to be re-admitted to international Rugby that when the Federation met in May, their representatives actually agreed that this would be done.

Accordingly, with war only two months away, the Four Home Unions resolved:

At a meeting of the Representatives of the Four Home Unions held in London on July 7, 1939, to consider relations with the French Rugby Federation, correspondence from that body explaining their actions was considered. In view of the decisions and undertakings of the French Rugby Federation, the Representatives of the Four Home Unions decided to recommend to each Home Union that they should resume relations with the French Rugby Federation.

There is no doubt that this decision was influenced more by the imminent war with Germany than by anything the French had done to 'put their house in order'. Indeed, it is hard to avoid the conclusion that the French *maison de Rugby* was just as much a house of ill fame as it had ever been, because although all four home countries resumed international matches against France in 1947, and British clubs took themselves across the channel with renewed enthusiasm to sample the delights of a country where food rationing had been abolished and where the pound sterling was still as strong as the local wine, there were several tricky moments. In 1953, the Scots arrived in Paris and told their hosts quite bluntly that if a certain former Rugby League player was not removed at once from the French team selected to play them, they, the Scots, would go straight back home.

Even before that, in 1951, the International Board was again so concerned about the state of the game in France that it wrote another letter to the French Federation, recalling the conditions of acceptance laid down in 1939. Amateurism was still very much an ideal for clubs with no money, referees were still subject to abuse and threat of physical violence and foul play was not properly controlled, or punished.

In particular, the International Board regretted that the French club championship was still flourishing like the green bay tree and so in 1952, the harassed French Federation officials announced that their executive committee had decided unanimously to abolish it. This never happened, because once again the outraged French clubs simply would not allow it to happen, but it now looks as if only that promise of action prevented the Four Home Unions breaking off relations with France again for the 1953 international season.

The Four Home Unions were still tut-tutting away in 1957, and asking for assurances, etc., and the French under the astute M. Renee Crabos, were still tut-tutting away in unison, and saying that it was all very difficult, and a thousand regrets, and promising to be, if not good boys, at least better boys next year.

By 1958, though, the International Board, to all intents and purposes, had given up the struggle to reform the French. Perhaps they were aware that the game in some of their own countries had always had a good few motes in its eyes, and the motes were multiplying rapidly. At all events, the French must have smiled infinitely Gallic smiles of contentment when, early in 1958, they received the following letter from the International Board.

Dear Monsieur le President,
First of all, I wish, on my own behalf and on behalf of the members of my Board, to thank you and your colleagues in the French Federation for all the kindness and hospitality extended to us during our visit to Paris last month.

All members of the Board who were in Paris agree that the meeting was fruitful and has strengthened those feelings of mutual understanding and respect which are so desirable in international relations, not least in the field of amateur sport.

The members of the Board were very glad to take note of the assurance which you offered that whatever decisions or principles the Board might see fit to make or adopt so as to secure uniformity in the Rules against Professionalism would be followed by your Federation.

They were also glad to have on record the agreement between the Home Unions and the French Federation, which was worded as follows:

'Representatives of the Four Home Unions met representatives of the Federation Française de Rugby in Paris today. The circumstances of Rugby Football in the present stage of rapid extension and other matters of common concern were carefully discussed with complete unanimity of view. The Meeting confirmed and emphasised the previous decision not to approve participation by representative teams or by their Clubs in any new competition or tournament of an International character whatever the venue.'

I feel I should add, without presumption, that we were gratified to learn from the talks with you that the primary object of policy of yourself, M. le President, and of your Federation is to maintain and cultivate the friendship and confidence of the Four Home Unions and that your domestic administrative measures continue to be directed to the support of that policy.

As an exercise in the enunciation of a policy of masterly inactivity, it could not have been bettered either by Stanley Baldwin or James Callaghan. It must have been a good weekend.

From that moment in 1958, the attitude in Britain towards professionalism in Rugby football and towards the principle of club championships began to slide towards the position defended so tenaciously by France, rather than the other way round. All France did was to go on doing precisely what they had always done, and ever so gradually, most of the Four Home Unions found themselves doing the same. Only a few of the clubs in England and Wales yet offer their players the lucrative opportunities in business which the rich patrons of French clubs do, but the practice is undoubtedly spreading even in Britain and in most other respects, the British player is now as much involved in club championships and twilight professionalism as his counter-part in France.

The French must have permitted themselves one final Gallic smile of infinite contentment when, in 1978, after 66 years of trying, their umpteenth application to join the International Rugby Football Board was finally accepted, and they were admitted as full members.

The re-admission of France to international Rugby was one of the three most profound influences on the game when it moved into the second half of the twentieth century. The other two both involved extraordinary improvements in communication, first the technical miracle of television and its unparalleled spread across the world, and second, the advances in air travel made possible by the colossal sums of money spent on aircraft development in the second world war.

France brought a new dimension to the world of Rugby. At first it was simply a question of style and ambition; marvellously flamboyant handling by a succession of invariably brilliant backs who had grown up with the confidence of invariably playing attacking Rugby with a dry ball on a dry ground. However it went even further than that. France swept aside the convention that forwards were only workhorses whose job it was to win the ball and then just run along faithfully in support while the *prima-donnas* behind the scrum luxuriated in their running and handling skills. French forwards showed that as far as they were concerned, there were no demarcation lines when it came to handling the ball. Even their locks started running and they joined in with such spectacular enthusiasm that they sent the game tumbling headlong towards the concept of what became known as 15 man Rugby.

It is true that the extravagance of this concept meant that many of the forward disciplines were ignored, or allowed to lapse, but it may have been that the French were unconsciously reacting, in the way that nature has, to a world where their forwards had always been at an enormous physical disadvantage. Without the benefit of infant welfare, and with the highest rate of infant *delirium tremens* in the world, their menfolk at that time simply did not grow big enough to match the physique of the Anglo-Saxons. So their forwards learned to handle and run instead.

France also stopped being imitators of the Anglo-Saxons, and became significant innovators instead. They thought about the game with sufficient depth to evolve the lineout peel and they extended the principle to the back of the scrum, where they introduced the churn. Their play lacked the steel of really solid team-work, but as more and more people saw it either through television or in person, and as France went on tours of the Southern hemisphere for the first time, that play influenced the whole world.

By no stretch of the imagination could a French forward be called a 'donkey', which was what the forwards of the 1959 British Lions called themselves with an engaging disparagement. Even such an unashamedly physical specimen as Alfred Roques, that great balding bull of a French prop, adored being involved in handling movements, and so did every other French forward.

7 The end of the Springboks' reign, and Ireland's golden years

International Rugby did not start again after the war until 1947, but the game had enjoyed a colourful existence throughout the hostilities. Both Rugby Union and Rugby League players were able to play in the same teams in the Services, with the result that the greatest players in the world were able to turn out and play if they happened to be posted near at hand, or if they had a commanding officer interested in the game.

Bleddyn Williams joined the RAF early in 1942 as a youngster almost straight out of Rydal School, and he always recalls with gratitude the pleasure and the knowledge he derived from playing alongside Rugby League heroes like Willie Davies and Gus Risman. 'They had a profound influence on my career,' he says, and as Bleddyn Williams became one of the greatest centre-threequarters the game has seen, British Rugby can only look regretfully yet again at the split which has divided it for so long.

Those war-time games did more than keep Rugby football going, because they poured the whole world of Rugby, both professional and amateur, into the same melting pot. The benefits deriving from it, in social and playing contacts, and in the exchange of techniques, were of value to all the Rugby playing countries of the world for years to come.

Rugby posts were dug into the ground in so many strange places in the world and so close to the front lines that the Germans and Japanese must have thought that they were some strange new radar aerials! The New Zealand Division once played a game against the South Africans in nothing but sand in the desert of North Africa.

Rugby football had been re-started after the first world war by an Inter-Services tournament involving all the major countries of what was then the Rugby-playing world, and the commanding officer of the New Zealand Division, General Freiburg, had the idea of raising a New Zealand army team to tour the British Isles when the second world war ended in 1945.

That team was captained by Charlie Saxton, himself an All Black whose play at scrum-half was one of the most significant influences on the teaching of the game in that position. General Freiburg obtained permission from the New Zealand Government to organise the tour, and they also guaranteed the team's expenses!

'That would be the strangest selected team that I think there has ever been,' said Charlie. 'Players were allowed to nominate themselves to be interviewed by selectors. The New Zealand Division was stretched from Trieste in the North of Italy over to the base in North Africa. It was a tremendous area to cover, and there were New Zealanders all over the place. But the selectors sorted out the players somehow. They sent forty of us to Italy straight away to practise and then they sent a further twenty down after a series of trials in Austria. It was every bit as good as an All Black team, although I was the only All Black in it at the time. Mind you, there were some great players in it. A lot of them subsequently became All Blacks, and I think all except two played for their provinces. Fred Allen, Neil McPhail, Jack Finlay, Johnny Smith, Bob Scott, Johnny Simpson – they were all there. They did a great job on tour in Britain and France and Germany, and then when they got back home, they did a great job for their provinces. It was a tremendous contribution to New Zealand Rugby, and it lasted a long time. Eric Boggs was one of the players in that Kiwi side of 1945 and yet he was still selector and coach of Auckland in 1977.'

Bleddyn Williams has equally fond memories of the Kiwis. 'That was the first time that players of my generation in this country saw really organised forward play. At that time, our forwards generally played the game off the cuff. Their game was much more loose, and I must say I enjoyed it immensely, but there is no doubt that those Kiwis showed us the way we would have to go. They were one of the better New Zealand sides, too, because they did not confine the game to their forwards. They used their backs, and they had some great players there. Johnny Smith, for example, was probably the best centre I ever played against in my life.'

The Kiwis were highly successful in Britain. The only international match they lost was against Scotland. They should have gone to South Africa as All Blacks almost as soon as they returned home but New Zealand's planned tour had to be postponed until 1949 and so the first major tour after the war turned out to be that of Australia to Britain, Ireland and France in 1947–48. The Wallabies had had to wait even longer for their tour than the Kiwis, because a full Australian team had arrived in Britain in 1939 at the time war was declared. They went back home without playing a match. Most of the players went to war instead.

Only one of the 1939 team was selected for the 1947–48 tour. He was Bill McLean, a member of a famous Australian Rugby family, and he came back as captain. However, he had the misfortune to break a leg early in the tour and the captaincy was taken over by Trevor Allen, who startled the crowd at the international against England at Twickenham by scorning the time-honoured convention of waiting for a ring of players to surround him while he changed his shorts, which had been torn, and then throwing the old ones in the air. Australians had no time for modesty. Allen took his shorts off as he stood in the open field and, with his buttocks gleaming and his jock strap clearly visible, he trotted twenty yards to receive his new shorts from an attendant. And that before Royalty, too! It was a sign of changed attitudes to come, but at the time, it caused more comment than Australia's thoroughly convincing victory, rounded off by a magnificently athletic try by Colin Windon. Australia beat Ireland and Scotland as well on that tour, and looked anything but a poor relation in Rugby football.

They were short of money, though, and when they let it be known that they would like to raise some cash so that they could play in America on their way home at the end of the tour, an extra match was arranged against the Barbarians. This was such a success that it has been a feature of every major tour of the United Kingdom since.

The Barbarians were formed in 1890, the same year as the International Board, and the club had developed a series of holiday fixtures, against Leicester at Christmas and with four games in Wales at Easter, to augment other special occasions. The Barbarians invited the best players from all four of the home countries to play in these games and consequently became an elite not far short of full international status.

The Barbarians beat Australia 9–6 in that first match, which was played at Cardiff. Above all, the Australians were happily provided with the money they needed, and by the time they returned to Australia, they knew that their achievement in beating Ireland would be remembered as something special, because later that season, Ireland won the Triple Crown for the first time for nearly fifty years.

That began the greatest period in the history of Irish Rugby. Ireland had a genius of an outside-half in Jack Kyle, a man who hated training, and they found a loose forward combination which was able to turn his promptings to profit. As Tommy Bedford says, great loose forwards tend to come in threes, because a top class back row is a precise blend of differing functions and talents, but there is no doubt that Jim McCarthy, Bill McKay and Des O'Brien produced exactly the right mix of ball-winning, ball-playing, speed, strength, tenacity and sheer unquenchable spirit that Ireland needed.

Kyle was an unobtrusive player. Cliff Morgan recalls that when he went out to play against him for the first time, he had been keyed up for days, and in his mind, had gone over and over the different facets of Kyle's play. 'But when I got out on the field at St Helens, nothing happened,' he says. 'Then, just when I had been lulled into a false sense of security, Jack suddenly took off and went past me to score a try which saved the game. What a player!'

While Ireland were climbing the heights with two Triple Crowns in successive seasons, New Zealand were plunging back into the depths. They had thought that the team-work and the playing personalities developed by the Kiwis at the end of the war would enable them to

Okey Geffin, the South African prop, whose goalkicking did so much to destroy the 1949 All Blacks.

challenge the world supremacy of the Springboks, but when the All Blacks, captained by Fred Allen, went to South Africa in 1949, they discovered that their fond hopes of glory were empty dreams. The All Blacks lost seven matches and drew three others on their 24 match tour. Even worse, they were beaten 4–0 in the test series.

New Zealand's problem was much the same as it had been twelve years earlier. They could not match South Africa in the scrummage. The years that New Zealand had spent in defending an outdated 2–3–2 scrummage formation were still taking their toll. The country just had not acquired that depth of knowledge of scrummage technique which was built into every province in South Africa.

The All Blacks were big enough to admit their deficiencies and they tried to repair them by taking instruction from the South Africans themselves, but you just cannot write a masterpiece within a matter of weeks of learning the alphabet. New Zealand had their problems with goalkicking, too, whereas South Africa were magnificently served by the bulky Transvaal prop, Okey Geffin. Injuries debilitated the team, and what they saw as home town refereeing demoralised them. This was to become a familiar tale of tours not only in South Africa, but New Zealand as well.

Geffin first played against a New Zealand team of sorts in a prisoner of war camp in Poland during the war, and even in bare feet, the goal-kicking of this squarely built Jewish boy gave the New Zealand inmates shivers of apprehension. The enormously talented Jewish people have rarely been noted for any very ardent participation in sport anywhere in the world, but curiously enough, they have a great tradition of eminence in South African Rugby, and Geffin had already attracted attention as a young goalkicker in Johannesburg just before the war. This was hardly surprising, because he once kicked twelve conversions out of 13 attempts in a match!

In those days, he was known as 'Ox' Geffin. He had no christian names on his birth certificate. 'How could I have Christian names,' he smiled later 'I was a Jewish boy.' Geffin shook his head and said regretfully, 'It cost me thirty rand to have my birth certificate altered to make it official that I am Aaron Okey Geffin'.

Geffin looked anything but a highly co-ordinated ball-player, which made it all the more ironic that he should have done so much to defeat an All Black team containing Bob Scott at full-back. Scott was an absolute artist of a player, as he demonstrated four years later on the All Blacks' tour of Britain, but in South Africa he suffered the tortures of the damned with his goalkicking.

The other great influence on the series was Hennie Muller, the Spring-bok number 8. Fred Allen, who went on to coach the All Blacks in one of the most successful periods in their history, captained that New Zealand team in South Africa as a midfield back and he still speaks about Muller with such rueful admiration that it is clear that the Springbok number eight's stature as a player was every bit as dominating as anyone who has played in that position before or since.

Muller achieved incredible standards of fitness for an amateur Rugby player and he carved through the New Zealand midfield like Genghis Khan on one of his better days. Muller wrought so much destruction that the All Blacks developed an absolute phobia about him, and when the Springboks backed this up by choosing a ferocious tackler like Ryk van Schoor in the centre, Muller was given plenty of loose ball to pick up as well. With their scrummage in a mess and with the team hopelessly outgunned at goalkicking, it was small wonder that the All Blacks lost.

In the first test match, Geffin kicked five penalty goals to give South Africa a victory so reminiscent of those later to be achieved by Don Clarke for New Zealand – and with the same outraged reaction from the opposition about the refereeing! The 15 points Geffin scored broke Gerry Brand's individual record of 14 points in an international match. Many years after, the referee, Eddie Hofmeyr defended with some spirit the decisions that had enabled Geffin to kick his way into the record books, and said that on one occasion, indeed, he had hesitated about whether to give South Africa a penalty try. Fred Allen growled, 'If he had awarded a penalty try, I would have taken the All Blacks off the field'. Not for nothing was Fred Allen known as 'The Needle'.

Before that game, the Springboks were a little uncertain of their current standards. They had not played major international Rugby for eleven years whereas the All Blacks had several players who had toured with the New Zealand Services team and who had also played against Australia in 1946. However, once Okey Geffin had given South Africa victory in the first test, the Springbok selectors, including Danie Craven, made some judicious changes and then sat back to watch their team pull right away under the astute control of fly-half Hannes Brewis. Like most of the leading South African fly-halves since Bennie Osler, Brewis supported his forwards mostly by kicking, but he confounded New Zealand utterly in the second test by scoring a brilliant individual try that won South Africa the match and gave them control of the series. He started with a dummy drop at goal from a scrum, a double back quickly to the blindside and then gathered himself as if to place a diagonal kick into the corner for his wing. As the defence hesitated, Brewis side-stepped, accelerated into the gap and dummied the cover defence on the line to score. Hannes Brewis had an international career that spoke for itself. He played in ten test matches for his country and South Africa won them all.

The 1949 series against the All Blacks established that South Africa were even further ahead of the rest of the world than they had been in 1937. The All Blacks were shattered. The New Zealand public could scarcely believe it.

Nevertheless, any notions that the All Blacks had lost their place as number two in the world of Rugby were firmly dispelled when the British Lions went to New Zealand in 1950. The All Blacks won the series 3–0 with the first test drawn. Inspired by Bleddyn Williams and Jack Kyle, the British backs played some beautiful football, particularly after the Welsh prodigy Lewis Jones had been flown out to join the team as a replacement for the injured Irish full-back George Norton. Jones was a magical full-back, with the most deceptive change of pace, but the Lions' forwards simply had no idea of how to match the organisation of the New Zealand pack.

Bleddyn Williams himself says, 'The game against Otago really hit us. I had never seen anything like their rucking in my life before, and neither had any of our forwards. We could hook the ball all right in the scrums, and we could win some ball in the lineout, but we simply could not match the ball-winning ability of the New Zealand forwards in the loose. We had no idea of how to match them. This opened all our eyes, and when we came back from that tour, we preached the gospel around Britain as long and as hard as we could. We tried to tell people how important it was for a pack to play as a unit like the All Blacks, particularly as far as rucking was concerned.

'I was only a back, just watching the whole exercise, but what impressed me so much was that the New Zealanders never concerned themselves with scratching for the ball, as we did. The ball stayed dead on the ground and the whole eight of their forwards went over the top of it

Bleddyn Williams

and left it in a stationary position for the scrum-half to pick up at his leisure. Now what better situation could a scrum-half be in than that – moving forward on to a stationary ball with all the opposition buried in front of him or cleared out of the way so that they could not interfere with what he wanted to do? That's what impressed me so much, but it depressed me that it took us about ten years to get it through the heads of the people in this country.'

Working in Otago, two of the greatest coaches in the history of the game, Vic Cavanagh Senior and Vic Cavanagh Junior, had taken Dave Gallaher's ruck and developed it into one of the most devastating attacking weapons in the game. The wetter grounds in the South Island suited the concept of the ruck, with a ram of forwards smashing over the top of the ball as soon as the opposition tried to contest possession. The sheer physical impetus of this stratagem either knocked the opposition off their feet or hurled them into disarray, and the two Cavanaghs spent their lives developing the technique. In effect, it was a running scrum, and they devised the body positions and the packing patterns of the participating forwards and worked out from experience what were the most effective follow-up plays. In the beginning, the ruck was a chance happening, but Vic Cavanagh and his son soon saw that it could be deliberately induced and used as a hammer to strike a blow and commit the opposition to physical contact almost wherever the attacking side chose.

The British forwards who played on the 1950 tour all confessed afterwards that it was a humbling and discouraging experience to be confronted with such daunting organisation as that built into the All Black pack. At the time, all the New Zealand forwards seemed to their visitors to be giants among men, but as the years passed, and the Lions forwards who played in 1950 acquired a sense of proportion about what had happened, they all agreed that one All Black forward stood out as the central rock in the citadel, and that was 'Tiny' White. For what he achieved in that series, and for what he achieved later, White must clearly be ranked among the half dozen greatest locks of all time.

Unfortunately, Lions teams have never been as representative of the best of British Rugby as the All Blacks and Springboks are of New Zealand and South Africa, because in Britain a Lions tour has never carried with it the national and social significance that All Black and Springbok tours have in New Zealand and South Africa. In those two countries, it is almost unheard of for a leading player not to be available to be chosen for a tour, whereas in Britain, there has never been a tour when all the best players were available. Ron Jacobs, one of the best props in Britain since the war, never made a Lions tour because of his commitments as a farmer; Gerald Davies went on only two tours when he could have gone on four; in 1938, players of the eminence of Cliff Jones, Wilf Wooller and Wilson Shaw were among many who simply could not spare the time.

Despite that, the Lions returned from their tour of New Zealand in 1950 thinking, 'If only . . .' They felt that British Rugby had enough skills and talent in the backs, and enough individual ability in the forwards, to make at least a shared series a possibility in New Zealand, providing enough work was done to develop the necessary organisation in the pack.

The forwards of the four home countries were not able to afford themselves the luxury of thinking like that the following year, when South Africa toured Britain. The Springboks were only beaten once and that was when Alan Grimsdell kicked some remarkable goals for a London Counties team captained by Johnny Matthews at Twickenham. In the internationals, South Africa won all their games, including the match against France, and in the course of winning them they inflicted upon Scotland the heaviest defeat sustained by any of the major countries in modern international Rugby. The Springboks won 44–0 and left Scottish Rugby absolutely devastated. South Africa scored nine tries, seven of them by their forwards, and Okey Geffin converted seven of them. Years after, Dr Danie Craven, the manager of the 1951 South African team, regretted the immensity of Scotland's humiliation. 'We should not have done that to them,' he said. 'We took away their pride and left them with nothing.'

'Tiny' White, the great New Zealand lock, storms away from a lineout in the match against Ireland in 1954.

Norman Mair, who incidentally was dropped by Scotland at hooker for that game, expresses the feeling exactly. 'It had the same effect on Scottish Rugby as an air crash might have had if it had involved the whole national team. People forgot that the previous season we had beaten Wales 19–0. That was a bit of a freak, certainly, but at the same time, we had scored try for try with all the other countries and up till then, things hadn't gone too badly.

'We won the Calcutta Cup in 1950 and we were still within a couple of games of England over all the matches played since 1871. Nobody really thought of Scotland as being weak – and then we lost this game 44–0 to South Africa.

'There was no preparation for the match, it was early season, a sunny dry day in November, the players weren't fit, there was no trial, we tried to go for a heavy pack, and of course, the forwards couldn't get about the field. It was one of those awful days when everything went wrong. The Springboks played absolutely magnificently. From that day on, Scotland really did lose their way. We lost 17 matches in succession and did not win again until 1955.

'We panicked right through. We went for a heavy pack one minute, and then a light, mobile pack the next. We just dithered. Arthur Dorward won 15 caps for Scotland, but for the first nine, he was in and out of the side seven times. You can argue whether A is better than B, or B is better than C, but you must have some kind of consistency in selection. The legacy of those awful years is still with Scotland today. There is still a slight inferiority complex which we've only occasionally managed to get rid of.'

Hennie Muller, who captained South Africa after Basil Kenyon had suffered an eye injury at Pontypool early in the tour, felt so sorry for Scotland as they were torn apart in the second half that he tried to give Angus Cameron, their captain, a bit of friendly advice. By that time, Scotland were past redemption.

Ireland also lost control of their game against the Springboks in the second half, though to nothing like the extent that Scotland had. At least Ireland had had an extra fortnight to step up their fitness training, because the annihilation at Murrayfield had left them in no doubt as to what was required. Ireland actually led 5–3 at half-time before succumbing 17–5.

Early in the tour, Cardiff had given the Springboks a game to remember. Their forwards had surprised the Springboks by having the better of both the scrums and the lineouts and their backs were so well led by Bleddyn Williams that they led until ten minutes from the end, when Hannes Brewis the South African fly-half, placed a diagonal kick perfectly for Chum Ochse to score the winning try.

South Africa found it much harder to beat Wales 6–3 and England 8–3 than might have been supposed from their victories over Scotland and

Ireland, but Bleddyn Williams is in no doubt that the 1951 Springboks were the best side he played against.

'They were fully equipped. They were superb up front, with forwards like Jaap Bekker, Chris Koch, 'Salty' du Rand, Ernst Dinkelmann and that great back row of Basie van Wyk, Stephen Fry and Hennie Muller and they had a very sound player at fly-half in Hannes Brewis. They also had Tjol Lategan in the centre, a marvellous player, and Ryk van Schoor, who could tackle like a ton of bricks. 'Chum' Ochse on the wing scored some wonderful tries, and Johnny Buchler at full-back was as safe as houses.

'Even more important than that, of course, was that the Springboks were prepared to use all the equipment that they had at their disposal, whereas the All Blacks were not. South Africa had good backs and they used them. It has always remained a mystery to me that the All Blacks never really tried to develop their back play until comparatively recently, when they found that their forwards no longer had the advantages of superior organisation which they always used to have over British packs.

'The Springboks showed the modern world how to scrummage and whatever may have happened in the 'thirties when Bennie Osler was playing for them, they showed us how to use that ball in the first two series after the war. The All Black forwards could match the Springboks with their play in the loose, particularly in their own country, and in 'Tiny' White they had a lineout forward who could beat anybody, but they never really used the ball they won. The Springboks did and that was basically the difference between the two teams. It was a question of attitude, and as a midfield back, I saw the difference very clearly.'

Williams himself certainly impressed the 1951 Springboks. He was such an absolute master of centre-threequarter play that Ken Jones, an Olympic sprinter as well as the winner of a record number of caps for Wales as a winger, even felt tempted to leave Newport and join Cardiff! The Springboks thought that there were only two players in Britain who might have got into their team, and Bleddyn Williams was one of them. The other was Roy John, also of Wales.

· Hennie Muller made an equal impression on his hosts. He ranged the country demonstrating just why he was the most significant number eight to play in international Rugby since Wavell Wakefield. By the time he had finished, he had any number of British players saying 'Amen' to the admiring and rueful judgment of Bob Scott, the New Zealand full-back, at the end of the All Blacks' tour of South Africa in 1949. 'I would say unhesitatingly that he was the greatest loose forward I have ever seen. He had great speed – he was very nearly as fast as our Peter Henderson, who was an Empire Games sprinter. His hands were good. He could kick well. He was always alert and he could last out a test match on a hard ground and a warm day without visible difficulty. As if all that wasn't enough, he was completely fearless and quite ruthless.'

The lessons taught by the 1951–52 Springboks made an even more profound impression in France, and quickly lead to a significant change in the balance of world Rugby power. South Africa beat France 25–3, and probably thought nothing of it, but a young French lock named Lucien Mias thought about nothing else. 'For me, it was a revelation. It showed the way ahead. I had played against England and Wales and we had lost, but I had not really grasped the importance of the team game, the power and the effect of the team game. It was after the Springbok match that I knew in which direction French Rugby must go.'

So once again, success by one country produced a catalyst in another. The Springboks, for their part, returned to their country to look forward to what would obviously be a much less demanding home series against Australia in 1953. Hennie Muller went through that series as captain of South Africa but he retired at the end of it. Muller's health had been of concern to Danie Craven for some time. The picture of his drawn, exhausted face as he received the congratulations of the Australian captain, John Solomon, after South Africa had won the third test at Durban gave some idea of the depths of the reserves that he drained with the mercilessly sustained running he did for his country. He died of a heart attack in middle age. Looking at that face, it is not difficult to see why.

South Africa, showing several changes from the triumphant team that had toured Britain, won that series against Australia, but not before the Wallabies had once again stolen a test match by persuading the Springboks to play a loose, running game that did not suit them. Australians

Hennie Muller leads the Springboks onto Murrayfield.

have always had the reputation of being the finest confidence tricksters in the world! South Africans are convinced that this is true.

The Wallabies' manager, the aptly named Wylie Breckenridge, waxed passionate in his pleas for open Rugby and easy-going refereeing throughout the tour. Like his predecessor twenty years earlier, he knew full well that Australia could never beat South Africa if the game was confined to the forwards and the kickers, and when Hannes Brewis was dropped after the first test, which the Springboks won 25–3, the Wallabies talked their opponents into a frame of mind which relaxed them just sufficiently to leave the door ajar. Before the Springboks knew what had happened, the Australians were through it and Garth Jones, a really sharp mover on the wing, had narrowly held off Hennie Muller in an agonising sprint to score the winning try at the end of the match.

The Australians had had plenty of practice at playing against the Hennie Muller style of loose forward defence, because they had played ten matches in New Zealand the previous year, and found the whole country burgeoning with aspiring Mullers. Despite that, the Wallabies shared the tests 1–1 with New Zealand.

It was in that year, 1952, that a young New Zealand full-back by the name of Don Clarke began to kick goals from all over the field for Waikato, but he was not chosen for the All Blacks' tour of Britain in 1953. The New Zealand selectors persuaded Bob Scott to make himself available again, and he played so beautifully in the trials that he was chosen.

The 1953–54 All Black team lost four matches on tour in Britain and France. Wales and Cardiff beat them, and so did their equivalents across the English Channel, France and South West France.

Bleddyn Williams played in both the Welsh victories. 'We had learned our lessons in New Zealand in 1950 and with all due respect, I do not think that the All Black forwards who toured Britain in 1953–54 were as good as those who played against the Lions in 1950. They still had 'Tiny' White, of course, but when we sat down before the Cardiff game and thought about it, we felt that we had the ability to beat them. With forwards like Sid Judd and C. D. Williams in the side, who were both very, very good footballers, and with a solid platform in the tight, we were quite sure that our forwards would raise their game, as they did, and we were absolutely certain that we could beat the All Blacks behind the scrum. That was how it worked out.'

This view of the All Blacks' deficiencies was borne out when Wales beat them, because New Zealand led 8–5 for a long time in the second half and had all the positions and possession they wanted to increase that lead. They never looked like doing so and Wales first broke out of defence to draw level with a penalty goal and then won the match when Clem Thomas, the Welsh flanker, dummied a pass and then cross-kicked from the left. Ken Jones was unmarked on the far wing and he scored a try by the posts to win the match.

The All Blacks had only themselves to blame for losing that game, but they were not amused when they lost to South West France by a penalty goal kicked at the end of the match. The scores were level at 8–8 and a local referee was alternately enraging and astounding the All Blacks just as local referees in New Zealand have enraged and astounded British Lions from Whangarei to Invercargill. New Zealand had a scrum, and as Bevan bent to put the ball in it, the referee blew his whistle for a penalty kick. 'What was that for?' exploded Bevan, his eyebrows going through his hairline. 'Not straight,' said the referee. 'But,' shouted Bevan, waving the ball under the referee's nose, 'I haven't put the bloody thing in yet'.

Bevan's justifiable indignation, and that of his team-mates, could not disguise the fact that they had not succeeded in impressing their opponents in Britain and France to the extent that earlier New Zealand teams had. On the other hand, South Africa were clearly slipping from their pinnacle of unchallenged world supremacy. This impression was confirmed when the British Lions toured South Africa in 1955 and drew the series 2–2.

The Lions team was a strange mixture of world class players and others whose claims even to be considered for the tour were a little difficult to discern. Back in Britain, a winger called Peter Jackson had been allowed to slide back into something approaching obscurity after being given an England trial in 1951 and at least one flanker was preferred to Don White who was nowhere near White's class.

Once again, some of the leading players were not available, and once again, the choice of captain left most of Britain's senior players wondering how the decision had come to pass. The captain chosen in 1955 was Robin Thompson, of Ireland, who was surprisingly small for a lock, and the choice was presumably based partly on the persistent myth that Irishmen make intrinsically better captains than Englishmen, Scotsmen or Welshmen. Selection has never been the strongest point of British Rugby, because until recently, so few men have involved themselves in the coaching and preparation of teams, and therefore, the understanding of players. In 1955, coaching, as the All Blacks and Springboks knew it, was unheard of in Britain and consequently, the technique of analysing players and their characters was regarded as being slightly ungentlemanly. This noble spirit had some advantages, but it did ensure that the wrong choice of captain would be made more often than the right one, and it was a problem that was to recur.

With Courtney Meredith, Bryn Meredith and Billy Williams, the Lions were at least equipped with a front row that could compete with the Springboks, and if British Rugby had known enough about the game to build the back five of the pack into a comparably effective unit, there is no doubt that the Lions would have come back with the clean sweep of four victories that Jeff Butterfield, for example, has always felt was within its capabilities.

Butterfield on that tour was an artist of a centre-threequarter, a supreme passer of the ball and such a brilliant, unselfish footballer that Frank Sykes, one of his club wings at Northampton became so sick of running in unopposed tries that he pleaded, 'Jeff, for God's sake let *me* do a bit towards scoring some of the tries occasionally!'

Butterfield played in the centre alongside Phil Davies, a hurtlingly fast tank of a runner who might have been known as a crash-ball runner today except that it was his literally unswerving principle to run straight over the top of his opponents rather than into them. Tony O'Reilly, the Irishman whom life has so richly endowed with so many talents, played on the wing outside him. Among his gifts, O'Reilly numbers the most delightful use of the English language, and when he describes Davies' distinctly unpredictable use of the ball, he says, 'He threw the pass away like a toffee paper, but if you could catch it you had nothing in front of you but the turnstiles'.

In the middle of the field, the Lions had Dickie Jeeps at scrum-half and Cliff Morgan at fly-half, and the selfless way Jeeps worked the ball to Morgan, and the brilliance of Morgan's attacking running earned the admiration of Jeff Butterfield and almost the whole of South Africa. Butterfield, reflecting on the remark made to him by Frank Sykes, has since said, 'Cliff worked to make half a yard of space for me in the same way that I tried to work for Frank Sykes'.

Oddly enough, Danie Craven has said that in his view, the 1955 Lions would have been even more effective if they had chosen their reserve half-backs, Johnny Williams and Douglas Baker. Both were the absolute opposite of Jeeps and Morgan. Whereas Jeeps was a tough, shrewd, durable competitor and an orthodox server of the ball, Williams was a brilliant attacking runner at scrum-half. Baker, on the other hand, was a calm, composed link player, as far removed from the pyrotechnics of Morgan's running as a reading lamp is from Guy Fawke's night.

Whatever the truth of the matter, the most remarkable thing was that Jeeps was on the tour at all because at that point he had not been capped by England. From what we have been able to discover, there is not much doubt that Jeeps owed his selection to a Welshman, Haydn Tanner, possibly the greatest scrum-half of them all. Tanner was returning from a game in 1955 when he found himself sharing a railway carriage with two of the Lions' selectors. 'Haydn, who do *you* think is the best scrum-half in the four countries?' he was asked. Tanner was in no doubt. He took his pipe out of his mouth and said, 'The best scrum-half I've seen is a kid called Jeeps, playing for Northampton'.

The 1955 Lions were the first side to travel to and round South Africa by air, and they suffered the most depressing start to their tour when they were beaten by Western Transvaal in their first match. The failure was the familiar one of inadequate forward play and Eastern Province exploited the same weakness to beat them 20–0 a few weeks later. Any self-respecting international team should now expect to win all its provincial matches in either New Zealand or South Africa, but it is as well to remember that these were the days when British Lions managers, as soon as they set foot in either country, were apt to trot out the line, 'We're here to learn'. This never failed to infuriate J. B. G. Thomas, the widely travelled Rugby critic and sports editor of *The Western Mail*. Two defeats in the twelve matches leading up to the first test match would now be regarded as the kiss of death for a Lions team but in 1955 it was pretty good going. The result that really alarmed South Africans, however, was the annihilation of Transvaal by 36 points to 13. The Transvaal, and Northern Transvaal, are the pride of Afrikaaner Rugby. They reckon themselves to be the high veldt hard men, so essential to provide a bit of backbone to all those fancy dan English-speaking basketball players on the coast. But the Lions scored seven tries against them!

Sadly, the success of the Lions split South Africa down the middle, with the Afrikaans speakers on one side, and the English speakers on the other. The public vilification of the selectors and some of the players chosen sickened and distressed not only the men involved, but men of both Dutch and English origin who thought deeply about the game and loved it as much. In the circumstances, it was remarkable that the Springboks did as well as they did, because a touring team always has the advantage of superior organisation in the first test of a series, and yet the Springboks came from far, far behind at 23–11 to pull up to 23–22 and even have a

---

Cliff Morgan, the Welsh fly-half, passes to Ken Jones on the wing, in Wales' match against France in Cardiff in 1956.

kick at goal to win the match. The picture of Jack van der Schyff's dejection as his attempted conversion of South Africa's final try swings outside the left post was said to be a journalistic accident – the photographer either forgot to press the button on his camera, or got tangled up in the mechanics until it was too late to take the shot he had intended. Accident or no, that photograph earned Ivor Hanes far more money than if he had taken an orthodox picture. It also recorded one of the greatest moments in Lions' touring history.

Despite the pessimism of their fickle supporters, the Springboks were far from done for and that exceptional wing Tom van Vollenhoven scored three tries as South Africa won by the overwhelming margin of 25 points to 6 in the second test at Newlands. Van Vollenhoven went on to play in Rugby League in Britain and he was so good that he rivalled even the legendary Brian Bevan.

The Lions changed their tactics for the third test when Robin Thompson was injured and the team was captained by Cliff Morgan. They

The famous picture of Jack van der Schyff's dejection as his kick to beat the 1955 British Lions misses the left post at Ellis Park.

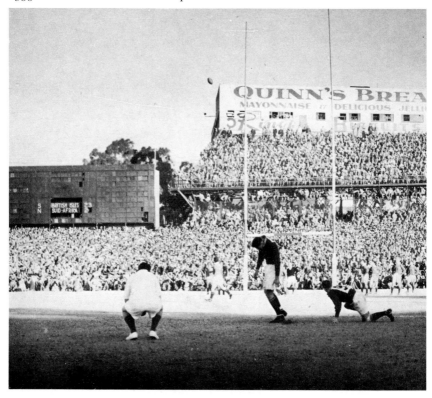

Salty du Rand, the Springbok lock, grabs Bryn Meredith, the Lions' hooker by the neck as Tony O'Reilly gathers himself for the pass and a sprint.

played much tighter, as the score of 9–6 indicates, but the point is, they won. It was as well that they did, because problems always compound as a team reaches the end of a long, hard tour. The effects of injuries build up as players realise that so little recovery time is left that they may not play again, and something of the unity of purpose and determination goes with it. Only the very best teams win the last match of a tour, and they have to dig deep into their reserves to do it.

The 1955 Lions did not win their last match. They dropped Phil Davies, which the South Africans thought a great mistake, and Tony O'Reilly was carried off injured in the second half. That was long before the time of replacements for injured players and the seven remaining Lions forwards could not cope with the Springbok pack.

Even before that, though, South Africa had taken command and the loss of O'Reilly simply meant that the Lions were left with no chance whatever of launching a recovery as dramatic as that which so nearly saved the first test for South Africa. In the end, the Springboks won 22–8, but they knew better than anyone that at long, long last, the British Rugby Lion was showing some signs of stirring from the sleep that had lasted from Queen Victoria's reign.

Looking back, in a conversation with Jeff Butterfield, Cliff Morgan said, 'I suppose it is fair to say that the 1955 tour was an absolute shambles if you compare it with the modern tactical approach?'

Jeff Butterfield replied, 'Absolutely right. That may sound a bit damning, because to a certain extent, we were fairly successful, but I think the cry from our hearts as we came back from South Africa was that we had played four test matches and had only won two of them, whereas with some sort of organisation, we could have won all four.

'When we went to South Africa, we really were naïve. We had no organisation at all. We had Scotsmen whose answer to all forward problems was "Thrree, two, thrrree, and drubble it with yoore feet". Yet the fact was that we played best on the high veldt where there was a lot of running and everything moved so fast. Strange as it may seem, we weren't half as good when we got down to the Cape where it was muddy and wet. We were still four countries, each one playing to its own little whims and its own little ways. And we never had enough ball.

'My first experience of that was in 1954 against the All Blacks. They did have backs, certainly; Bob Scott wasn't a bad full-back and Ron Jarden wasn't a bad wing but their back play really was very steady stereotype. On the other hand, what they did have was possession.

'I played for England and North East Counties against them and then I played for the Barbarians at Cardiff at the end of the tour, and the All Blacks had the ball all the time. This meant that we had to make far better use of what little ball we had. We had to run from difficult situations and we simply had to produce scores. How terrific it would have been to be in the situation where *we* had the ball all the time.

Right: Jeff Butterfield demonstrating his immaculate passing technique.

Below: Jim Greenwood's cover tackle is just too late to stop Tom van Vollenhoven scoring for South Africa.

'When we went on tour after that year, we still lacked any idea of how to co-ordinate eight forwards and to work them in with the back line. One thing, though, we did smile; the joy of the tour is something that South Africa gave to me particularly. I worry a bit that we may destroy this enjoyment with all the ultra-sophistication in coaching. After all, look at soccer. These guys never laugh. They are all aggro, and they are always trying to get at their own mates. They argue as much with their own team as they do with the opposition.

'Soccer may be a professional business, but the best business men in the world laugh sometimes. Look at the great O'Reilly, boss of Heinz world-wide and boss of an absolute empire in Ireland. He smiles occasionally, doesn't he? And Ken Chapman. He was the boss of a nice big company in Britain. He even laughs sometimes, and makes other people laugh. Even in business, you don't have to be aggressive all the time. If we couldn't laugh or say "Have you seen that bit of crumpet in the staff lift?", what's the point of it all?'

The 1955 Lions certainly had some laughs, on the field as well as off it. O'Reilly is one of the best raconteurs in a game which has produced a treasure-house of story-tellers and his amusing vignettes of his experiences in international Rugby have a wonderful eye for character detail pointed up to a sharpness of almost professional theatre by his ability as a mimic.

His stories about Phil Davies, for instance, are told with exactly the right balance of English public school drawl. The one about the toffee paper starts with Davies announcing to O'Reilly, 'Anthony, I think I'm going to have a run at your man', rather as a Colonel Blimp might announce to the gun next to him at a shoot that he has an excellent '47 Maison Lafitte that they might try at luncheon. O'Reilly then describes in graphic detail the reverberations and snorts and groans of agony as Davies, a big man, all knees and nose and elbows, uses his surprising speed to accelerate outside his own immediate opponent and run straight into, at, over and through the poor quavering wing who is supposed to be marking O'Reilly. 'When the noise had quietened down a bit and he had shaken the poor mangled wretch out of his studs, Phil threw the pass away like a toffee paper, but if you could catch it you had nothing in front of you but the turnstiles.'

O'Reilly's assessment of South African Rugby was equally acute. Asked what he felt about it, he said simply, 'Bruised'.

Expanding the theme, he said, 'I often say that there are three white tribes left in the world today. There are the Afrikaaners, the people of Israel and in a sense, the Northern Ireland Presbyterian. They all have their backs to the wall. They all feel threatened. They all have a wonderful history. They are all very productive people. South African Rugby reflects the *laager* intellect of the people.' (I don't mean Castle lager, of which we all drank at least 14,000 gallons while we were in South Africa.) I mean the basic feeling that it's them against the world. And so the game of Rugby football in South Africa has this characteristic, this defensive characteristic, this self-assertion. It is their claim to nationhood. It means more to them, it's not a game. It's an important expression of their way of life and their attitude to the surrounding forces. It brings a very purposeful quality to their Rugby. In recent years, the character of the Rugby community has changed as the farmers, the outdoors men, have become more integrated in the urban way of life. Their forwards do not have the same physical advantages that they once did. They are not so strong. But when they played us, it was like a military exercise, and it was done very efficiently.'

8 The All Blacks and France reach the promised land

South African fears that the rest of the world was beginning to catch up with Springbok Rugby were confirmed when South Africa toured New Zealand in 1956. Rugby football in those two countries has often carried with it a degree of national fervour which is unhealthy and the intensity of New Zealand's desire to beat the Springboks and so rid themselves of the All Blacks' status as second class Rugby citizens, which had then lasted thirty years, burned like acid into the gut of the whole country. The result was a series of such brutality that it made all the violence over which we wring our hands today seem like a childish squabble by comparison. If that series between New Zealand and South Africa in 1956 had been photographed with modern television techniques, it would have provoked a national outrage. New Zealand won their victory over South Africa, but at what a price.

The knowledge of what went on in that series, more than anything else, was probably the chief reason why the New Zealand Rugby Union prohibited live television of Rugby matches for longer than any other country where television was available, and why they insisted, in their agreement with the New Zealand Broadcasting Authority, that only a censored version of Rugby football should be presented second hand to the public.

The first test was a brawl from start to finish and the All Blacks won it 10–6. Then, to their dismay, they saw the Springbok front row begin to assert itself as South Africa won the second test 8–3 in one of Wellington's typical strong southerly winds.

New Zealand had suffered in the scrums for long enough to know that South African supremacy in the front row had to be challenged, and so it was, but not by the use of strength and weight and technical expertise. Instead, the All Blacks brought back Kevin Skinner, who had boxed for New Zealand. Skinner had not been available for the first two tests, and the whole of New Zealand awaited his return. They were not disappointed. In the third test, Skinner switched from one side of the scrum to the other so that he could play opposite Chris Koch and Jaap Bekker in turn. Afterwards, Bekker looked as if he had been in a road accident and the story goes that he asked innocently if Skinner intended to box in the

Kevin Skinner (left) the All Blacks' prop, tries to pull one of the Springbok forwards away as Johan Claassen, the great Springbok lock, closes in support.

Olympic Games in Melbourne.

'No' he was told. 'Skinner has retired from boxing.'

'Pity,' said Bekker. 'He would win his division.'

The Springboks did not complain in public, and in those days, only a very small number of people knew what had gone on, but it became a joke among the Springbok touring party that they would have to take boxing lessons.

Inevitably, the fisticuffs escalated to involve most of the forwards and there was retaliation, the nastiest of which led to 'Tiny' White being helped off the field after being kicked in the back in the final test.

The feeling between the teams was so bad that there was even talk of cancelling the game at Rotorua before the final test because Kevin Skinner was due to play for the local team and there were fears that the

Jaap Bekker's bruised and bloody face after one of the 1956 tests against the Springboks.

vendetta would become so vicious that it would be impossible to sweep it under the carpet.

It was all so sad, because that series featured two of the best wingers who have ever played Rugby football, Ron Jarden, of New Zealand, and Tom van Vollenhoven, of South Africa. Unfortunately, artistry rarely flourishes in a war. Only the guns speak, and New Zealand were fortunate that they had a siege gun goalkicker in Don Clarke to back up the machine gun battalion in their pack.

The Springboks met the young Clarke in the first match of their tour, and they were astonished as much by the strength and accuracy of his goalkicking on a wet and windy field at Hamilton as they were disconcerted by the defeat that Waikato inflicted upon them. Waikato scored in the corner in the first minute from a thundering forward rush, so the Springboks thought little of it when Clarke failed to convert. They began to sit up a bit though when he decided to kick at goal from ten yards inside his own half and only just missed, with plenty of height to spare, and they gaped in amazement when he dropped a goal from 45 yards and the ball cleared the top of the posts! Clarke also kicked a penalty goal and converted another try to give Waikato a 14–0 lead at half-time. Waikato lost their fly-half with a broken jaw in the first half and had to play the whole of the second half with only seven forwards, but they hung on to win 14–10. Donald Barrie Clarke had scored eight points and had begun an era.

Clarke did not play in the first two tests against South Africa. Pat Welsh, later to be a New Zealand selector, was the man chosen instead. Clarke came in for the third game, and within 15 minutes, had kicked two penalty goals and a conversion to stretch New Zealand's lead to 11–0. The Springboks scored two tries and converted them to pull up to 11–10, but they were driven back by Clarke's vast touch-kicking and New Zealand scored two more tries to win 17–10.

The final test was of a similar pattern. Again, there were incidents which would have left Rugby football with an impossible case to defend if they had been tele-recorded with the accuracy that is possible today, and again, perhaps just as significantly, Clarke gave the All Blacks the comfort of a six point lead with two long penalty goals. With the try then worth three points, that meant South Africa had to score twice to lead. Psychologically, that is a huge hill to climb. Clarke then closed the door in the second half by converting an extraordinary try by Peter Jones. South Africa scored a late try themselves, and converted it, but by then the match had been won and lost.

New Zealand therefore won the series 3–1, and felt their national pride restored, but even outside the tests, the Springboks' record was not nearly as good as usual. At least one of their provincial defeats could be attributed to home town refereeing, a subject which so incensed the South African manager, Danie Craven, that he spoke out about it in public, but

Don Clarke, a legendary goalkicker and full-back for New Zealand.

the feeling remained that the Springboks were not the force they had once been.

The 1956 series between New Zealand and South Africa was important for several other reasons. It began a period when New Zealand were impregnable in their own country, although they never managed to beat the Springboks in South Africa, and it began a period when New Zealand techniques of loose forward play and their concentration on second phase possession began to influence the world more than the traditional basics of scrummaging so powerfully developed by South Africa. That series also saw the emergence of some young New Zealand players who were to become giants in the game.

Apart from Don Clarke, a young lock named Colin Meads, from King Country, and a young prop named Wilson Whineray, from Canterbury, had their first real taste of international Rugby and looked forward eagerly to the years ahead. At the time, New Zealand wondered if they were about to decline in the world of Rugby, as the Springboks had, because at the end of the series against South Africa, some of their best forwards, including 'Tiny' White and Bob Duff had retired. As it turned out, their departure simply accelerated the development of one of the greatest generations of forwards in New Zealand's history.

South Africa's melancholy at their defeat by New Zealand in 1956 soon deepened. France went to South Africa on a short tour and beat the Springboks in a two-match series. It was the first time the Springboks had lost a series in South Africa for sixty years and the whole world sat up and took notice. The French were delighted as much by the new respect with which they were regarded as by the victory itself.

France were captained by Lucien Mias, by then a qualified doctor and a mature man. He had not played international Rugby for four years so that he could complete his studies, and in his time away from the game, he had given a great deal of thought to the way France could make better use of the country's marvellous individual talents. *Le team game* was the answer, as the Springboks had demonstrated it to him in 1952. So he played *le team game* right back at South Africa, and France won.

As Mias says, 'When I began playing for France in 1950, I was very much aware of the French team being a collection of captains. We had no sense of really belonging to each other. That really bothered me. There had to be deficiencies somewhere, because French postwar teams were technically good, and in individual terms, they were very good indeed. But the collective play was poor. There were certain matches when everything worked well, and that was marvellous. But there were other occasions when the English, with their stolid approach, but sound principles, caused us to lose.

'The four years I spent with my medical studies enabled me to sort out my ideas about Rugby football, and I felt that I wanted to prove them. After the defeats of the French team in 1957, my chance came to put my ideas into practice. With the same players of the year before, we transformed the indisciplined play of the team into a situation where they began playing for each other and thus established a team spirit. We found the secret of harnessing the real strength of a team, the co-ordinated strengths of individuals.

'No-one gave us much hope when we left for South Africa in 1958. They said that we were beaten before we started. We had some problems because the South Africans thought that we were a second class team, and from time to time we had to prove and demonstrate that we had both physical strength and spirit. It was particularly satisfying to win, considering that we had been beaten by 25 points only six years earlier.

'In the years before the war, the Catalan style of Rugby had been the vogue and was popular in France, but it wasn't Rugby. It was just a game with a ball – it was handball, or basketball, if you like. It wasn't Rugby, because Rugby is a game which requires physical contact. 1958 was the year when the lesson was learned and so that team in South Africa occupies a special place in French Rugby history.

'Apart from winning, the psychological revolution was most important for us, being Gallic, romantic European. When the Springboks had gone in 1952, ideas were exchanged between individuals and clubs in an attempt to find a new style, but success was only possible if each individual accepted certain constraints and responded psychologically and conformed to the demands of the group. The key word was unity. We had

Lucien Mias (right), talking to Peter Robbins of his days as captain of France.

to fashion a sort of family, especially the forwards. My only regret is that we could not follow through and pursue this revolutionary policy with the backs, and make them more expansive. We made colossal progress with our forward play, but in my opinion, there was still a complete world to explore in the backs.'

Despite that, France were still good enough to win the international championship outright for the first time in their history when they returned from South Africa, and the psychological revolution was not the only one which occurred in French rugby. In 1958, the game in France was at the beginning of what turned out to be a physical revolution, in which the traditional concept of the Frenchman being a stocky, nimble man of limited stature was overthrown.

Until the 1950s, France had never had a forward taller than 6ft 2in. This stemmed from lamentable infant feeding, but in the 1930s, government welfare schemes improved the diet of French children enormously, and as soon as they were given milk to drink instead of wine, they began to grow much bigger than they ever had before.

By the time France went to South Africa in 1958, France had a lock called Bernard Mommejat who was nearly 6ft 5ins tall. This was the beginning of the physical revolution which was to create a pyramid of such huge men in France that in less than twenty years, every one of the 64 clubs in the French championship had at least one forward who was more than 6ft 4ins tall, and some clubs, like Beziers had three. At the top of this pyramid was the French pack, which was so massive that it was the biggest the world had seen.

Rugby football has a way of constantly regenerating itself, and sometimes, as in the case of France, of suddenly producing spectacular new growth from an old branch, and so it was in the French team in South Africa in 1958. Just as Lucien Mias, as a young man, had watched and wondered at the 1952 Springboks, so in South Africa in 1958, a relatively obscure French prop called Raoul Barriere sat fascinated as a reserve for France and absorbed everything he saw. He did not know it at the time, but he was in the process of evolving a whole new Rugby philosophy. Twelve years later, when he had graduated from the junior teams to become coach of the Béziers first team, he set about building a playing structure which, at club level, eventually became unique in the world.

'The tour I made to South Africa really opened my eyes,' Barriere says. 'I learned a lot then because I was a reserve for many of the matches. That was unfortunate for me in a way, but at least I was able to observe much more than if I had been involved in actually playing the game. I learned a lot from our South African friends; particularly the seriousness of the game. I learned to respect the game. It was so important a game that it had to be approached properly. One must never make fun of the game. Rugby should not be treated as something mediocre. I also learned a lot about techniques; about preparation; about diet – all so important. I learned about a new way of life and it made me realise that Rugby football is a very serious business and that it must be kept so.'

British Rugby was gradually coming to realise the same thing. Until the late 1950s, no one in Britain had got further than talking about what ought to be done to make British forward play competitive enough to release the teeming talent then available behind the scrum. But when the Lions toured New Zealand in 1959, the cheerful extroverts in the party – usually in a slightly irresponsible majority on any Lions tour – had among them some thinkers who were also practical men and who determined to actually *do* something to improve British Rugby, rather than just talk about it, when they returned.

Chief among these was Jeff Butterfield, to whom must be given the credit for being involved in the first really effective coaching structure to emerge in Britain at senior level – that in the East Midlands of England. Butterfield had seen in South Africa in 1955 something of what needed to be done in Britain; 1959 in New Zealand merely confirmed that he had been right.

Ronnie Dawson, the 1959 Lions' captain, was another who saw, like Lucien Mias in 1952, what had to be done. So did Bryn Meredith, the brilliant Newport hooker, and Hughie McLeod, the Scottish prop. So did Syd Millar, the Irish loose head, and Ray Prosser, the Welsh tight head. So did Ken Scotland, a footballing genius who could play international class Rugby anywhere behind the scrum. Not all involved themselves in the coaching of the game as soon as they returned from New Zealand, but all of them learned, just as Raoul Barriere learned, and they stored their knowledge for the time when they would do something about it.

The starting point of this motivation was undoubtedly the first test against New Zealand. The Lions may have laughed about it afterwards, but all were outraged by the circumstances of that game. The Lions scored four beautiful tries. New Zealand did not score one. And yet . . . and yet . . . New Zealand won the match by 18 points to 17 because Don Clarke was given the opportunities to kick six penalty goals. Even now, twenty years later, the Lions players on that tour find it difficult to use the words 'winning' and 'losing' in connection with that game, because as Tony O'Reilly says, they were convinced that if the Lions had scored a fifth try, and the All Blacks needed eight penalty goals to win that match, then Clarke would have been given the opportunities to kick them.

Using his best New Zealand accent, Tony O'Reilly quotes with scornful laughter the relevant part of the speech made by Cuth Hogg, then president of the New Zealand Rugby Union. 'I am delighted to congratulate the New Zealand team on their victory toduy, which was guyned within the frimework of the rules.'

Despite their disgust at the refereeing, some of the senior Lions players still felt that the match had been thrown away, just as they felt that the second test was thrown away when the Lions were leading 8–6 in the second half. They attributed this to the inexperience of Ronnie Dawson as captain. Their view was that all the great Welsh clubs, and those in the Midlands of England, would have known how to win from the situations in which the Lions found themselves. They felt that instead of closing the game up, and kicking for position, as they should have done, the Lions pursued the mistaken tactics of keeping the game open, and they paid the price for it.

The Lions were well beaten in the third test, but won the fourth, by scoring three tries to nil when Bev Risman returned at fly-half after breaking his ankle. Most of the 1959 Lions are convinced that they should have won that series 3–1. Instead they lost it by the same margin.

By then, the Lions, like the Irish, were sick of moral victories. They wanted to win something for a change. They were fed up with being regarded as princely entertainers behind the scrum and as absolute dummies in it. They felt that even though Don Clarke's goalkicking was every bit as good as the legend, it ought not to have been beyond their capacity to organise a game to keep both Clarke and the home town referees out of range of their posts. In that, they were probably right, because in terms of individual talent, the 1959 Lions was probably the finest team ever to represent Britain. They lacked, perhaps, the highest class at loose forward, because of the tragic injury which cost Peter Robbins a broken leg in a sad moment of horseplay at Newport after the team had been chosen, but they had everything else. Everything, that is, except the organisation to make the best of a tight forward combination which had players of the calibre of McLeod, Meredith, Prosser, Millar, Marques, and R. H. Williams available to it.

Rhys Williams was that rarity among British locks, a world class player. Of all the positions in a Rugby team, lock forward has been that in which British Rugby has found it most difficult to match the forwards produced by South Africa, New Zealand and in latter years, France. But as Colin Meads himself says, Rhys Williams was a champion. Meads rates Rhys Williams and Johan Claassen as the best two locks he played against, with Benoit Dauga not far behind.

Even then, at the beginning of his international career, Meads made a deep impression on his opponents. Tony O'Reilly says that David Marques, very much a product of public school, Cambridge University, the Harlequins and England, once declared crisply after a match in New Zealand: 'You know, the thing I despise most about that chap Meads is the way the terminal traces of your jock strap hang out of the corners of his mouth at the end of each game.'

But if Meads impressed the Lions forwards, there is no doubt that the Lions' backs enchanted the New Zealand public. Tony O'Reilly himself set a record by scoring 17 tries, but he is the first to insist that there was only ever one name at the top of the entertainment bill, and that was Peter Barrie Jackson. A tall, pale wraith of a man, Peter Jackson was all subtlety and insinuation. His footwork and dummying defied belief and O'Reilly positively croons with admiration when he recalls the *leger-demain* and the *legerdepied* with which his tour room-mate baffled New Zealand and delighted his team. 'Honestly' says O'Reilly, 'there were times when the rest of us felt like clearing off and leaving him with three billiard balls and a one-wheeled bicycle to entertain the crowd. He was incredible.'

'In one match, I think it was in Auckland, he went across from one side of the field to the other, and then back again, like a shuttle on a loom,' (O'Reilly picks up Jackson's flat, slightly nasal Coventry accent, and breathes down his nose), 'before putting O'Reilly in for the easiest of tries'.

Peter Jackson, apparently about to kick in the match he won for England against Australia in 1958, but it could just as easily have been a dummy.

Peter Jackson had demonstrated his capacity for scoring unforgettable tries when he produced one to beat Australia in their match against England at Twickenham in 1958. It was not a particularly memorable tour, or even a very savoury one, and when England lost Phil Horrocks-Taylor, their fly-half, through injury, it looked very much as if Australia would win. However, England pulled Peter Robbins out of the pack, and played him in the centre, and with Jeff Butterfield at fly-half, they simply poured the ball towards Peter Jackson on the right wing. In the end, he won the match by scoring a try that for sheer grace and artistry would have done credit to Covent Garden.

That same year, Peter Jackson had scored a try for England against France in Paris which so rubbed salt into the wounds inflicted by a decisive England victory that it was undoubtedly the catalyst that made it possible for Lucien Mias subsequently to lead his country into the promised land. Jackson intercepted near the England 25 and made off upfield with that deceptively easy looking stride on the right wing. Desperately, the French cover turned and gave chase and Jackson knew, far better than they did, that the leading man would catch him. Accordingly, as he approached the French 25, Jackson eased ever so slightly to persuade the straining French coverer to commit himself to the tackle. Then, when he saw that the Frenchman was safely launched on his dive,

Peter Jackson slips past the French back row.

Jackson simply stopped dead and waited patiently for the wretch to slither past. Then he calmly trotted infield and scored between the posts.

That gave England a 12–0 lead and the insouciance with which it was done sent the French crowd berserk at their own selectors. They turned on them screaming '*Demission! Demission!*' (Resign! Resign!) It looked as if they would storm the barricades. This caused untold anguish to a senior and extremely distinguished English newspaper correspondent, who had married in middle age and had made Paris the first stop on his honeymoon. He had installed his bride in some style in the *tribune d'honneur* and the thought of having her lynched in retribution for a smashing England victory was more than he could bear. While all this was going on, Peter Jackson was gently strolling back with the ball to afford the England place-kicker what Jackson might have modestly described as 'the easiest of kicks at goal'. England won 14–0.

Jackson scored a similar try against New Zealand in the last test of the 1959 Lions tour. He beat Bruce McPhail, Kel Tremain, Don Clarke and Terry Lineen before scoring in the corner. As Tony O'Reilly says, 'Peter Jackson was a loner. Probably the most unique winger that ever played Rugby football. He scored tries which were quite breathtaking to behold. In terms of entertainment and in terms of effectiveness as a scoring player, he was the supreme example of the great joy of Rugby, which is running with the ball.'

He was all of that. So much so, that the argument about how you would fit both Peter Barrie Jackson and Thomas Gerald Reames Davies into the world's eclectic Rugby team will occupy the gods for all time.

British Rugby at that time was brimming with individual talent. Grammar schools and secondary schools across the country provided a solid base for the teaching of the game and the emphasis was almost entirely upon individual skills, rather than team organisation. In the Midland and West country towns of England and the towns and cities of Wales too, the game was taught in schools covering the whole social spectrum. The universities of Oxford and Cambridge were at the zenith of their power, able to provide places for gifted games players as well as academics, and strengthened immeasurably physically by the intake of men returning from two years of compulsory National Service. What is more, the blissful self-indulgence of the boyhood of the men of that generation had not been wasted by the almost total addiction to television which was to come later. In those days, television sets were owned by only a small minority. In Britain and France, the men playing the first-class game were growing bigger and stronger, simply as physical specimens. They had not quite caught up with the physical power of South Africa and New Zealand, but the process was under way.

Above all, the players of that generation enjoyed the game. They laughed a lot off the field, and sometimes they even laughed on it. Tony O'Reilly tells the classic story of the day Phil Horrocks-Taylor, fly-half for

England, ran past Mick English, fly-half for Ireland, to win the game. There was no moaning in the Irish dressing room afterwards, no recriminations, but the other Irish players did ask English what had happened. 'Well, the Horrocks went one way, and the Taylor went the other, and I was left holding the hyphen,' mourned English. How could anyone be cross after that?

Oxford and Cambridge Universities also broke out of a period of attrition with a memorable match in which Onllwyn Brace, a fair-haired, darting man from the Welsh valleys with magic in his feet, played the game of running scrum-half which Danie Craven had envisaged as a possibility for Johnny Williams and the 1955 British Lions. The basis of the game was an extempore series of scissors or dummy scissors, in which the foil to Brace's dramatic improvisation was the soundness and intelligence of Mike Smith at fly-half.

Soon after Brace left Oxford and Iffley Road, Ken Scotland illuminated that fine, fast surface at Grange Road, Cambridge, with successive exhibitions of footballing talent and versatility which are remembered still. But Brace and Scotland were just two of a royal academy of Rugby talent at the Universities. In the clubs, too, there were brilliant hookers like Ernie Robinson of Coventry, and Bryn Meredith of Newport; tremendous props like Hughie McLeod of Hawick and Ray Prosser of Pontypool and Ron Jacobs of Northampton; formidable loose forwards like Johnny Gardiner of Coventry, Don White of Northampton, and Reg Higgins of Liverpool, and enough backs in Wales to fill three Lions' teams.

Far, far beneath these luminaries, but enjoying the game just as much, was the infinitely various world of junior Rugby, though some of the physical specimens playing it were so ancient that they would have been distinctly flattered to be associated with anything junior. This world was revealed in all its humour by a young writer called Michael Green, who served part of his apprenticeship in journalism travelling around with that great Northampton team of the 1950s, surely one of the strongest club teams ever to play the game. Green borrowed an idea used in another context and began to write about the world of Coarse Rugby. It was an hilarious adventure, like most of the slightly zany lives lived by all the assorted physical and athletic misfits who took great pleasure in trying and failing to play the game. It was a world of its own, and Michael Green opened a window on it.

This world had no frontiers and the escapades of its inhabitants have passed into the folklore of the game. The Old Millhillians once misbehaved themselves on an Easter tour of the West country, led by Bill Gibbs. From time immemorial, touring Rugby clubs have encountered these little difficulties with local hotels, and on this occasion, the management firmly asked the Old Millhillians to leave. This they did, but because of the Easter holiday, found it impossible to find alternative accommodation. Accordingly, W. D. Gibbs, who became the 48th president of the Rugby Football Union, and who was then Mayor of Bromley, telephoned the hotel he had just left and enquired if, by chance, they had any accommodation available. He explained that he was the Mayor of Bromley, and he had a civic delegation with him.

The hotel manager was delighted. 'Well, it just so happens. . .' he said. So His Worship the Mayor, complete with Rolls-Royce, sailed back to the hotel and booked the entire party back in again. It was some time before the hotel management discovered what had happened, but they smiled and put up with it.

The staff of the imposing North British hotel in Edinburgh did the same after Peter Robbins had led Coventry on a Scottish tour which still brings wrinkles of anguish to the extensive forehead of that club's distinguished president.

Coventry had played in Glasgow and had celebrated their victory by cutting a swathe right across Scotland to Edinburgh. The fact of Coventry winning was not surprising, because they were then one of the most powerful club sides in the world, but they were not noted for their spirit of adventure when it came to touring. Robbins had other ideas, and was relaxing in the state room of the North British at half past seven in the morning, enjoying a bottle of best claret and reflecting on a memorable night, when he was joined by one of Coventry's more earthy forwards.

A waiter materialised out of the background, and asked the newcomer if he would like some refreshment. 'I'll drink what the skipper's drinking,' he said.

Back came the waiter with the claret, which he offered for inspection before lovingly easing the cork out of the bottle. He then poured a little of the wine to be tasted.

At this, the earthy gentleman in question leapt out of his chair, and jerked the terrified waiter two feet off the ground by his collar and tie, and snarled, 'You pour me as much as the skip's got, or I'll smash yer face in'.

Danie Craven also maintains that part of his slight baldness is due to the hair he lost worrying about some of the brighter escapades of a joint Oxford and Cambridge team on tour in South Africa a few years after. These culminated in something of a disaster when a bed was being lowered from the seventh floor of a hotel in Durban, with the idea of manipulating it back in to another bedroom on the sixth floor. For some reason, it has always fascinated touring Rugby teams to empty completely the room of one of their fellows.

The bed-lowering operation is always a tricky manoeuvre, partly because the furniture removers are invariably giggling uncontrollably at the time, and this one went down with all hands. The bed escaped their grasp and crashed to the ground below, narrowly missing a fearfully expensive Mercedes motor-car, and mercifully failing to kill any of the passers-by. However, the hotel manager was not amused.

The next morning, the manager of the team rushed to present his apologies. He led a solemn deputation which assured the hotel manager that the damage would be paid for, that the culprit had been discovered and that he would be sent home at once in disgrace. The chances were that the culprit would be sent down from his University and his career ruined! The hotel manager subsided from righteous indignation to sympathetic horror in about five minutes, and the South African Rugby Board picked up the bill.

Another memorable moment occurred at a buffet lunch in Pretoria, when one of the team asked in a resonant Scottish accent whether the assembled company had seen his particular party trick, which was to whip the table cloth from under all the glasses and bottles and plates of things in aspic with one flick of the wrist, leaving all the glasses and bottles and plates of things in aspic standing on the table. The local worthies said, no, they had not seen that, though they had always wanted to do so. They gathered round, not hearing the patter of tiny feet as various large undergraduates suddenly found their presence required elsewhere. When the audience was comfortably in position, the would-be conjuror ripped away at the table-cloth, and sent the whole lot crashing on the floor.

'Oh dear,' said he. 'Failed again.'

The laughs extended to the field of play, too. On one occasion, R. C. B. Michaelson, recently captain of Cambridge, was isolated upfield, far ahead of his support. From the rear, the stentorian voice of J. J. McPartlin, recently captain of Oxford, bellowed, 'On your own'. Michaelson looked round desperately, and saw that he had no alternative. He put his head down and ploughed on, before being cut down by about four 15 stoners all tackling him in different directions at once. It took him some while to recover consciousness, and as he blinked up into the African sun, he saw McPartlin bending over him and saying disapprovingly through pursed lips, 'Greedy!'

9 The development of touring

Oxford and Cambridge Universities had already toured Argentina and Japan, and by 1960, the development of air travel was opening up the whole world to the possibilities of Rugby tours. International encounters of one kind and another began to tumble over each other. South Africa wanted more matches against the four home countries, and so the concept of the short tour was evolved.

Scotland began it by playing three matches in South Africa in 1960, including a test which they lost 18–10. Ireland followed Scotland to South Africa in 1961, Wales went in 1964 and England completed the cycle in 1972.

This encouraged the projection of similar tours in New Zealand, and Australia. England toured New Zealand in 1963 and 1973, Wales went in 1969, Scotland went in 1975 and Ireland in 1976. Australia hosted tours by Ireland in 1967, Scotland in 1970, England in 1975 and Wales in 1978.

There were two distinct curiosities about the pattern of results which emerged from these international tours. The only one of the four home countries to win a test in either South Africa or New Zealand was England, despite the fact that over most of the period in question Wales was consistently the most successful of the British teams. Wales, in fact, were beaten so heavily in South Africa in 1964 that it caused a complete reappraisal of the Welsh Rugby Union's attitude to coaching and to the structure of the game in its country.

England on the other hand, while going from bad to worse in the international championship in Europe, not only managed to tour South Africa unbeaten, and win the test against the Springboks 18–9 at Ellis Park, but even managed a decisive victory over New Zealand at Auckland in 1973. Wales, in 1969, had lost two tests to the All Blacks at Christchurch and Auckland almost as heavily as they had lost to the Springboks in 1964.

The other oddity about the short tour results was that Australia, traditionally the weakest of the seven major countries comprising the International Rugby Football Board, only lost one test when playing at home, and that was against Ireland in 1967. Australia beat Scotland in 1970, beat England twice in 1975 and even beat Wales twice in 1978 after

Wales had won the five nations championship in Europe by beating all four of the other countries. Over the years, many strong All Black teams have learned how difficult it can be to win in Australia because of the local conditions yet both England and Wales made the mistake of under-estimating the size of the task and quickly paid the price.

The four home countries also began a series of tours to the Argentine, although much to the annoyance of the hosts, the England tour there was cancelled in 1973 because of the threat of terrorist acts against the touring party. England fixed up a short tour of New Zealand instead and astonished everyone by beating the All Blacks after suffering a disastrous run of defeats in their provincial matches.

The Argentine also gave notice of potential development. The game in that country operates from a more limited base than it does in all the other countries with major international pretensions, but as the cycle of tours against the home countries progressed, it became obvious that the Argentines were gradually producing a nucleus of players who were individually good enough to compete in any company. This view was shared by South Africa, who did as much as anyone to encourage international Rugby football in the Argentine, and by France, who found the Argentines useful short tour opponents.

The attitude of the overseas unions to the concept of short tours was vastly different. Australia were prepared to take whatever opportunities they could to increase their participation in international competition, but South Africa and New Zealand were more cautious. South Africa did tour Ireland and Scotland in 1965 but with such disastrous results that New Zealand were confirmed in their instinctive distrust of such ventures. South Africa's tour in 1965 was made at the beginning of the Southern hemisphere's season when their players were relatively unfit, and thereafter, New Zealand took good care never to make the same mistake. When the All Blacks did finally agree to make a short tour, fourteen years after Scotland initiated them, it was arranged for the end of the season in the Southern hemisphere and the beginning of the season in Europe. This meant that the New Zealand players only had to maintain their level of fitness and to maintain the team-work and player development that they had established in the previous five months whereas the European sides were at the disadvantage of being at the beginning of all these three annual processes.

New Zealand were wise to protect their interests in this way because it could be argued that South Africa's tour of Ireland and Scotland in 1965, when they did not win a match, was psychologically the end of an era of Springbok supremacy which had lasted for nearly fifty years. South Africa went on winning home series, particularly against New Zealand, but teams in other parts of the world realised that what the French had started in 1958 they could all achieve. The legend of Springbok invincibility was shattered, and the All Blacks stepped happily into the void.

The All Blacks dominated the decade of the 1960s with a team that became one of the most powerful in the history of Rugby football, but the one thing they could not do was win in South Africa. They failed in 1960, at the beginning of their years of glory, and they failed in 1970, at the end.

Within a matter of weeks of the end of Scotland's short tour of South Africa in 1960, the All Blacks arrived for a major tour of that country. After their success against the Springboks in New Zealand in 1960, and after France's success in South Africa in 1958, the All Blacks thought that at last they would achieve their heart's ease. It was not to be. The Springboks won the series 2–1 despite some magnificent goalkicking by Don Clarke which won one test and drew another. Clarke did the job that Bob Scott blamed himself so bitterly for failing to do in 1949, and set a record for points scored on tour in South Africa, but it was still not enough. The Springbok selectors did their homework yet again, and analysed the All Blacks with their usual thoroughness in the proliferation of games that New Zealand have always foolishly undertaken before the first test.

South Africa undoubtedly had the makings of another outstanding Springbok team and that impression was confirmed when they left Cape Town at the end of their series against the All Blacks to begin a tour of Britain, Ireland and France. That was the last time the Springboks travelled by sea, and to those well-wishers who happened to bump into John Gainsford as they stepped on board the *Windsor Castle* in Southampton for the opening Press conference of the tour, the 1960–61 Springboks appeared the most likeable and civil of tourists. Unfortunately, Gainsford was in a very small minority when it came to public relations, and in a miserably wet winter, the touring party withdrew into itself both on and off the field.

The Springboks were captained by the young lock forward Avril Malan, then nothing like as mature as he was to become later. They also had a formidable front row in which Pict du Toit was a tight head prop of such iron strength that he was able to break almost every front row he played against. With Johan Claassen alongside Malan in the second row, and Doug Hopwood playing like a titan at number eight, the Springboks were able to beat all but two of their opponents in the forwards and the appallingly bad weather gave them the excuse for not letting the ball go much further.

The team also had a cheerful young extrovert named Frik du Preez playing as a loose forward and emergency goalkicker. At that age, he had something of the exuberance of a puppy, but when he acquired more of the gravity traditionally associated with Springbok forwards, he became one of the greatest forwards of the age.

That South African team had many other talents, which it did not fully explore. Some of the most gifted England wingers of the time confessed that Jannie Engelbrecht was the one winger who put the fear of God into them and little 'Mannetjies' Roux, in the centre, had enough explosive ability to fill a man twice his size. Lionel Wilson, too, was the essence of soundness at full-back and John Gainsford, the most articulate of the English-speaking contingent in the backs, was one of the best centres of the post-war era. Those watching from outside the Springbok camp felt that there was a dichotomy between the English backs and the Afrikaans forwards which was resolved in the forwards' favour, and that as a result, the backs did not enjoy either themselves or the tour nearly as much as they might have done.

Not that the Springboks' results were poor. They beat all the home countries, including an England team which was then coming to the end of a remarkable period of success in the international championship. Doug Hopwood scored the try that beat England, just as he had anchored the pack in a tremendous battle against the elements in the match against Wales at Cardiff.

The only opponents who met the Springboks on equal terms were the Barbarians and France. The Barbarians put together a team to beat the Springboks at their own game, which they did, and the match was made memorable by a remarkable tackle in which Haydn Mainwaring, the Barbarians' burly Royal Marines full-back, met the equally burly Avril Malan head-on after the Springbok captain had broken clean through with the ball. Mainwaring hit Malan so hard with a combination of a tackle and a shoulder charge that he knocked him yards into touch and laid him out. As a piece of symbolism, it could not have been equalled. The two men met, alone in midfield, like knights in the lists, and the young champion of South Africa was not only unhorsed but laid out cold.

That was the only match that the Springboks lost on tour, though they were held to a 0–0 draw by France. The French admitted afterwards that their tour of South Africa in 1958 and their study of the Springbok team in Britain had convinced them that it was necessary for them to demonstrate at the very beginning that French forwards were as virile as South Africans. 'We had to show that we were with them in a physical sense,' they said. Accordingly, the first few minutes were among the most explosive in Rugby history, and Gwynne Walters, the tiny Welsh referee, had to call the two captains together. Walters, who was usually meticulously dressed in a striped blazer, barely came up to the chests of the two players as he lectured them in his high tenor voice, but Malan, his back as straight as a guardsman answering a charge from his commanding officer, and Francois Moncla were left in no doubt that Mr Walters would send off their players one by one until none was left if that turned out to be necessary. The game then settled into a hard, evenly balanced struggle, but it was essentially a fair one. The French felt that they had made their point.

France left almost at once for a tour of New Zealand, and although they achieved nothing like the same unity of purpose, either on or off the field, as they had under Lucien Mias, and although their results did nothing like justice to the talent available in their country, they still produced enough glimpses of authentic flair to persuade a man like Fred Allen that France had something significant to contribute to the world of Rugby. Allen was soon to become coach of an All Black team at the peak of its country's Rugby power, and so the influence of France upon his thinking was one of the greatest importance to the development of the game.

The All Blacks pack was beginning to develop the players who were to carry New Zealand to the heights – Colin Meads and his brother Stan, Kel Tremain, Waka Nathan. Not quite the same class of forward was available in the front row, but even there, a young prop named Ken Gray was beginning to make his way up through the grades in local football in Wellington.

In 1962, New Zealand toured Australia and Australia toured New Zealand and in between the British Lions toured South Africa. The All Blacks won all their games in Australia, including one at Quirindi by 103–0, but some Australians were left shaking their heads at the turn of events which had led to scrum-half Des Connor playing for New Zealand after first playing international Rugby for Australia. It is an ill wind that blows no-one any good, however, and the loss of Connor enabled Australia to bring in a young scrum-half called Ken Catchpole who was to become the greatest scrum-half of modern times.

The Lions, not so well equipped behind the scrum as the 1959 team, made a tremendous effort both in selection and in their preparation to match South Africa's forward strength, and they succeeded to an extent which probably surprised even themselves. The first test was drawn and the Lions are convinced that only another piece of deplorable home town refereeing prevented them from winning the second. They subjected South Africa to the indignity of being pushed far over their line from a five yard scrum and Keith Rowlands touched the ball down but the referee would not give a try. All the Lions in that scrum will know to their dying days that a perfectly fair score was not granted, but instead of leading 1–0 in the series, with every hope of at least sharing the rubber, the Lions found themselves one down and on their way to a 3–0 defeat.

That series saw the development of Dawie de Villiers, at scrum-half for South Africa, and Frik du Preez confirmed the massive promise he had shown when beginning his international career in Britain two years earlier. Du Preez was an astonishing player, possibly the only lock of modern times who had every one of the skills necessary to the completely equipped forward. He could jump a truly remarkable height in the lineout, he could scrummage, he could kick, he could maul, he could tackle, he was hard, he could handle, he could pass and as if all that was not enough, he was as quick as almost any back in the world and could sustain his extraordinary pace for more than half the length of the field. He was also a fine place kicker. Even Colin Meads never came near that sort of natural talent and none of the other locks of recent times, with the single exception of Benoit Dauga, could manage more than four of du Preez's ten marks of greatness. All du Preez lacked was the ability to motivate himself consistently. The gods had been so kind to him that sometimes he played as if it did not really matter; but when he *was* switched on, and when he *was* really trying, no one, as they say in New Zealand, could come within coo-ee of him.

England went on a short tour of New Zealand in 1963 and were beaten in the second test by what they regarded as a mixture of pure gamesmanship and hometown refereeing. Don Clarke dummied to kick at goal from a mark ten yards inside his own half. By doing this, he persuaded the England forwards on the mark to charge too early, but instead of Clarke being penalised, as he should have been, the England forwards were penalised instead. This gave Clarke the advantage of kicking the ball

Frik du Preez, beginning his remarkable 50 yard run to score against the 1968 Lions.

from a placed position, instead of having it held above the ground by a team-mate until the moment of the kick. That in turn enabled Clarke to kick the goal and win the match 9–6. This was the sort of device that helped New Zealand and South Africa to preserve their records in their own countries for so long, and it was just one more step along the road towards neutral referees.

While this was happening, Australia toured South Africa and did something which New Zealand have only once been able to achieve and which only the Lions have been able to surpass. They beat South Africa in two consecutive tests and shared the series.

The Australian captain was John Thornett. Their inspiration was Ken Catchpole. Thornett was a long serving prop and a most likeable man who knew how hard the game could be in South Africa because in one of Australia's own early ventures into the world of short tours, they had taken the mother and father of a hiding at Ellis Park in 1961. On that occasion, Australia had caught the full blast of backs like Engelbrecht and Roux in the prime of their powers and confidence. South Africa scored eight tries that day, and won 28–3, and Thornett confessed afterwards that the Australians' pack went backwards so fast that it was in danger of trampling their own scrum-half, Ken Catchpole, to death!

Ken Catchpole, of Australia, the greatest scrum-half of modern times.

Thornett therefore took great satisfaction from the success of the Australian coach, Alan Roper, in building a competitive pack. That gave Catchpole the chance to control the game, and although he could not play in the first test because of injury, his brilliance in the next two, both of which Australia won, showed just why it was that every other scrum-half of Catchpole's time inclined their heads in deference to the master at the mention of his name.

It is hard to believe that even Haydn Tanner passed better than Catchpole. The speed with which he served the ball to his fly-half was uncanny. Indeed, it was so remarkable that one felt that one had to look and look and puzzle over it, like a really testing crossword, to work out just how he did it. He had great strength in the forearms and wrists, of course, but eventually it became apparent that the secret of his pass was his positioning. He always seemed to take up a position so that the ball came to him handily on the side away from that to which he wanted to pass. This meant that he never had to make a backswing. This had already been built in to his pass by his positioning and then he used a body pivot like a golfer to give the power platform necessary for the final snap of hand and wrist action to send the ball on its way. Catchpole himself, at a barbecue at Wilf Cohen's house in Sydney at the time of the England

Phil Hawthorne, the Australian fly-half who developed his game so brilliantly as a result of Catchpole's service.

tour of Australia in 1975, agreed that positioning was the element of the game upon which he had concentrated most in the work he did to develop his speed of pass.

This pass was a fly-half's dream. It enabled a youngster named Phil Hawthorne to develop his own game to something near world class and a whole succession of Australian backs gorged themselves on the fruits. For several years, this provided a platform for Australia to achieve results which ought to have been far beyond their capacity, considering how modest their forward resources were.

Catchpole was not only a brilliant passer. He was a profoundly re-sourceful footballer as well. He could kick beautifully, he could defend and his Rugby intellect was so sharp that he automatically took charge of the games he played in. He was not physically powerful, but before his career was ended prematurely by an injury sustained in a test against New Zealand, Kenneth William Catchpole was the scrum-half king.

Australia has always been an amazingly fertile Rugby country, con-sidering the demoralising drain of players to Rugby League. They have a knack of producing players which is unequalled anywhere, and there was a lock called Rob Heming in Ken Catchpole's Australian teams of the 1960s who would rank with the best of all time as a lineout jumper. He displayed an athleticism which was so startling that it is a pity that the modern media have not followed Dave Gallaher's advice in 1905 and filmed the technique of Heming's jumping and the sheer mastery of Catchpole's passing. This is the way the skills should be taught to the young, because schoolboys learn so much better by imitation.

When Catchpole was at his peak, his play was relished by a young scrum-half developing in New Zealand called Chris Laidlaw. Thanks to the example set by Charlie Saxton, New Zealand has been blessed with technically sound scrum-halves for as long as anyone can remember, but a heritage of that kind does depend upon regular contact with players of the highest international class, and Chris Laidlaw came along at the time when New Zealand most needed a new scrum-half to set fresh standards. Laidlaw provided those standards, and with his development of the spin pass, he gave scrum-halves everywhere another dimension of the game.

In the early 1960s, the All Blacks were completely absorbed by the ruck and all its associated techniques, and almost the whole of their game was directed towards deliberately creating situations where the im-measurably superior rucking skill of their forwards could be exploited. Therefore they developed the concept of committal play; of absorbing the opposing defence by deliberately committing it to the tackle, and using each point of check as a platform to set up another ruck, and therefore another loose ball. The focal point of this committal play was the centre where, instead of seeking to beat the opposition by the traditional skills of passing and running, New Zealand used a big, powerful man, built like a flank forward, to run straight into the opposition midfield defence to set up a ruck. On the 1963 tour, the man the All Blacks used for this crash running was Ian MacRae.

This type of play had various advantages. It played to New Zealand's strength in the ruck; the forwards knew exactly what was going to happen and therefore could organise their own running and support play more efficiently; it was safe, because it kept the play tight; and it put the opposition defence under such pressure in their own half of the field that the percentages alone ensured that Don Clarke would be given relatively more chances of using his remarkable skill and strength as a goalkicker.

This committal play was augmented by a policy of kicking from half-back. Again, this kept the ball in front of the forwards and forced the opposition to catch under pressure. Again, it was percentage Rugby. It depressed beyond measure those with grander visions of Rugby football as a handling and running game but it was undeniably efficient and it might have survived as the technical basis of the game, at least in those parts of the world where Rugby is played on largely damp or wet fields, if the laws had not been changed and if the concentration on rucking, at the expense of scrummaging, had not sown the seeds of New Zealand's own eventual defeat.

In 1963, the All Blacks did produce one world class prop out of nowhere in Ken Gray. His development on tour was one of the most remarkable features in a remarkable display of growing All Black forward strength, but it was undoubtedly an anachronism. Against Ireland, Wilson Whineray, the New Zealand captain, had a desperately uncomfortable afternoon against a young prop of iron strength named Ray

Chris Laidlaw, playing his first game at scrum-half for New Zealand, beats Herrero, the French flanker, with his new spin pass.

McLoughlin, who was to contribute so much to British tight forward supremacy eight years later. New Zealand beat Ireland by only one point, 6–5, and no matter how hard they tried, the All Blacks could neither quench McLoughlin nor discourage him.

Whineray is considered by New Zealanders to be one of their greatest captains. A courtly and highly intelligent man, he had a maturity and a facility for leadership which is rare among players, and he was a champion loose forward, but he was undoubtedly fortunate to have his own fairly modest ability as a scrummager covered by such a juggernaut of a pack. Ken Gray, Colin and Stan Meads, Kel Tremain and 'Waka' Nathan would be on the short list of forwards good enough to play for anyone, anywhere, at any time in the history of the game. New Zealand revelled in their ability, and that brave and loyal country had every justification for doing so.

The All Blacks lost only one match on tour in 1963–64, and that was against Newport. Dick Uzzell dropped a goal for Newport to give them a 3–0 victory, but the two men who came out of the match with most to remember were Glyn Davidge, the Newport number eight, and Earle Kirton, the young All Black fly-half.

Newport decided that on a wet day, they would block the All Blacks' superiority in the ruck by collapsing on the ball in such numbers in the loose that the referee would have no choice but to re-start the game with a scrum. As the New Zealanders indignantly and repeatedly pointed out, this was a technique which was strictly illegal, and was always penalised as such in New Zealand, but in Britain it was a grey area of the law where, for the moment, playing technique had crept ahead of refereeing consciousness. The technique soon became known as 'killing' the ball, but then, the expression was unknown.

The man who did most of the killing was Davidge, and he himself was very nearly killed in the process. The All Blacks quite naturally disapproved of what he was doing, and as the referee was not prepared to stop him, they did everything in their power to discourage him. After the match, his back was red raw with stud marks and weals. Davidge did not complain. 'They could kick me as much as they liked,' he said. 'We won, me old flow, didn't we?' ('Flow' was short for 'flower'. It was a habit of the cheerful Davidge to call almost everyone 'flower').

On the other side of the coin was the fate of Earle Kirton. He was blamed by his own countrymen for the defeat. He played in only eight more games on tour and was sent off into a limbo which lasted four years. In a country like New Zealand, this was very much worse than a prison sentence. It says much for his tenacity and strength of character that he came back and played so well on the 1967 All Blacks' brilliantly successful tour of Britain and France that he answered all his critics.

At that time New Zealand had never won all four international matches on a tour of Britain and they did not do so in 1963–64, because

Scotland held them to a 0–0 draw. However, that was scant comfort for British Rugby, and even less was forthcoming when the Barbarians played the All Blacks at Cardiff in the last match of the tour. The Barbarians' selectors seemed almost to have a conscience about the way they had beaten South Africa three years previously, and produced a team which played so appallingly loosely that the All Blacks won by 30 points. The match ended in a great wave of nostalgia when Wilson Whineray dummied through from 30 yards to score a try but those with the interests of British Rugby at heart simply felt a sick despair. The Barbarians' selection and the play of the team was all so bad and so naïve that it seemed as if British Rugby would never come to terms with the realities of what had to be done. Fortunately, like so many pits of despair, this match did provide a significant catalyst for the future, and even within the Barbarian club, it began to be appreciated that the teaching of Dave Gallaher's 1905 All Blacks was as relevant as ever – team organisation and method were the essential platforms for the utilisation of individual brilliance, and they would always defeat individual brilliance on its own. Even in their domestic fixtures, the Barbarians were learning that the team play of opposing clubs was improving to the point where it was becoming increasingly difficult to succeed against them with 15 individuals, no matter how talented. There was always a slightly patronising element, no matter how unintentional, about the concept of fifteen international players coming together for a bit of a jolly to show the peasants how to play, and in the next ten years, the tumbrils of Barbarian Britain were to become increasingly full of the heads of the aristocrats as the peasants built themselves a playing revolution.

The All Blacks went home from that tour of Britain to prepare for their series against the Springboks the following year. New Zealand forward play was at its peak, but in a three match series against Australia, they lost the third test by the quite embarrassing margin of 20 points to 5. Once again, Ken Catchpole proved that in at least one position, Australia were supreme, and once again, Rob Heming showed that when it came to lineout jumping very few forwards before or since have been able to put as much daylight between the soles of his boots and the ground.

South Africa, for their part, entertained Wales for a short tour, though it is doubtful whether Wales would agree that 'entertainment' was a suitable description of what happened. The Springboks were about to undergo the most damaging decade in their history, but they still found enough of their old power to crush Wales 24–3. Wales collapsed in the last twenty minutes and returned home not only chastened but uncomfortably aware that they could no longer survive on the cult of the individual. They had to follow the path trodden by Dave Gallaher and develop the science of team organisation. They knew that the Rugby Union had commissioned a major work on coaching and they awaited the result with interest.

Later that year, though, South Africa were beaten again in their own country, and again they were beaten by France. It was such a poor match that it recalled that beautifully dry observation once made about a University match between Oxford and Cambridge by Arthur Smith, who had captained Cambridge in 1958 and who had captained the Lions in South Africa in 1962. 'It was a case of two poor teams having an off day,' he said. 'There was much less in the match than met the eye!' Wales would have gladly settled for such poverty, because they have never beaten South Africa in all the years the two countries have been playing Rugby Union football.

The defeat by France brought South Africa swiftly back to earth, and even worse was to follow. In 1965, the Springboks made their own first tentative venture into the new world of short tours and suffered an unmitigated disaster. They played five matches in Ireland and Scotland, including two tests, and did not win one of them.

This was not altogether surprising, because the Springbok selectors had chosen Doug Hopwood as captain but their recommendation was not accepted by the South African Rugby Board. That august body appointed Avril Malan instead. Naturally, this caused a great deal of ill feeling. The status of Hopwood as a player was beyond reproach, and he had been an extremely successful captain of Western Province. Whatever the rights and wrongs of the issue, the side played so badly and looked so demoralised that enormous damage was done to South Africa's Rugby image. They did not look a bit like world champions. They looked very, very ordinary and very, very vulnerable. Psychologically, this was of incalculable value to British Rugby, which still had to get used to the idea that it might have the resources to be capable of finishing higher than last in the world of major international Rugby.

It was a bad year for South Africa, because on their return from Ireland and Scotland, they set off for a major tour of Australia and New Zealand during which they lost five tests out of six. Once more, they made an unpromising beginning by decreeing yet another change in the captaincy. Avril Malan was dropped and the job was given to the Springboks' young scrum-half, Dawie de Villiers. This caused much less dissension, but it did not help South Africa's results. They lost both tests to Australia as well as their match against New South Wales on their way out to New Zealand and subsequently played with such a lack of spirit against the All Blacks that Colin Meads found them unrecognisable as the foes who had so often shattered the steel of New Zealand. The Springboks did win the third test at Christchurch when Tiny Naude, one of their locks, summoned up enough strength and concentration at the end of an exhausting game in mud and slush to kick a wide-angled, immensely difficult penalty goal to give his side a 19–16 victory. The recovery was even more remarkable for the fact that South Africa were losing 16–5 at half-time.

'Tiny' Naude turns away in triumph after kicking the goal that enabled South
Africa to beat New Zealand in the mud at Christchurch.

Two tries by that formidable centre John Gainsford inspired South Africa, but the Springboks could not sustain the mood and they were beaten comfortably in the final test. For once, New Zealand found South Africa unable to compete consistently in the forwards, but the All Blacks always feared the Springbok backs, and especially Gainsford. He had a magnificent physique and an unquenchable spirit. Danie Craven always said that Gainsford was one of the few backs who could do a series of interval sprints in training and somehow dig down into his guts to produce his fastest time for his last run.

Gainsford was even prepared to take on the legendary Meads! Gainsford himself recalls with a laugh that once he was so outraged by something that Meads did in that 1965 series that he raced up the field and jumped on Meads as he lay on his back on the ground and pummelled him with his fists for all he was worth. 'Colin just caught my wrists and held me like a vice and laughed up at me. "Now you know what test Rugby is all about, son," he said.'

On that tour, South Africa did not only suffer disaster on the playing field. While the Springboks were actually in New Zealand, Dr H. F. Verwoerd, then Prime Minister of South Africa, let it be known that as far as he was concerned any All Black teams touring South Africa would have to be all white, just as they had in the past. He was not prepared to accept a racially mixed New Zealand team containing Maoris.

For the first time in their history, New Zealand refused to accept that condition of selection, and although they regarded their matches against South Africa as being for the championship of the world, and consequently cherished them almost as much as the game itself, they said in effect, 'If we can't bring our Maoris, we won't come'. And so the New Zealand tour of South Africa in 1967 was postponed, and the All Blacks went instead on a hurriedly arranged 16-match tour of Britain and France. This was such a success, from every point of view, that after ten years of thinking about it, the International Board came to the conclusion that there might be something in it after all, and decreed that all future major tours should be of roughly the same length, instead of 24 or 26 matches, or even longer, as they had been in the past.

Before that, though, New Zealand played a home series against the British Lions, and won it 4–0. The game played by the Barbarians against the All Blacks in 1964 had been bad enough from the point of view of British Rugby, but the series in 1966 was the worst in British history. It had only one merit, and that was that it was so bad that it made a few more thinking players determined to improve the understanding of the game in Britain and it made the committee of the Four Home Unions define the functions of manager, assistant manager and captain so that there could be no doubt that in future the assistant manager had supreme authority for the playing preparation of the team. On previous Lions' tours, the assistant manager had been not much more than an odd-job man, part-time secretary, and part-time baggage man, but in 1966 the intention was that John Robins should use his ample physical education qualifications to coach the team. This intention was frustrated by the captain, Mike Campbell-Lamerton, who insisted that the Lions captain should retain all his previous authority. The result was such a playing disaster that some of the leading players became thoroughly impatient with the squabble and all its attendant circumstances. 'The manager should have sent the pair of them home,' said one.

The manager, Des O'Brien, did no such thing, and the team – split at the top and split in the middle by the formation of various rebellious factions – limped round New Zealand writhing in the death agonies of British Rugby Past. It could even be argued that such an immensely damaging trauma was necessary to prod British Rugby into accepting that Dave Gallaher had been right in 1905, and that Rugby football was indeed a team game which could be improved out of sight by organisation and intelligent use of detailed tactics. If so, British Rugby can only be grateful to Mike Campbell-Lamerton and John Robins, because they paid an appalling price in loss of tranquillity in their private lives.

The day the 1966 Lions left for New Zealand, they went to Twickenham to watch the finals of the Middlesex sevens. The tournament was dominated by a young student playing in the backs for Loughborough Colleges. His name was Davies. He was Welsh. His middle Christian name was Gerald and he played with such a breathtaking mixture of footwork, artistry and sheer blistering pace that no one was in any doubt that a great new star had been born. Seven-a-side tournaments are notoriously unreliable as vehicles in which to judge the abilities of players in the fifteen-a-side game, but the watching Lions were just as certain that this young man, Thomas Gerald Reames Davies was a player of extraordinary talent as the ecstatic crowd. It was remarked at the time that some of the more fortunate of the Lions' selections among the midfield backs almost ran up the steps of the aircraft that evening, in case the selectors changed their minds and asked Gerald Davies to go instead! Not that he could have turned the tide of New Zealand forward superiority in that series, any more than Peter Jackson could in 1959, but, like Jackson, he would have thrilled an awful lot of people on the way.

In 1966, the New Zealand pack was probably at its peak. It had Ken Gray and Ed Hazlitt propping Bruce McLeod. It had Colin Meads and Stan Meads at lock, and it had Waka Nathan and Kel Tremain flanking Brian Lochore at number eight. If the lineout of the day had been a contest of jumping, that particular All Black pack may not have rated much above average, but the lineout of that particular day and most others was a contest of organised law evasion – knowing, as Kel Tremain once said, whose turn it was to push and whose turn it was to jump. No one did that better than the forwards of the 1966 All Blacks.

The only British player who really rated against them was not a forward at all, but a young Irish midfield back named C. M. H. Gibson. He joined the tour late so that he could take his examinations at Cambridge University, but whether he was playing fly-half or centre, he persuaded New Zealand Rugby enthusiasts from 90 mile Beach to Bluff that he was really something special.

That tour demonstrated more clearly than anything that what British Rugby had been doing up to then was nowhere near good enough, and in the process, it made some significant converts to the missionary work that was so necessary in the four home countries, but it did it in different ways. Ray McLoughlin, for instance, thought that the New Zealand way was essentially practical and essentially right. Don Rutherford, the England full-back, acknowledged the power and technique of New Zealand loose forward play but said that he thought Rugby was to be enjoyed, and he did not enjoy playing Rugby in New Zealand.

It was to be another eight years before the Lions had sufficient raw physical power to intimidate an opposition pack. In 1966, it was the All Blacks who did all the intimidating, and in a contact sport, this has a significant effect on the psychology of match play. By then, Colin Meads had achieved the status of a colossus in the game, both as a player and as a ferociously hard competitor. As far as British Rugby was concerned, he

'Gerald Davies, a breathtaking mixture of artistry, footwork and sheer, blistering pace . . .'

was the biggest of the baddies and although New Zealand Rugby players do not yet wear black hats, they do wear very large black shirts. The stories of physical one-upmanship on that tour always involved New Zealand players, rather than Lions, and the pick of the stories always involved Colin Meads, rather than anyone else.

Thus it was that there was an enormous hullaballoo when Colin Meads, a big man in every sense, flattened David Watkins, the tiny Lions' fly-half. The story went that Ken Kennedy, the Lions' hooker, derided Meads for his action, and asked him why he did not pick on someone his own size. 'But he hit me first,' protested Meads. 'Where?' asked Kennedy scornfully. 'On the knee?'

No doubt the playing background that produced incidents of this sort was one of the reasons why Don Rutherford, a full-back, did not enjoy playing in New Zealand. Ray McLoughlin, on the other hand, was a front row forward who not only relished the fray and all the slings and arrows of outrageous fortune that went with it, but who could see that there were areas of forward play, and particularly the front row, where British players could beat New Zealand. Both had a justification for their view and this was important, because their views became more and more influential in the technical revolution which was to reshape British Rugby and which was given its greatest impetus by the debacle of the 1966 Lions tour of New Zealand.

Rutherford had an arm broken on tour, and spent the subsequent time before he returned home studying the game in such depth that the Rugby Union eventually appointed him as their coaching administrator, although, being the Rugby Union, and not the English Rugby Union, they called him something different!

By then, and to their great credit, the Rugby Union had already commissioned the compilation of a coaching manual, based on the work which had been done for three or four years in the East Midlands of England by an Englishman, a Scotsman and a Welshman, Jeff Butterfield, Bob MacEwan, and Ray Williams. This was the first major work on coaching produced by any country, and it formed the basis for all the others that followed. The manual described and illustrated the individual and the unit skills of the game, and at the same time, it created a new language, at least for European readers. Much of the credit for the dramatic impact of expressions such as 'snap shove' must go to Bob MacEwan, who had such a gift for communication that it is hard to escape the conclusion that those newspapers in Fleet Street that specialise in the projection of four letter verbs missed an editor of distinction when Bob MacEwan decided to concentrate on shoe manufacture!

Ironically, the teachings of this coaching manual were largely ignored in England to begin with. The manual defined a whole new world to be conquered, but few of the major clubs could see any reason for doing things differently from the way they had always done them before, and without their example to enthuse others, it was left to a few keen school-masters and to the emerging countries to seize avidly upon the literature becoming available so they could improve their knowledge of the game.

The one area of Britain where this new coaching Bible was treated as the gospel was Wales. Their experience in South Africa in 1964 had persuaded them that their coaching of the game needed to be placed on a sounder footing and they embraced the new philosophy with such enthusiasm that they were soon reaping most of the benefits for which the Rugby Union should have had the patents. It was most noticeable to those involved in this technical revolution that Welsh players were infinitely more interested in technique than the English. Even the Scots and the Irish had men among them who were sufficiently interested to master the details of the new crafts. English players, certainly at first-class club level, lagged nearly three years behind and there was a damaging reluctance for English international or near international players, coming to the end of their careers, to put on track suits and go out and learn enough about coaching to be able to help the rising generation. They preferred to stand in the bar and criticise. This lack of involvement contributed to a lack of continuity, a lack of reliable player evaluation, a lack of capability in the field of selection and even to a lack of understanding of the modern game. This was a crippling handicap to English Rugby. In 1963, England had come to the end of a century of being number one in the British pecking order at Rugby football, and the lack of enthusiasm for coaching, with a few notable exceptions like 'Chalky' White, at Leicester, simply made the task of recovery harder and harder. As international Rugby stretched out into the 'seventies, it became more and more evident that England had been left so far behind because of the failure of its first-class clubs that over a period of twelve years, Wales could expect to beat them five times out of six. Even countries like Ireland and Scotland, with infinitely slimmer resources, achieved runs of success against England which were too consistent to be explained away as historical accidents.

However, it remains a fact that having led the way into the world of organised coaching in Europe, England were the last to explore it, and they have paid the price. They cannot complain. The chance was there for the taking in 1966, and they had in the Midlands and the West Country clubs which could and should have provided the basis for the new technology.

Those clubs then were only concerned with the next week and the next match. They were not even very interested in the visit of Australia. After all, who were Australia? Catchpole? Hawthorne? Never heard of them! Australia was a second division team.

Judged simply by results, this disparaging assessment proved fairly accurate, because Australia lost thirteen of the thirty matches they played in Britain and Ireland. The Australians' problem was that they were not quite good enough in the forwards, but despite that handicap, they beat both the first division countries at that time, England and Wales, and they also had a profound influence on Carwyn James, then developing his career as a coach. It was the 1966 Australian team in Britain, and their back line more than any other which convinced him of the value, the effectiveness and the beauty of quick finger-tip passing from the scrum-half to the wing. The 1966 Australians also convinced him that the key to the operation was the scrum-half. The way Ken Catchpole wasted not an inch nor a split second in the delivery of his pass however the ball came to him and from whatever situation made a lasting impression on James. He had never before seen a scrum-half as technically accomplished as Catchpole who, like Clive Rowlands of Wales, was made captain of his country on his international debut. The combination of Catchpole with Phil Hawthorne at fly-half had done as much as anything to produce a period of remarkable success for Australia at international level. They showed, as John Hipwell and Alan Maxwell showed in New Zealand twelve years later, just what could be achieved by a brilliantly fast and accurate transfer of the ball. They gave Welsh and British Rugby a lot to think about, particularly Barry John and Gerald Davies, two young Welsh backs winning their first caps.

10 The influence of the 1967 All Blacks

In 1967, England toured Canada, after losing badly in a series of practice matches against provincial teams beforehand, and Cardiff became the first club side to make a short tour of South Africa at the specific invitation of the South African Rugby Board. The Cardiff tour was interesting for another reason, too. On the Lions tour of New Zealand the year before, the Welsh players had grouped themselves together to such an extent that, after reading Des O'Brien's tour report, the tours committee of the Four Home Unions resolved that in future, Welsh players would not be allowed to room together on tour. It so happened that in 1967, Cardiff had a team full of brilliant young backs who were all practically certain to be chosen for the British Lions tour of South Africa the following year, and as most of them were West Walians, and therefore very Welsh, the Four Home Unions' edicts about the dangers of Welsh clannishness and Welsh homesickness were especially relevant.

As it turned out, there was no cause for concern. Thanks to such innovations as package holidays to the Costa Brava, the younger generation of Welshmen had got over the old Celtic feeling that foreign parts began at Newport and that to all intents and purposes, the river Severn was the river Styx. Gerald Davies, Maurice Richards, Gareth Edwards and Keri Jones sailed through the tour with every sign of outgoing enjoyment. Obviously, some were of a more serious nature than others, and three of them frequently spoke in Welsh, but there was none of the moping that had caused so much trouble in New Zealand the year before. With John O'Shea to make them laugh, and a group of supporters who were determined to enjoy themselves at whatever the cost to their livers, constitutions and pockets, it was a very happy tour. Cardiff lost badly to Northern Transvaal in the final match, as so many other teams have done since, but they had a great day when they topped 40 points against Eastern Province, and Maurice Richards himself scored 19. In those days, he was not only a left winger with a mesmerising run; he was also a goalkicker of some pretensions.

Cardiff had not been home three weeks when the Four Home Unions tours committee met in London to appoint the manager and coach of the 1968 Lions in South Africa. This type of forward planning was an innovation. Néver before had a British Lions touring management been appointed a year in advance of the tour. The idea was to give the manager and coach a whole domestic season in which to get to know each other and to get to know the players they wanted for the tour.

The committee appointed David Brooks of England as manager and Ronnie Dawson of Ireland as coach, and thanks to the unhappy experiences of Des O'Brien and John Robins the year before, neither of them was left in any doubt as to their own precise area of responsibility.

They had an eventful season to study, because New Zealand had declined to tour South Africa without their Maoris, and at short notice, had managed to arrange to tour Britain, Ireland and France instead. This turned out to be a marvellous bonus for British Rugby, because the All Black team was so powerful in certain specific areas that it was exactly the technical stimulus the players of the four home countries needed. In addition, the All Blacks played a type of Rugby which was far more expansive than anything New Zealand had attempted for forty years, and for that, everyone could thank their manager, Charlie Saxton, and their coach, Fred Allen. Both had been associated with the New Zealand Services team which had toured Britain and Europe at the end of the war, and they were lucky enough to inherit a pack which was capable of fuelling almost any type of Rugby football, no matter how ambitious.

When Saxton and Allen revealed their plans to their team, some of the senior players like Colin Meads were frankly sceptical. An All Black pack was a very exclusive club and the New Zealand forwards who belonged to it had been used to playing in a team designed to bring the play back always to them. Saxton and Allen wanted to involve all 15 players in a form of total Rugby. Admittedly, there would be areas of concentration, and specific moves designed to employ the remarkable talents of full-back Fergi McCormick, but basically, the idea was to involve everyone. Meads and the rest of the heavy mob pursed their lips and shook their heads in doubt but eventually agreed to 'give it a go'.

The result was thoroughly absorbing. The pack was marginally past its towering peak of two years previously, but it was still good enough to take care of most of the one-off teams put up against it, and in doing so, it provided Fred Allen with the platform to express his own view of the game. For at least 60 years, New Zealand had played in nothing like the same style, but by making such a commitment to attack, the 1967 All Blacks did the game of Rugby football throughout the world a service which even they probably did not appreciate.

The All Blacks played 15 matches in Britain and France and won 14 of them. The other game, against East Wales, in Cardiff, was drawn. The team set new standards of technique, which were understood better than ever before because of the impact of television. Their coach, Fred Allen, was an incisive and articulate character and above all, their leading player, Colin Meads, was of the stuff of which legends are made. Until that tour, Rugby football in all of Britain, except Wales, had been rather a dress circle game, somewhat remote and somewhat upper class, but the 1967 All Blacks played Rugby for the gods, as well as the front row of the stalls. In doing so, they achieved the projection of the game to the masses in a way that had never been done before.

There were anomalies, of course. It would have been altogether too depressing for European Rugby if there had not been. Ian MacRae, for instance, had practically nothing to contribute to the style envisaged by Fred Allen and therefore, he had a miserable tour and should not have been selected. It was encouraging for British Rugby that he *was* selected because it was a mistake, and it was heartening to know that such an efficient management as that possessed by the 1967 All Blacks could make mistakes. Similarly, it made no sense to have Chris Laidlaw as one scrum-half, and Sid Going as the other. Both were masters of their own particular game, but Laidlaw played to the backs, and Going played to the forwards. Again it was a mistake, but it was an encouraging mistake for the All Blacks' European hosts. The difference between Laidlaw and Going has been analysed in New Zealand where, thanks to the rueful remarks made by various fly-halves, it has borne in upon the natives that every fly-half who played outside Laidlaw in an All Black trial went on to greater things, whereas almost all those who played outside Going did not. This is not to disparage Going. Loose forwards loved him, but he was not the type of scrum-half needed by the 1967 All Blacks.

There were some pretty ordinary players elsewhere in that New Zealand back division, too, but they had their deficiencies covered by a superb pack and the football played by Laidlaw and Earl Kirton at half-back, and by the immense resource shown by Fergi McCormick at full-back.

As in the case of every team touring Britain and France, the 1967 All Blacks were also materially helped by the fact that every team they played was a scratch team. These teams had no past, or future, in the way that provincial teams have in New Zealand and South Africa. They had only a present. They existed only for the hour, or to be more precise, for the hour and twenty minutes. Then they were no more.

Thinking of that factor, which is so vital in a team game, perhaps history has over-rated the 1967 All Blacks. They arrived early in the British season, before any of the home teams were properly fit, and yet they beat Midlands, London and the Home Counties, that team which sounded so much like a British railway before the days of nationalisation, by only 15–3. They beat the South of England, who would be confidently expected to lose by 50 points to anyone these days, by only 16–3. They beat West Wales 21–14. They beat South West France 18–14. They beat Monmouthshire 23–12. They drew 3–3 with East Wales. They beat the Barbarians 11–6, and had to come back from the dead to do it.

Knowing what we know now about those teams, and the way they were selected and prepared, it is not all that impressive a record, but more

Sid Going, All Black scrum-half. Loose forwards loved him.

than anything else, it was the statement of faith in 15-man attacking Rugby, after years and years of ten-man attrition, that made the 1967 All Blacks so important in the development of the game.

They were hesitant themselves for the first half hour of their tour. In their first match, against a weak and badly selected North of England team playing within the confines of the dog track at the White City, Manchester, they saw their opponents miss four kicks at goal before they scored themselves and they led only 6–0 at half-time. After that, the All Blacks found some confidence and went on to score six tries and win 33–6. There was one symbolic moment in the game, in the second half, when Colin Meads pulled the ball in to his chest with one hand, dropped his other shoulder and, with his eyes glittering, charged into the North pack. It took five men to stop him and he laid the ball back like a precious stone on a velvet cushion for Sid Going to pick up. A North of England committee man – sadly all too typical of the game in England then and now – turned round in the stand and asked in a loud voice, 'Now what does he think he's achieved by that?'

Meads, of course, had taken out more than half the North's pack, and the All Blacks found themselves positively festooned with overlaps when Going moved the loose ball, but such was the ignorance in England about the technique of the game at that time, that a man who had some influence over decision-making had no inkling at all of what advantage Meads had achieved for his side.

The 1967 All Blacks reached their peak in the first half hour of their match against England at Twickenham. The football they played was such a marvellous blend of power, skill; purpose and tactical shrewdness that they scored 18 points, and Peter Larter, one of the England locks, confessed afterwards, 'I thought they were going to score fifty'.

England were spared that humiliation because the All Blacks relaxed. With a try still worth only three points, England would have had to make at least four scores to overhaul their opponents, and even more unlikely, they would have had to do it while New Zealand scored nothing. Both teams knew that this was about as likely as Colin Meads finishing last in a selection from the 16 forwards on view and that knowledge inevitably coloured the rest of the game. In the time remaining, England did in fact score 11 points, while New Zealand scored only five, and Bob Lloyd had the considerable personal satisfaction of becoming the only opponent on tour to score two tries against the All Blacks, but it was all something of an anticlimax. The game had been won and lost, and the game in Europe would never be the same again.

Unfortunately, the All Blacks could not play Ireland because an outbreak of foot and mouth disease in England restricted travel, but they went on to beat Wales and Scotland without any difficulty. They beat France, too, but not before Colin Meads had had his head badly cut by Alain Plantefol's boot studs, and not before the All Blacks had been made to work very hard indeed. The All Blacks were surprised by the quality of the play throughout France. After their visit in 1964, they had expected their games to be much easier.

The All Blacks were also surprised when they returned to Cardiff to play East Wales, in the last match before they played the Barbarians at the end of the tour. Injuries forced the All Blacks to field a team some way short of their best, and East Wales had enough strength in their pack and outside it to give the All Blacks a nasty fright.

In the front row, East Wales had John O'Shea and Jeff Young, who were powerful scrummagers, and in the back row they had John Hickey and Tony Gray, a combination of implacable competitiveness and real pace. East Wales also had the young Barry John and Gareth Edwards at half-back, and John Dawes and Gerald Davies in the centre, so they had an excellent balance of footballers capable of squeezing most of the advantage from any situation. Both sides scored a try in their 3–3 draw.

The All Blacks had an even bigger fright against the Barbarians. With ten minutes left, the Barbarians were leading 6–3 and their full-back Stewart Wilson was taking a kick at goal, none too difficult, which would have put them ahead 9–3 if it had been successful. Wilson missed, but it did not seem important as the Barbarians won a loose ball in defence and Gerald Davies broke clear with only Fergi McCormick covering across.

Of all the players in the world whom you would have backed without hesitation to score every time from that sort of situation, Gerald Davies would have been top of the list, because he had brilliant footwork as well as unmatchable pace, but McCormick somehow stopped him. It was one of the greatest pieces of defence in modern Rugby and it was even more remarkable for the fact that he had done almost exactly the same thing in the same sort of situation earlier in the match to stop Keri Jones, who in full stride was as fast as Davies.

Even then, the All Blacks felt they would lose. As 'Waka' Nathan, one of their great loose forwards, said years afterwards, 'We were dead. There was no way that we could win that one, but then that guy Stewart Wilson kicked for touch on the wrong side of the field, away from his forwards, and missed, and that let us in for the try to win the match.'

It had been an eventful tour. Quite by chance, because of the haste with which the tour had been arranged following the postponement of the All Blacks' tour to South Africa, the International Board had discovered almost the ideal length for a major tour. The New Zealand players thoroughly enjoyed it, because they were all back home by Christmas and because the tour did not make unfair demands on employers or on *locum tenens*, of whatever trade or profession, who were standing in for the All Blacks while they were away. The imminence of the international matches – New Zealand's game against England was the fourth match of their tour – concentrated the minds wonderfully and did away with the interminable build-ups which had always taken the edge off touring teams in the past. The players who were any good were fully employed, and those who weren't were soon back home and out of their misery. The tour had lasted ten weeks and in retrospect, one of the most remarkable things about it was that it took the International Board exactly ten more years to accept what they had discovered by accident in 1967, and that was that major tours should be restricted to a maximum of ten weeks.

The tour also saw the emergence of television as a major factor in the world of Rugby football, and at no time was this more apparent than in the All Blacks' match against Scotland at Murrayfield, when Colin Meads was sent off the field for dangerous play. Almost at the end of the match, Meads had followed through after a loose ball and had aimed a lunging kick as David Chisholm, the Scottish fly-half, went to pick it up. The referee, Kevin Kelleher, of Ireland, deemed it dangerous play because he felt that Meads was indifferent whether he kicked the ball or Chisholm. As Mr Kelleher had already given Meads a formal warning after an incident earlier in the match, he had no alternative under the laws of Rugby but to send him from the field.

The incident was replayed over and over again on television, and this technique enabled people to form opinions which no doubt would have been very different, if like Kevin Kelleher, they had had only their own instant visual impression of the incident to guide them. There is no doubt that slow motion replays of incidents like this, and those depicting playing skills, have helped very considerably in the understanding of the game and its problems, and as long as television technique is regarded in that light, it is of value. But it is as well to remember that under the laws of Rugby football, the referee is the sole judge of fact, not the television camera, and although, being human and fallible, he may make mistakes, they have to be accepted. The referee may well learn from his mistakes, and so may the players and everyone else, but they cannot be undone.

Not that Kevin Kelleher did make a mistake. He had far more justification for doing what he did than the New Zealand management, Charlie Saxton and Fred Allen, who afterwards tried to pre-judge the disciplinary hearing by choosing Meads for the next match in advance of its decision. They had time to think about what they were doing, and they still made the wrong decision, so their understanding of Kevin Kelleher's position should have been even more sympathetic.

Ironically, the All Blacks had chosen Kevin Kelleher to referee the match against Scotland because they thought he was a softer and more tolerant referee than another Irishman, Paddy D'Arcy, who by quite some distance was the best referee in the world at that time.

The All Blacks objected to the fact that in one of their provincial games, Paddy D'Arcy had exposed the fact that their play in the lineout was a massive and deliberately organised assault on the laws of Rugby football and he had penalised it as such. In this, he was supported completely by the evidence of television which in turn was indebted to the fact that in Bill McLaren, the BBC had discovered a commentator with such a profound understanding of the technique of the game and the laws that he impressed even a critic as trenchant as Colin Meads. There is no doubt that like Michael Green, Bill McLaren opened a window on the world of Rugby football and millions of players and spectators had a better view of the game as a result.

The play of the 1967 All Blacks in the lineout fairly took the breath away of the first-class playing community in Britain. They had never seen organised cheating like it, but they were very quick to copy it and in no time, everyone was putting into practice organised obstruction. One of these techniques was called the one-step theory. Teams playing against the All Blacks were soon aware that their opponents all advanced one step sideways as the ball was thrown in from touch, which meant that when all the barging and ricochetting had finished, the odds on the ball coming down on the side of the All Blacks had been appreciably shortened.

Scotland's game against New Zealand provided the most controversial moment of the tour, and it also provided the funniest story. Again, one of the players involved was Colin Meads, and the story illustrates better than anything the awe in which he was held both as a player and as what might be euphemistically described as a competitor.

According to the story, the forwards were forming up for a lineout when there was an interruption in the play while a player was attended for an injury. Meads used the few moments of respite to address some succinct words to Erle Mitchell, whom he was marking in the lineout, and who was playing his first game for Scotland. Apparently, Meads went into some detail as to what he was going to do to Mitchell for the rest of the game. He left nothing to the imagination. Hiroshima would have been a squib by comparison.

Mitchell told the story to his team-mates afterwards, and they listened round-eyed in amazement. At the end, one of them asked breathlessly, 'And what did you say to him, Airle?'

Mitchell replied, 'I told him to bugger off, but I have tae admit, I did'na say it in a very loud voice!'

The influence that the 1967 All Blacks had on the playing of the game was just as profound in both the short and the long term as their organised disregard of the laws. Chris Laidlaw's beautifully controlled spin pass at scrum-half set youngsters everywhere trying to master the technique. Even new international players like Gareth Edwards realised that their passing was inadequate in the light of what Laidlaw was doing, and set to work to try to add the spin pass to their repertoire. The ability to imitate is strongest up to the age of 15. After that it becomes much more difficult, and although Edwards eventually acquired sufficient confidence to spin pass off his right hand, he never did acquire the confidence to do it off his left. This is why the instruction of technique is so essential at schoolboy level. If players are not fully equipped in the skills by the time they leave school, they never will acquire them.

Team organisation is a different matter. That can be acquired at any age, and the innovations introduced by the 1967 All Blacks quickly became adopted world wide. The use of the full-back in attack on the short side, and the very short ball given from fly-half to centre, or from one centre to another, to make a subtle change in the line of run, were soon copied. The practical demonstrations of the All Blacks' rucking technique were also absorbed and digested even more completely than they were in 1963–64, because the All Blacks in 1967 were playing a game that was infinitely more attractive for the players. It was also more attractive for the spectators, but that is not very important in a game like Rugby football. Techniques must appeal to the players. Even the cheating of the 1967 All Blacks circled the globe like Asian 'flu, and provided a new dimension of difficulty for referees everywhere.

Technically, British Rugby was still in its infancy, but it was a period of great excitement and great happenings. The game was being written about and televised in greater depth, it was being thought about, and inevitably, some of the minds doing the thinking were original minds and were shaping the excellence of British Rugby which was to follow so quickly upon all this effort.

Gareth Edwards, scrum-half for Wales, caught in a bad position on his weak side and therefore having to dive pass.

Inevitably, too, the thinkers and the analysts were disparaged. The Rugby Football Union's centenary history, published in 1971, makes no reference at all to the way the game in Britain was dragged out of the dark ages by people who had the eyes to see. No reference was made to the production of the coaching manual. Those who suggested that things could be done better by doing them differently were sneered at. But this disparagement and these sneers were irrelevant. They were a part of the fuddy-duddy past.

The players, particularly those in Wales, were interested in the new techniques, and they applied themselves to mastering them in such a way that they set new standards for at least the next decade and dominated the European championship throughout that period.

Very little of this had time to bear fruit before the 1968 British Lions set off to tour South Africa. Consequently, Ronnie Dawson, the appointed coach, was in the unfortunate position of those brave and gallant souls who went to their deaths a day or two before the Armistice on November 11, 1918. They knew, as Ronnie Dawson knew, that the great day was coming, but it had not quite arrived, and in the meantime, they and he had to go out and do their best to survive.

The 1968 Lions won all but one of their provincial matches, and saw very clearly that South Africa had been reduced to a very thin crust of 16

On this occasion, the ball comes in such a way that Edwards is able to turn, and although he is still on his wrong side, he is able to deliver a spin pass.

or 17 players who were of international calibre. After that, there was a horrifying drop in class. However, the Lions could not break that crust, and they lost the series 3–0, with one match drawn.

Looking back, one can only have sympathy with Ronnie Dawson, because no one could have tried harder to make British Rugby face reality and to bring it into the second half of the twentieth century. His dedication was total, and such was his personal level of fitness that he was able to run Keith Jarrett into the ground when he sought to show that young player that his attitude to the tour was not sufficiently responsible.

Unfortunately, that criticism could have been applied to many other players besides Keith Jarrett. It was an irresponsible tour, and this cut the ground from under Dawson's feet. Indeed, the poor behaviour of the team caused such concern in South Africa that Dr Danie Craven subsequently revealed that one of the major provinces actually proposed that the 1968 Lions should be sent home. In view of all this, it was a miracle that Ronnie Dawson achieved as much as he did. By the second half of the tour he had even built a competitive pack, but he had to concentrate his energies so much on the forwards to do so that in the end, the backs let him down and lost the third test which was there for the taking in Cape Town.

Once again, therefore, the Lions were left pursuing the old cult of the individual and it was not good enough to win a team game. As ever, there were some memorable individual performances, such as a try scored by Gerald Davies against Boland at Wellington, but in the tests, the Lions never produced that irresistible surge of team effort that the All Blacks had displayed so magnificently the year before.

The forwards of the 1968 Lions, like other Lions teams before, did have a good front row. Tony Horton, John Pullin and Syd Millar were good enough to scrummage against anybody, and so was John O'Shea, but O'Shea did not make as much of his tour as he should have done, and he lived to regret it. The 1968 Lions also had some brilliant individual talent in the backs, with Gareth Edwards and Barry John, Mike Gibson and Gerald Davies. Unfortunately, the young Barry John had his collarbone broken in the first test, and was not able to follow up the remarkable progress he had made in the first month of the tour. Still, it would have stretched credibility to believe that even a series of virtuoso performances by the young Welsh fly-half could have made up for the Springboks' superiority in the back five of the pack. Frik du Preez, Tiny Naude, Tommy Bedford, Jan Ellis and Thys Lourens carried too many guns in too many places for their opponents.

Whether a more disciplined approach by the 1968 Lions would have brought them into contention in the series will never be answered, but the fact is that they were their own worst enemies off the field. No doubt other British touring teams had broken up hotels and had made public nuisances of themselves, because sadly, that was one of the least attractive traditions that British Rugby has inherited from its public school and Services connections, but in 1968, it was an anachronism. The time for that had passed. It was time for British Rugby to apply itself and win something. The journalists and broadcasters covering the tour turned a series of Nelsonic blind eyes to what was happening, but some of them felt only a sadness that a team could be capable of such immature self-destruction and that in doing so, it could undermine the work done so selflessly by Ronnie Dawson.

When the 1968 Lions returned to Britain, their manager, David Brooks, voiced the consensus of opinion that British teams touring South Africa and New Zealand would always find it hard to win from within the traditional structure of British Rugby. He pointed out that in both New Zealand and South Africa, there was a logical progression from club, to province to national level, and that there was organised competition in both those countries at all levels. This meant that although they did not play nearly as much Rugby as British players, the leading players in New Zealand and South Africa regularly played Rugby of a higher quality, and therefore had to produce their best football more often. British Rugby had far greater playing resources than either New Zealand or South Africa, but wasted them by not teaching the game properly, and by not instituting a club and provincial structure which would sift the talent and channel it to the top.

This overdue statement of the obvious infuriated those who had contentedly presided over the mediocrity of British Rugby for so long. Indeed David Brooks was told testily by a former president of the Rugby Union that 'the game can do without whippersnappers like you', even though Brooks himself had been a member of the Rugby Union for three years. In any case, it had long been clear that the objectors were doing no more than fulfil the function of King Canute. There was nothing they could do to stop the tide, and if they had been administering the game properly, they would not only have known that, but would have long since cut the channels to make proper use of the water.

However, the objectors let it be known that competitive Rugby, at least in England, and Scotland, would only be introduced over their dead bodies. Yet within two years, the Rugby Union had been forced to hurriedly arrange a club cup competition in England, in an attempt to head the clubs away from their determination to institute a system of club leagues. This cup competition flourished immediately and confounded all those who had opposed it because it produced none of the carnage and foul play so confidently predicted. Two years after that, the Scottish Rugby Union introduced a system of club leagues, with promotion and relegation, to cover the entire country. Initially, the Scottish Rugby Union opposed the leagues, but their clubs were determined to have them, and they found that they were part of a constitution which required the Union eventually to obey their wishes. Once that was established, the

Union gave in with good grace, and organised the leagues both efficiently and with commendable despatch. Like the cup in England, the Scottish Leagues flourished and immediately became a vital part of the clubs' season.

Within less than five years, therefore, cups and leagues had been introduced successfully throughout England and Scotland, and all those who had opposed them were still alive, and mostly still in office. It was so sad, and even worse, it was unintelligent, because it put the objectors into a position from which they could not withdraw without loss of dignity. There seemed little doubt that the world of Rugby was about to move into an era of great change, and so it was only common sense to remain as flexible as possible to adapt to that change, and make the best of its merits.

1 The Lions awake

The two countries in which the portents of change were most apparent were Britain and South Africa. Despite their victory in the 1968 series against the Lions, it was clear that the Springboks were living on borrowed time. Their Rugby had no depth of quality and sooner rather than later, that lack of depth was bound to be exposed. Similarly, the game of Rugby in Great Britain was making a rapid advance because of the development of organised forward play. There was a much greater understanding of the realities of forward play in Britain, both among the players themselves, and among the new breed of coaches who were devoting themselves to the study and improvement of the game. Until the middle 'sixties, coaching in Britain was almost unheard of outside the schools. For nearly a hundred years British Rugby had mostly embraced the comfortable and stupid philosophy that it was not necessary to try to add to the sum of knowledge about the game after a boy left school. Captains were responsible for the tactical development of the game, such as it was, and because captains as astute as Wavell Wakefield were so much of a rarity as to be almost an historical freak, the ignorance of the mechanics of the game was positively frightening.

That began to change very quickly as more and more players, former players and schoolmasters began to involve themselves in coaching, and as a result, the built-in advantages which South Africa and New Zealand had enjoyed for nearly 70 years soon disappeared. This became apparent almost within the space of six months in 1969.

In the middle of the year, Wales went as European international champions on a short tour of New Zealand. The itinerary was beautifully designed by New Zealand to advance the cause of the All Blacks, but from the point of view of Wales, it was absolutely suicidal. Even to consider such an itinerary, never mind accept it, showed a naivety of which no one could ever accuse New Zealand, because, very sensibly, they only accepted touring commitments which gave their team some chance of doing itself justice. Wales played two tests against the All Blacks, the first only eight days after sitting in an aircraft for 36 hours and flying non-stop to Auckland. Predictably, they lost to a great All Black team which was just coming to the end of the road. Wales also lost the second test, when the

New Zealand full-back Fergi McCormick, took the opportunity to set a world record for points scored in an international match, but even though Wales lost a game in which their players were disappointed with the refereeing, they were only out-scored by three tries to two, and their young back division gave notice that even with less than half the ball, they would be capable of beating New Zealand in the not too distant future.

This glimpse of daylight broadened into the dawn of a new era later in the year, when South Africa toured the United Kingdom. The tour was disrupted throughout by political demonstrations which were to become familiar with any sporting engagement involving South Africa, but that did not alter the fact that for the first time, British teams playing the Springboks all went on the field expecting to beat them rather than trying just to keep the score down.

That was apparent in the first match of the tour, when the Springboks lost to Oxford University at Twickenham. The match was moved from Iffley Road, in Oxford, to London because the University's ground was much more vulnerable to demonstrators than Twickenham. With large parts of the ground fenced off, and a huge police presence, the atmosphere of the game was slightly unreal, but no one could mistake the skill and the determination with which the All Black scrum-half, Chris Laidlaw, then studying at Oxford, and captain of the University, directed his team, and no one could fail to discern the footballing presence of a young forward named Peter Dixon.

This match set a pattern for the tour. The Springboks were constantly under pressure, both on the field and off it. They bore the political demonstrations with remarkable stoicism, even though some thoroughly revolting and obscene acts were perpetrated against them, and they did not use these demonstrations to make excuses for their difficulties on the field. As the Springboks said, the demonstrations were as disconcerting for the home teams as they were for the tourists, and the demonstrations were certainly not the reason why South Africa could not win one of the four international matches they played on tour in Britain.

Indeed, at the end of the Springboks tour, Avril Malan, by then their coach, had the courage to voice his considerable misgivings about the advantages which he thought the technical revolution had given to British Rugby in relation to South Africa, and he had the foresight to predict that the Springboks would soon find themselves at an even bigger disadvantage in relation to British Rugby. These opinions were not popular in South Africa, and Avril Malan was promptly fired, but at least he eventually had the satisfaction of being proved right in every respect.

The effort that impressed him above all others was that of Llanelli, who, as Malan said, 'Played so far above themselves that it was almost unbelievable'. Llanelli scored a try that day in which the ball was handled 21 times by 14 different players. The Springboks won narrowly in the end, but their coach and all their players will remember the intensity of the occasion as long as they live.

All the Springboks did do on that tour was preserve their record of never having been beaten by Wales. Indeed, South Africa would have won the game at Cardiff if they had succeeded in kicking the ball into touch at the end, because the referee, G. C. Lamb, said that he intended to end the game the next time the ball went out of play. South Africa were then leading 6–3, but Wales gathered themselves for one final assault and Gareth Edwards, chased desperately by a mud-caked Hannes Marais, dived over to score near the left corner flag to draw the match.

The conditions in which the match was played were appalling. The Arms Park was an ooze of mud and water, almost devoid of grass. The pitch had always been used every week by the Cardiff club, even when the Welsh Rugby Union decided to play no more international matches on the sandy, well drained field at St Helens, Swansea, and instead to play them all at Cardiff. The move made the soundest of economic sense, because of the vastly greater receipts from a match at Cardiff, but the playing traffic on the Arms Park was so heavy that the pitch was easily the worst international playing surface in Europe. Even in the 1920s, Wavell Wakefield said wryly that the knack of playing well at Cardiff lay in playing with the tide!

Not a Saturn rocket launch pad at Cape Canaveral, but simply the sockets which hold the posts at the re-built stadium at Cardiff Arms Park.

This prompted the Welsh Rugby Union to begin the huge task of re-building the stands and re-surfacing the pitch after installing a proper drainage system. A smaller ground for the Cardiff club was built next door, on what had been the ground of the Glamorgan cricket club. That club moved across the river Taff to Sophia Gardens.

Ken Harris, one of the most astute men ever recruited by the Welsh Rugby Union, was their treasurer at the time, and he had the task of seeing the work through. As he says, he had already seen considerable changes in his own period of office. 'When I became treasurer,' he smiles, 'the late Eric Evans was the secretary of the Welsh Rugby Union, and he ran it from the back bedroom of a house on Rumney Hill. The tickets for the international matches were laid out on the bed! We've come a long way from there, a long way.'

'The first major step in putting our finances right was to move all the international matches to Cardiff. This increased our income sufficiently for us to build the first of the new stands. Then we realised that we had to improve the pitch. We wanted a pitch worthy of the quality of the play that we were accustomed to seeing. There had been times when the players were unrecognisable because of the mud; times when you could see the waves on the water standing on the ground.

'Since then, we have spent £2,750,000 on the ground, and we are planning to spend another £750,000. It is a big business now. The work, of course, is far from finished. I don't know whether I shall see it completed. Perhaps I might, as a geriatric old gentleman. My wife says she is sure that I will want to be buried under the thing. I did make a suggestion in fun some years ago that for £1,000, people could be buried under the pitch and we would put a plaque up in the stand! This, of course, would improve the turf enormously!!'

The Springboks who played at the Arms Park in 1969 would have found it hard to believe the transformation which was wrought. The work, initially, was financed by a debenture scheme thought of first by Scotland. Looking back on it, Ken Harris says, 'A lot of people said that no-one would lend us £50 for ten years, free of interest, on condition that they could have a ticket at whatever price we cared to charge them. Well, they did, and those debentures are now being advertised for £1,500.'

Within four months of the end of their desperate rearguard action in Britain, South Africa had to regroup and prepare for a tour of their country by New Zealand. The South African government, with a new Prime Minister to replace Dr H. F. Verwoerd, accepted that they were not entitled to dictate the racial composition of sporting teams visiting their country and so for the first time, New Zealand toured South Africa with a complement of Maoris. Some of the New Zealand players thought that at least one of the Maoris was fortunate to gain selection, and had only done so because he *was* a Maori. This form of inverted racialism soon manifested itself elsewhere as one of the expressions of human conscience, and Dr Danie Craven himself acknowledged that it represented one of the greatest dangers in South Africa itself as their sport moved inexorably towards multi-racialism.

Until comparatively recently, All Black teams always found South Africa to be a tantalising mixture of an earthly paradise – easily the best place in the world to tour – and a footballing purgatory, at least at international level. Speaking of the country, Colin Meads himself once said smilingly, 'We'll come back here to tour every year, as long as we can play all our matches out of Durban!' A lot of players in a lot of different countries shared his view, and still do.

As far as the Rugby was concerned, New Zealand thought that in 1970 they would, at long, long last, manage to win a series in South Africa. After all, the Springboks had just been pounded to defeat in Britain, whereas they, the All Blacks, had beaten Wales, Britain's strongest team, without any difficulty. The All Blacks had lost Ken Gray, who declined to tour because of his political objections to South Africa, but they had nearly all the other players who had contributed so much to New Zealand's eminence through the 1960s, including Colin Meads.

By then, Meads was effectively the Godfather in the world of Rugby. He bestrode it, a mixture of goodie and baddie, according to your outlook. He played the greatest football of even his career as New Zealand roared round South Africa before the first test. At least, he did until he had his arm broken by a deliberate kick in one of the provincial games. The whole of the first-class game in South Africa knew who had broken Colin Meads' arm, and knew that it had been done deliberately, and although some said, 'Those who live by the sword, die by the sword', they were not proud of what had happened. There is no doubt, though, that the injury had a profound effect upon the international series. Meads could not play in the first three tests, and should not have played in the series at all. He was fit enough to play, a long way short of his best, in the last test, when he wore a protective guard on his arm. By that time, New Zealand were already 2–1 down in the series and their dreams had been shattered. Still, they felt that if they could win the last test, their honour would be satisfied. They were denied even that satisfaction. South Africa won another fiercely fought game and took the series 3–1.

Once again, New Zealand had accepted too many preliminary games before the first test, and so the South Africans had been able to analyse every detail of their game. In most analyses, the realisation of plans is often an accident, and no analyst could have predicted the success of Ian McCallum, the new Springbok full-back, as a goalkicker. He had a decisive influence on the series, just as another Springbok goalkicker, Gerald Bosch, was to decide a series against New Zealand six years later. In the tactical field, the Springboks' plan could scarcely have been simpler. If you are playing against a team which is basically better than you are, then all you can do is defend, and hope to turn that defence into a weapon of attack. This is what South Africa did.

By then, Avril Malan had been replaced by his fellow lock forward from the 1960–61 tour of Great Britain, Johan Claassen, as coach of South Africa. He chose a powerful centre named 'Joggie' Jansen as the key to his defence. Jansen's tackling, backed up by superb loose forward play by Piet Greyling and Tommy Bedford, had a decisive influence on the midfield, though how much of this was intentional and how much a happy accident, we shall never know.

It has been proved often enough that a prophet is rarely honoured in his own country, and that was demonstrably true of 'Joggie' Jansen. When the British Lions left South Africa in 1968, one of the touring party was asked to name his eclectic team of South Africans from all those players the Lions had met. When he mentioned the name of Jansen, who had not played in the tests, the South African interviewer asked incredulously, ' "Joggie" who?' Well, two years later, the whole of South Africa knew who 'Joggie' was.

South Africa's victory did not invalidate Avril Malan's argument. That was proved conclusively within the next four years. In that time, the British Lions won in New Zealand, England won in both South Africa and New Zealand, and the British Lions smashed South Africa in their own country.

Tommy Bedford, the brains of a superb loose forward combination for South Africa.

Naturally, many wishful thinkers in South Africa thought that Johan Claassen heralded a new Springbok dawn, just as many wishful thinkers in New Zealand thought that Fred Allen was mad to get out as coach when he did. The All Blacks' record in South Africa in 1970 and against the Lions in 1971 and against England in 1973 proved just how shrewd Fred Allen was. He knew that the show was over and he went back to his dressmaking. The Springboks' record against England in 1972 and against the Lions in 1974 showed just how right Avril Malan had been.

Those years also showed just how rapidly the world of Rugby was expanding. Fiji had toured Britain in 1970 as part of the Rugby Union's centenary celebrations, and had smashed a full strength Barbarians' team – in effect almost the British Lions – to such an extent that they had materially affected the selection of the Lions team to tour New Zealand in 1971. Fiji had demonstrated their potential on a tour of Wales in 1966, and when they returned to Britain four years later, they put together such a brilliant exhibition against the Barbarians that Fiji won 29–9 and players like Phil Bennett, then reserve fly-half for Wales, and Keith Fielding, the brilliantly fast England wing, never recovered from the damage done to their defensive reputations.

Bennett had played in Fiji the year before at the end of Wales' tour of New Zealand and Australia and so he knew the danger that the Fijians presented. They dislike the chores of hard work – even to the extent, as they cheerfully admit, of allowing themselves to be outbred by the Indians in their own islands – but they love the personal dramas and the fun that can be had from handling and running with a Rugby ball. In the heat and the humidity of Suva, a different world from the hot aridity on the other side of the central mountains, every vacant piece of ground at lunch-time and at the end of the day seemed to be occupied by a group of youngsters playing touch Rugby; handling, running, dummying and passing quite beautifully. Fiji had lost to Wales because their lack of fitness made them collapse at the end. Also, guided by some coaching from Fred Allen, they had tried to play a disciplined game which was beyond them. But against the Barbarians at Gosforth in 1970, they played their natural, running game in a way that gave notice that one day, they might be capable of beating the British Lions, which is exactly what they did on a famous afternoon in Suva seven years later.

Argentina had already visited South Africa in 1965, and helped enormously by that brilliant South African coach, Izaak van Heerden, had surprised both the Springboks and themselves with the strength of their game. England toured Japan and the Far East in 1971 and were considerably disconcerted by the unorthodox play of the Japanese. This embarrassment was quickly dissipated when the Japanese later toured England and Wales, and it was discovered that fifteen good big 'uns will always beat fifteen good little 'uns, providing they play the game sensibly and play to their physical superiority. Nevertheless, the improvisations introduced by the Japanese to offset their lack of height and weight quickly became a part of the world game.

Tonga, too, sent a team from the Pacific Islands, and showed that they had at least one player, their captain, Sioni Mafi, who was good enough to compete with anybody. The first-class careers of players from that part of the world seem to be much shorter than those of Europeans, but for at least two years, Mafi was arguably the best number eight in the world. The Welsh number eight, Mervyn Davies, of course, was much better known, and when Ireland's Ken Goodall sadly went to Rugby League, Davies earned his top ranking among the major Rugby playing countries, but as Mafi showed in Britain, he was good enough to jump any-where in the lineout – not just at the back – he was quick enough to hold off the fastest of the Welsh backs in a 30 yard sprint, he was strong enough to scrummage well as a lock and he was a devastating tackler. He was almost a one-man team, and although that inevitably placed unfair pressures upon him, he was good enough to withstand them.

Mervyn Davies had come to the front on the Welsh tour of New Zealand in 1969. He had made extraordinary progress as a loose forward with the London Welsh club, just as John Taylor had before winning selection for the 1968 Lions, and when Davies went to New Zealand in 1969, he passed that most searching test of a player; he played really well

---

Sioni Mafi (far left) of Tonga, one of the finest number eights in the history of Rugby.

in a losing team. In later years, Mervyn Davies filled out a little more physically but at that time he was a tall, thin, gangling player who seemed most unlikely to be able to withstand the buffetting inevitable in forward play in New Zealand. Not only did he withstand it, he positively thrived on it, and in the space of a month, his game visibly grew in stature.

Not that Mervyn Davies expected to be first choice number eight for the British Lions. That place, at least for the next two Lions tours, seemed certain to be occupied by Ireland's Ken Goodall, possibly the finest number eight to play anywhere in the world since the war. He played the most extraordinary game for Ireland against Wales in Dublin in 1970 and nothing looked more certain than that he would play forty games for Ireland as a number eight, and another thirty as a lock. The civil disorders had just started in Ireland, though, and he thought that there would not be much future in being a schoolteacher in Londonderry, so he joined Rugby League. To Doug Smith and Carwyn James, who in 1970 had just been appointed manager and coach of the Lions team to tour New Zealand the following year, the loss of Goodall was the hardest blow they had to bear. The only putative Lion who received the news of Goodall's departure with equanimity was Mervyn Davies. 'I never would have got into the test team if he had been around,' he grinned. 'I was glad to see the back of him!'

Mervyn Davies, who came to the fore on the Welsh tour of New Zealand in 1969.

12 Colin Meads and the 1971 Lions

Nothing epitomised the world wide expansion of the game better than the Rugby Union's centenary celebrations. The Rugby Union have always had a reputation for doing these things well, in a style which is a cut above everyone else, and on this occasion, they lived up to that reputation. Apart from the early season tour by Fiji, they invited a team of undoubtedly the best players in the world to play a short tour of England at the end of the 1970–71 season, and the tour was a great success. It was of considerable value to Doug Smith and Carwyn James, because it provided them with an opportunity to see the leading New Zealand players, including Colin Meads, who seemed likely to follow Brian Lochore as captain of the All Blacks against the Lions the following year.

The centenary celebrations also included a world congress, and this was the most valuable and imaginative concept of all. Representatives of 49 countries met at Cambridge, and the contacts established at that congress accelerated the expansion of the game beyond measure.

The actual playing of the game was also expanding because of a dramatic revision of the laws. The post-war game had become increasingly defensive, with low scoring matches of six or nine points the rule rather than the exception. There were no restrictions on touch-kicking, and so teams sought to advance to attacking positions by kicking for touch. There was also an element of safety in this but it did produce international matches in which there were nearly 100 lineouts, and the futility of this was nicely expressed early in the 1960s by Bill Nicholson, who was then the manager of the hugely successful Tottenham Hotspur football club. 'There must be something wrong with a game in which the players seek to make progress by kicking the ball off the field,' he said. Rarely has a nail been hit more squarely on the head, and the whole business came to a sorry climax in 1965, when Wales played Scotland at Murrayfield, and won a match containing 111 lineouts. In its way, it was a tactical triumph for Clive Rowlands, the Welsh scrum-half and captain, whose immaculate touch-kicking had contributed so much to the poverty of the play. He said before the match that he thought Scotland would try to play the game to their forwards, and particularly to their powerful scrummaging locks, Mike Campbell-Lamerton and Frans ten

Bos, who had contributed to a famous Scottish victory over Wales. He was also right when he said that neither Campbell-Lamerton nor ten Bos had any chance at all against Brian Price, the Welsh lock, as a lineout jumper, and so he, Clive Rowlands, intended to kick for touch even more than Scotland, confident that Price would beat the Scots at their own game. That is exactly what happened, but it did make for a watershed in the world of Rugby.

By doing so, it gave a powerful stimulus to the movement agitating for a revision of the laws. First, the International Board required players to keep behind the hindmost foot at the scrummage, and then they required all backs, except the scrum-half, to stand back ten yards from the lineout. They also introduced the Australian touch-kicking dispensation, under which a player was not permitted to gain ground by kicking the ball direct into touch outside his own 25. These changes revolutionised the playing of the game. Backs who had acquired the sharpest of handling, passing and running skills under the pressures of close marking both by opposing loose forwards and by opposing backs, suddenly found that they had space to use those skills, and as a result, the international season in Britain in 1971 was the most spectacular in the history of the game.

The culmination was the match between Scotland and Wales at Murrayfield. It was full of marvellous Rugby, and late in the second half, Scotland were leading 18–14. That score in itself was a revelation after so many barren years, but Wales had not finished. They launched a series of desperate attacks, one of which ended with Barry John being pushed into touch near the Scottish line. It was Scotland's throw into the lineout, but Delme Thomas won it and Wales whipped the ball across field to Gerald Davies, who scored a try halfway between the posts and the corner flag. That made the score 18–17, and the Welsh flanker John Taylor, only an occasional kicker, stepped up to try to make the conversion to win the match. By then, too, the law requiring another player to hold the ball above the ground until the moment of the kick at goal had also been repealed, and so Taylor was able to place the ball to his satisfaction and examine the task before him. There have been few more dramatic moments in Rugby football. Taylor had been given the kick because he was a left-footed kicker, and used the new style of instep kick which had been encouraged by the introduction of lighter boots with soft toes. By cutting across the ball with the instep, instead of following straight through with a hard-capped toe, the kicker could curve the ball in its flight. From the right of the posts, the shape of the curve suited a left-footed kicker.

Knowing this was one thing. Putting it into effect was something else. The whole crowd held its breath while Taylor looked up at the posts and back down at the ball. Then when he made his kick, and the Welsh supporters saw that it was flying true for goal, the whole ground erupted with noise. Strong men watching television screens all over the country either rejoiced or despaired. Joe McPartlin said it was the greatest conversion since St Paul! It gave Wales victory by 19 points to 18.

It also made sure that a large proportion of the British Lions team to tour New Zealand in 1971, would be made up of Welsh players. In the end, thirteen were chosen, which rather disappointed Carwyn James, because he had thought that one or two more might make it! At the interview the previous summer, when the tours committee of the Four Home Unions had appointed him, in the confident and accurate expectation that he would fail to be elected as a Welsh nationalist MP in the forthcoming general election, Carwyn James reflected that a utility player, who could deputise at scrum-half or flank-forward, might be very useful. He had Clive John in mind, the brother of Barry John. One of England's representatives on the tours committee was Cyril Gadney, and the great man looked up and asked innocently, 'You have an Englishman in mind, of course?' The coach did not succeed in carrying the selection committee with him at the end of the season, and neither could he persuade them that Phil Bennett (also, curiously enough from his own club at Llanelli) had put sufficient distance between himself and that awful afternoon against Fiji to justify selection as a utility back. Bennett had begun his international career as a replacement player on the wing, and had played in most of the positions in the threequarter line. As it turned out, both Phil Bennett and Clive John would have been useful members of the Lions team in New Zealand, but neither was selected.

Fortunately, the team that was chosen was as well equipped as any British Lions team since 1959, except, perhaps, in the second row, where New Zealand were beyond reach with Colin Meads and Peter Whiting. It was a surprise to the Lions to see that in New Zealand, Whiting was regarded with a distinctly patronising air. He was considered to be a softie, and was given a fearful working over in the All Black trials. The Lions judged him to be a magnificent lineout forward, and the ideal partner for Colin Meads, and their judgment was vindicated over and over again. Eventually, it was even accepted in New Zealand.

Meads featured large in the Lions' planning. By then, he had acceded to the captaincy of the All Blacks, but even before Meads' appointment was confirmed, the Lions' coach felt that he would be the key figure in the psychology of the series. Accordingly, he studied Meads closely in the games which had been arranged so conveniently to celebrate the Rugby Union's centenary. Meads was frightened of no-one. He revelled in taking on opposing forwards to find out how hard they were. He used physical pressure to the point of intimidation. He only respected those who could stand up to him. He truly was the Godfather, an analogy to the Mafia made even more compelling by the all black playing uniform worn by his country.

He had an inbuilt resistance to those who tried to impose law on the game. His presence was such that he effectively refereed many of the games in which he played, or he did if he could. He took on the referee in the same way that he took on the opposition, and he probably did it for the same reasons, and enjoyed it as much.

Meads was always superbly fit. He was a good handler and a great rucker. He was nothing extraordinary as a lineout jumper, or even as a scrummager, because his own instincts were halfway between being a tight forward and a loose forward, but it was significant that the opponents he always respected most were not forwards of brilliant talent like Frik du Preez, in whom he might have seen something of himself, but the really tight forwards, like Johan Claassen and Rhys Williams. When you looked at him, either as a coach or an opponent, you knew you were looking at a unique figure. He was utterly uncompromising. It was as if God had distilled in him the essence of competition. He accepted the Adam in himself and admitted that there were moments in his career which he regretted.

He was the product of a unique environment. Boys in Wales wanted to be Barry John. Boys in New Zealand wanted to be Colin Meads. He came from a breed of hard men, of farmers, like the South Africans, for whom he has such respect. He gloried in being a part of that breed. He always had a mind to Rugby when he set about the daunting physical work on his farm. That work meant that he spent hours on his own in conditions of absolute solitude and it gave him a great deal of time to think.

Colin Meads had tremendous pride in his country, tremendous pride in being an All Black. His views on the game were conservative and as a

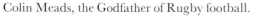

Colin Meads, the Godfather of Rugby football.

member of a team, he had a natural acceptance of the authority of his coach and his captain. His relationship with Wilson Whineray was revealing for its absolute obedience to playing authority. Meads was the last of the great forwards who had this acceptance.

He was an implacable opponent, but in no way a small man. Deep down, he is warm and sincere. No one tried harder on the field, but when the day was done, he was generous in defeat, and even more important, he was sensible and restrained in victory. Even then, it was evident that he represented the essence of 'us' to all New Zealanders against the 'them' of the rest of the world. He was larger than life. He still is. Even then, it was apparent that we would not see his like again.

Colin Earl Meads represented a mountain for the 1971 Lions to climb, both physically and psychologically, but fortunately for them, not all the signs were as discouraging. Even in 1967, on the All Blacks' triumphant tour of Britain and France, there had been just a glimpse of looseness in their play. This looseness was covered by Ken Gray, but by 1971, Gray had retired. By then, too, the All Blacks were without Kel Tremain and 'Waka' Nathan, and they were struggling to settle on the third man in their loose forward combination. They did not have the same calibre of personalities, either.

This must have been evident in South Africa in 1970, and for that reason it was surprising that Ivan Vodanovich, the All Blacks' coach in that losing series, did not send a papal letter to all the provincial coaches in New Zealand urging upon them the need to tighten the country's forward play. Simply by tightening their scrum, New Zealand would have tightened their whole approach. Nothing would have been simpler, because the All Blacks must be the easiest Rugby squad to teach in the whole world. They will do anything that you want and they will work at it because they enjoy it. A prop like 'Jazz' Muller, for instance, was immensely heavy and strong, but his technique was inadequate.

Part of this stemmed from the refereeing in New Zealand. The refereeing of any country mirrors the strengths and the weaknesses of the game in that country. New Zealand refereed the ruck well, so their players rucked well. New Zealand did not referee the scrum at all, so their players scrummaged abysmally. Their foot-placing, their binding, and their scrum-feeding were all wrong.

The scrum therefore became the area of physical contact that was the hub of the Lions' planning with regard to the forward play, and because of the quality of British props then available, it was possible to achieve domination. This was vitally important, because one of the beauties of the scrummage in Rugby football is that it is primeval. It is an eyeball to eyeball contest. Therefore, the sight of Colin Meads and his scrum in retreat in the second match of the tour, against the symbolically named King Country, was a tremendous encouragement to the Lions psychologically. So was the sight and feel of Meads and the All Black pack almost running backwards in the second test. New Zealand won that test by the most decisive score of the series, but to the Lions' coach, it was immeasurably more encouraging than the first test, which the Lions won. He felt that New Zealand were fifteen points the better team in the first test, even though they lost it, and it was hard to see how they could be outmanoeuvred. The Lions' scrummage domination in the second test gave them a platform off which they could build. All they had to do was fill up the holes.

It would be hard to overestimate the contribution made by Ray McLoughlin to the Lions' forward effort. He talked the forwards through the early weeks of practice scrums, and all the forwards were learning all the time. Foot placement. Binding. Use of legs. Use of arms. Body position. Angle of packing. Changes of position. How to exert pressure, and when.

For a coach who was a back, this sort of technical assistance was invaluable, and it should always be built into team selection wherever possible. In addition to that, McLoughlin was a bulwark in the community of senior players. If the senior players are all right, and all of a mind, the tour that they are on will be all right. The All Blacks learned that lesson the following year in Britain, when they did not choose Meads and when, in his absence, other players let themselves down and let All Black Rugby down. They did not have enough pride in their blazer and their tie and their jersey. Colin Meads had this pride born in him. So did Ray McLoughlin. It had been a long road since 1966 and McLoughlin was glad to be back.

The Lions derived other benefits from McLoughlin's work with the scrummage, too. If a pack scrummages well, it tends to ruck better and it tends to maul better. The forwards can also look their opponents straight in the eyes, because they know they are better in that special theatre which Rugby football has evolved to demonstrate, in a recurring set-piece, the virtues of physical strength and technique.

In other areas of the game, though, the Lions had to face realities. They were fighting a tradition of All Black pride. They were fighting a tradition of nice guys coming second. According to Meads himself, in an interview with Terry McLean of the *New Zealand Herald* which produced perhaps the most memorable remark of the tour, Lions forwards in the past had given New Zealand's captain the impression that they believed in fairy tales. The Lions had to correct that impression as well.

Remembering the lineout play of the 1967 All Blacks, and remembering Meads' methods in the Rugby Union's centenary games, the Lions' coach decided to make such a mockery of the illegal practices as to make the All Blacks' continued use of them both embarrassing and difficult. He knew that the Lions could not really compete with the All Blacks in the lineout, except through Mervyn Davies in that vital area at the back, so they had to conduct a holding operation, with all the assistance they

Ray McLoughlin, the Irish prop who contributed so much to British forward play. A visionary ahead of his time.

could get from propaganda. Hence the expression 'get your retaliation in first'. Hence the careful attention drawn at all the early Press conferences to the fact that as the Lions were in the lineout of Rome, they intended not only to do as the Romans did, but even to practise it. The stratagem worked so well that in the end, the International Rugby Football Board rushed to re-write the lineout laws. They made a mess of it in the process, but we will come to that later.

The Lions also had to fill up the holes in their defence at the side of the scrummage, and at the same time provide the support essential behind the middle jumper in the lineout. For these reasons, they chose a big man to play as a blind side flanker, and they chose a fast, outstanding tackler to play on the open side. The Lions were fortunate to have a choice between Derek Quinnell and Peter Dixon on the blind side and John Taylor and Fergus Slattery on the open.

Much pointless dogma is talked and written about loose forward organisation. Whether a team organises its flankers to play on a left and right basis or open and blind should depend only on its resources and the needs of the situation. The Lions had to play a big man on the blind side in 1971 to counter Sid Going and to take a little of the edge off Peter Whiting and it worked.

In many ways, it was easier for the Lions to plan their game than it was for the All Blacks. At that time, New Zealand Rugby was jammed firmly between two stools. It felt itself committed to play the running game spread out before the world with such success by Fred Allen and Charlie Saxton in 1967, but without a passing scrum-half like Chris Laidlaw, they were not in a position to play that game. It was a difficult situation for Ivan Vodanovich, because he was undoubtedly in the shadow of Fred Allen, but he should either have picked another scrum-half instead of Sid Going or played a different game. In the end it was comparatively easy for the Lions to counter Sid Going, a point which was made again when New Zealand toured Britain the following year and were beaten by Llanelli at Stradey Park. All Llanelli's plans were centred on containing Sid Going, but when the All Blacks rested him, and played Lyn Colling instead, Llanelli had to reshape their thinking and found it much harder to come up with a solution.

The realities of dealing with the situation as it existed in New Zealand in 1971 shaped the rest of the Lions' play. The last thing the Lions' coach wanted was second phase play, whether artificially created or otherwise, because the All Blacks were supreme at that phase of the game. Accordingly, the ball had to be moved as wide as possible and as fast as possible from the New Zealand forwards. This did not apply only to the test matches. It applied with just as much force to the provincial games, because all the powerful New Zealand provinces were capable of out-rucking the Lions.

This was what made the contribution of the Lions' midfield and full-back so crucial. It is all very well having the notion of moving the ball rapidly from A to F, but it will not bear much fruit if B, C, D and E cannot pass. Happily, both John Dawes and Mike Gibson were supreme passers of the ball and J. P. R. Williams came into the line so well from full-back that Gerald Davies and David Duckham were able to make use of their skill on the wings.

Similarly, the Lions had to make use of any ball that New Zealand kicked away. They had to develop the counter-attack and they had to develop the confidence to use it under pressure. The All Blacks and the provincial teams had a tendency to overkick when trying to hoist the ball into the box behind the forwards on the blind side wing, and so the Lions wings had to stand deep so that they were in effect playing as three full-backs. Then they could support each other in their counter-attacks. This had its greatest moment in the match against Hawke's Bay, when J. P. R. Williams caught a narrowly missed kick at goal behind his own posts and launched a surging counter-attack which ended with Gerald Davies scoring a try between the posts at the other end of the field.

Davies was then in the blazingly high summer of his powers, and in the match against Hawke's Bay, he gave such a comprehensive demonstration of the range of his skill that it was as if the fates had decreed that he should be given one chance to compress the magic of his career into one afternoon. He took that chance by scoring four tries, three of them as a wing and one of them in his old position as a centre. All were exquisite examples of the most beautiful of the running skills.

For the first five years of his career, Gerald Davies had played as a centre. It was from that position that he scored the most memorable try of the Lions' 1968 tour of South Africa. This was in the Lions' match against Boland, in the Cape Province, and running with the ball from a lineout in his own half, Davies saw that the opposing outside centre had come up too fast in defence. This meant that the Boland defensive line was dog-legged, and Davies made a searing break on the outside before twice side-stepping the cover and running on for seventy yards to score.

Strangely enough, the final try that Davies scored against Hawke's Bay in 1971 was very similar. He had moved into the centre after an injury to Mike Gibson, and when Duncan, in the Hawke's Bay centre, came up too fast in defence from a scrum near his 25, Davies streaked past MacRae on the outside and side-stepped the full-back to score by the posts.

By that stage of Gerald Davies' career, centre-threequarter play had become much more physical and as he was small and lightly-built, he had accepted advice to move out to the right wing. Initially, he was rather reluctant to accept this advice, because he felt he would see much less of the ball. Towards the end of his career, his fears in this respect were fully justified, but at that time, John Dawes was playing in the centre in the Welsh team and he was such an unselfish player and such a supreme passer of the ball that Gerald Davies was persuaded that there was a whole new world waiting to be conquered on the wing.

The way he conquered that world was one of the supreme satisfactions to be had from watching British Rugby in those few fleeting years when it was at its zenith. Thomas Gerald Reames Davies met all Dave Gallaher's exacting requirements as a back. He had scalding pace and breath-taking acceleration and he had the rare gift of being able to side-step at pace off both feet. Bleddyn Williams insists that very few players have ever been gifted with a true side-step, which is the ability to execute the manoeuvre without perceptible loss of pace, but Gerald Davies was unquestionably one of them.

Being so lightly built, Davies had to develop the instincts of the forest animal. He knew his body was fragile, so he had to depend on speed and alertness and quickness of thought and footwork. Fear is an important element in the make-up of such a player, just as it is in that of the forest animal. It heightens perception, and the adrenalin secreted adds to the surge of acceleration.

Gerald Davies also played the game with his head. He was aware of the possibilities offered by variation in the length of his stride. He learned what paid and what did not pay and he remembered. He learned to stay out in defence and mark his man and to leave the inside man for the

Gerald Davies, the instincts of a forest animal, but always keeping the ball available.

cover. He could read the game because he had acute footballing intelligence. His positional work and his assessment of the possibilities of counter-attack were excellent. He was a killing runner-in of tries and yet, he knew when he was not going to score and invariably contrived to make the ball available for his support. Mick Molloy, who played in the second row of the pack for Ireland for many years, once said ruefully that he had lost count of the number of games he had played at club and national level in which his own team and all its aspirations had been dashed by one devastating run by Gerald Davies. Wales made nothing like the use of him towards the end of his career that his talents demanded, and for that his opponents all over the world were eternally grateful, but he was that rarity in any sport, a player whom all his rivals acknowledged as the master.

Carwyn James treasured him, as he did all his other gifted backs, but he knew that if those gifted backs were to have the chance to express their skills, the Lions' forwards would have to come to terms with the realities of rescuing every scrap of possession, often from a position of weakness. He knew that on many occasions, the Lions would not be rucking in the ideal situation of going forward. Frequently, they would have to ruck or maul in retreat, and so it was important that they should know how to do it and that they should practise it regularly. That practice alone paid dividends in the first test, when the All Blacks were so much the better side, and yet the Lions got away with a victory.

Finally, the Lions were helped by the fact that there were players in the team who had been to New Zealand and who knew what it was all about. Gareth Edwards and Barry John had toured New Zealand in 1969 and had been rated as nonentities. Their coach was delighted. He knew that two years later, Edwards and John would want to prove themselves, and they did. By the seventh match, when the team played quite beautifully and destroyed Wellington, the Lions felt that they were capable of a genuine roar. Even the brutal match against Canterbury a fortnight later, in which they lost their two test props for the rest of the tour because of injury, did something for the Lions. In one way it was a disaster, the low point of the tour, but after darkness there has to be light, and that match made the Lions more determined than ever to prevail. 'We shall overcome,' they sang. And they did.

3 Wales triumphant

Nineteen seventy one was the year British Rugby came of age. The Lions won the series in New Zealand by two matches to one with one drawn. They won all their provincial games, too. The only regret was the draw in the final test at Auckland. The Lions could and should have won that match. The All Blacks had given everything in the second half, when playing into the wind, not only to hold off the Lions but even to threaten to snatch victory, but in the last ten minutes, they were exhausted. The Lions forwards found the game going their way again and Barry John at fly-half drove New Zealand into their 25. Oddly enough, though, he was content just to keep them there. No one has ever had a greater awareness of the moment for the kill than Barry John, nor a sharper sword with which to put the opposition out of its misery, but instead of taking, with that essential Celtic relish, either or both of the two chances that presented themselves to win the match, he went through cricket's equivalent of blocking out for a draw. In one way, it was uncharacteristic. In another, it was in keeping with his capacity for the unexpected. He had done something similar early in the game when he took a kick at goal from almost in front of the New Zealand posts, and suddenly decided to lie the ball flat and kick it with his toe instead of hooking it over with his instep. He missed the kick. The Lions did not have to forgive him. Indeed, it did not even occur to them that the 'King' might require forgiveness. He had already done so much on tour that they were eternally in his debt.

His kicking in the first test had won the series, not so much for the points he had scored from two penalty goals, but for the way in which his line kicking had destroyed Fergi McCormick, the New Zealand full-back. McCormick was unquestionably one of the greatest full-backs of the postwar era but he outraged the Lions' coach by the way he played for Canterbury.

As a result of injuries inflicted in that match, the Lions lost both Ray McLoughlin and Sandy Carmichael for the rest of the tour. The Lions went off to Blenheim to lick their wounds, and the coach played a game of snooker with Barry John and told him quietly that he did not want to see W. F. McCormick ever again. Barry John responded with an exhibition of line kicking in the test match the following week that will be remembered by everyone who saw it. He pulled McCormick from one side of the field to the other with a string of merciless kicks that almost cut the lines. McCormick in fact did incredibly well to get as close to them as he did. It was a miracle of positioning and running for him to be able to get near enough to the kicks to stoop and reach for them, but they were almost always just out of his reach, and as he slithered and fumbled, he looked like a player who had come to the end of the international road. So he had. He never played for New Zealand again but the Lions' coach always felt that it was this decision above all others that made sure that the Lions would win the series and that New Zealand would lose it.

The 1971 Lions based their game in New Zealand on the brilliant passing and running of their backs, and on vastly superior goalkicking. Ironically, they did not achieve their objective in the test series because in those matches, the Lions forwards only once won enough of the ball for their backs to play as they did against the provinces. That was in the first twenty minutes of the third test on their favourite ground at Wellington, when the Lions scored 13 points with such effortless ease that a glum New Zealand spectator groaned, 'Jeez. They're gonna score fifty.'

They did not score 50, because the New Zealand forwards pulled themselves together, even though they had the unfortunate Brian Lochore playing in the second row as an emergency replacement for the injured Peter Whiting. Unwisely, Lochore was persuaded to come out of retirement to play because originally the New Zealand selectors thought that Colin Meads might not be able to play either, and they would need another captain. It would have been hard enough for Lochore at the height of his powers to move up from number eight to the second row and put together an effective game in that most demanding of positions as a middle jumper. Starting from where Lochore started in 1971, it was unfair both on a fine man and on his reputation as a player, because it was a mistake which worked very much in the Lions' favour.

For the rest of the series, the Lions backs had to make do with what ball they could get from the excellent front row of a solid scrummage and from Mervyn Davies at the back of the lineout. Colin Meads was in no doubt that the contribution made by Davies was decisive.

The performance of the Lions against Wellington, when they scored nine tries, and their victory in the series persuaded New Zealand's coaches and players that artificially created second phase possession had been outdated. The way to play was to counter-attack and to create space for the wings to run, just as the Lions did.

The 1971 Lions were exceptionally well equipped to play the ball to their wings. The All Blacks badly wanted to crush Barry John with their loose forwards, because they knew that he was the hub of the Lions' confidence, but they just could not reach him. Gareth Edwards' pass from scrum-half was so powerful that it put Barry John out of reach.

The classical school of thought holds that the essence of midfield play is to preserve space for the wings, and indeed, the highly respected New Zealand coach, Vic Cavanagh, said that this was the feature of British Rugby he admired most. This school of thought insists that a brilliantly *fast* pass, rather than a *long* pass, off both hands is the essence of top quality scrum-half play, and that the essence of the subsequent play in midfield must be to achieve penetration and to check the opposing defence by running straight and using close support runners.

Clearly, that type of play was unsuited to both the scrum-half and the fly-half of the 1971 Lions because it was not in their nature to play like that. They had compensating strengths and very formidable they were too, but the balance of the Lions back play still depended on the speed and quality of the passing in the centre and the timing and placing of the full-back's run into the line. In all three respects, the 1971 Lions were magnificently served. John Dawes, the Lions' captain, was one of the finest passers the game has known, and he had outside him two supreme footballers in Mike Gibson and J. P. R. Williams. Their work made sure that whatever might have been lacking in speed of transfer or angle of run when the ball got to them, it was brilliantly re-shaped to make the most of the running skills of Gerald Davies and David Duckham on the wings.

John Dawes, captain of the Lions in 1971, and one of the finest passers of the ball the game has known, about to give a scissors pass to J P R Williams.

Dawes had played as a scrum-half and as a flanker at school, and this helped to give him a vision of the whole game which is extremely rare among players. Flankers and centres have become interchangeable as midfield back play has become more physical in recent years – John Taylor made the change very successfully in the opposite direction – but very few flankers have ever been gifted with Dawes' supreme ability to time a pass. There was much discussion when the Lions' team was chosen as to whether Dawes was good enough as a player to command a place in the test team. He had not always been appreciated in Wales, but both Doug Smith and Carwyn James were in no doubt that he would be the essential link in the chain, as well as a calm and sagacious captain. They shared the view of Stuart Watkins, the Newport and Welsh international wing who had toured New Zealand with the 1966 Lions and who at the time was one of the monarchs of Welsh back play. Dawes had been dropped by Wales, but Watkins said emphatically, 'If anyone is starting a fund to get John Dawes back into the Welsh team, the first pound comes from me, and the next fifty quid comes from the next fifty wingers in Wales.' Watkins treasured Dawes' ability to play to his wing and indeed, as a timer and as a deliverer of a pass, Dawes would rank close to Bleddyn Williams and Jeff Butterfield as the best the British game has known in modern times. Dawes was also ahead of his time in that he was especially

Mike Gibson, technically the most completely equipped player of them all.

gifted as what was in effect a player-coach and the magnificent London Welsh team of the late 1960s and the early 1970s bore tribute to his work.

Another of the players in that London Welsh team was J. P. R. Williams, then following his whole family's involvement in the study and practice of medicine. He inherited another quality from his family, too, that of an inbred competitiveness. It was not in his nature to accept being a number two. It was never necessary to motivate him, either. The steel and the determination were built in. He would not accept defeat.

There have been many more skilful and more artistic full-backs than J. P. R. Williams, and any number who were better equipped as kickers of the ball, but none who were more resolute. In many ways, he resembled Gareth Edwards. Both had gone to the same school, Millfield, where both had developed their competitive instincts. Williams lacked the classical armoury of the full-back, in that as a youth he was a full-back without a kick, and Edwards lacked the classical armoury of the scrum-half, in that he was a scrum-half without a pass.

However, the community of schoolboy sports stars at Millfield was an extraordinary elite, gathered together by Jack Meyer, the headmaster, and both Williams and Edwards had their thirst for competition sharpened. It was entirely appropriate that Williams should have won junior Wimbledon as a schoolboy tennis player. He literally hurled himself into every game in which he played, and although Fergi McCormick towered above him as a kicker when Williams emerged in international Rugby on the Welsh tour of New Zealand in 1969, the major changes in the laws which were introduced in 1970 to restrict touch-kicking, suddenly made John Williams a world class player. Like Edwards, he also worked hard on his deficiencies, and although he never approached the class of Bob Scott, or Terry Davies or Bob Hiller as a classical kicker, he nevertheless became a sound and effective one. He even dropped a colossal goal from near the halfway line to help the Lions draw the last test against New Zealand in 1971.

The greatest help in the development of J. P. R. Williams, however, was the fact that while he was a young medical student in London, he found the ideal expression for his play in the beautiful Rugby consistently produced at the time by London Welsh. It is hard to imagine that there was ever a safer or a more courageous full-back than J. P. R. Williams. There was never a more adventurous full-back, either, or one who more enjoyed that adventure, but at the same time, he never lost sight of the essential defensive virtues of catching and tackling and covering.

Mike Gibson, for his part, was technically the most completely equipped player of them all. There was nothing that he could not do, except perhaps believe that he was as good as he really was. He knew what he could do, and yet paradoxically, he lacked self-confidence. Other players with half his ability would have been insufferable. His attitude, in the team sense, was almost one of diffidence. This was born of years of playing an inevitably restricted game for Ireland; of making do with scraps of possession and making sure of avoiding mistakes. With the 1971 Lions, Mike Gibson rediscovered the joys of instinctive Rugby. By then, he had already made two Lions tours, but he enjoyed his days of high summer in 1971. He enjoyed playing alongside Barry John, and marvelled at his self-confidence. He enjoyed anticipating the defensive gaps in Barry John's game and filling the holes. He was also a tremendous competitor, who had a genuine appetite for training. He worked unceasingly at his fitness, and smiled at Barry John because he did no such thing.

The intensity with which Mike Gibson lived and loved the game can be measured by his gift of almost total recall of every match in which he has played. Carwyn James once tried to recall the number of times Gibson had put the 1971 Lions into attacking positions either from defence or from threatening situations, but eventually gave up because he lost count.

The intensity with which Gareth Edwards played the game was of a different sort. He started playing Rugby football as an athlete, a very competitive athlete. From a boyhood spent in fairly humble circum-stances in Pontardawe, he was given a scholarship to Millfield, which widened his horizons beyond measure and introduced him to an entirely different world. He lived in a community of gifted games players, and as a natural competitor, his determination was reinforced. He could have played international Rugby in many positions, and ironically, might have found the game easier to play if he had chosen to settle in a midfield position rather than at scrum-half. His athleticism and his strength were remarkable. They earned him try after try at international level.

Early in his career, his game at scrum-half was deficient in its passing, and he was made to realise the extent of the deficiency by the perform-ance of Ken Catchpole with the 1966 Australians, and by that of Chris Laidlaw, with the 1967 All Blacks. As a mature player, he set to work to try to develop a spin pass, and was still practising it hard when he toured South Africa with the British Lions in 1968. He did eventually develop a very long spin pass off his right hand, but never had confidence in trying the delivery off his left. This type of pass, which relied on length rather than speed of delivery, shaped the play of the fly-halves outside him. They explored the possibilities of the room it offered them, rather than the time. Barry John alone had the strength of character to dominate him as a partner and to curb his voracious appetite for going for the line and for running with loose ball. Barry John helped him to mature in his judgment as to when to run and when to pass, although after John retired, the occasional despair of Gerald Davies on the Welsh right wing was evidence that perhaps the balance of judgment had tilted again towards Edwards' natural instinct to take on the opposition. From either a scrum or a lineout near the opposing line, Edwards was explosively dangerous. If the defence did not stop him before he reached the gain line, either Edwards or his support would almost certainly score.

These backs achieved the highest expression of their ability in the match against Wellington, but they were never able to reach the same peaks in the test series because New Zealand won so very much more of the ball. To that extent, New Zealanders felt that they had been the victims of a massive confidence trick; that the Lions had built an image of playing a spectacular, open game, and yet had won the series by kicking and by playing as tightly as any dour All Black team had in the past. At the end of the series, the New Zealand players themselves said ruefully that in their view, even the New Zealand journalists and broadcasters had been conned by the Carwyn James magic! The Welsh were obviously Merlins when it came to imagery. The reality was very different.

The point was, of course, that nothing would have pleased the Lions more than if their forwards had won so much possession that their backs could have played the game as they chose. They demonstrated that clearly enough when, playing as the Barbarians, they beat the All Blacks at Cardiff two years later. In 1971, in New Zealand, they had no choice. Colin Meads and his forwards were much too good. In terms of possession, the 1971 Lions were beggars, and they had to choose the only way to victory open to them.

The impact in Britain of the achievements of the 1971 Lions surprised even the players. The phlegmatic British sporting community came as near as it ever will to a ticker-tape welcome, and in Wales, at any rate, the returning heroes went back to their villages in motorcades.

The focal point of this adulation was Barry John, who not only broke the scoring record for a tourist in New Zealand but practically doubled it. Typically, he sensed the type of welcome that would be waiting if he went back to Wales by an orthodox route, so he slipped home unobtrusively and went to ground. Again, no one laid a finger on him.

This was one of the most extraordinary features of his play. He did not have either the scalding pace or the startling acceleration which is almost indispensable to a back, but his running had a ghost-like quality which made him infinitely elusive. He achieved this partly by variation of pace and by the variation of the length of his stride and partly by mesmeric use of the ball or, his hips or, his shoulders, or his feet. One New Zealand flanker confessed ruefully, 'Barry John rolled his eyes, and I fell over'.

Barry John was not a classical passer of the ball, but in the words of Mike Gibson, one of his greatest admirers, 'he got it there'. Barry John also had staggering self-confidence and he was a merciless exploiter of individual weaknesses in the opposition. He was a beautiful kicker, too, and he was left-sided in so many activities that he kicked very well off his left foot. He was fragile in build, and so, like Gerald Davies, he had the same awareness of physical danger as a forest animal. Perhaps this helped him to find as much time and as much space as he did. Certainly he had the rare gift of being almost able to transcend the game in which he was playing and to regard the opposition almost with pity. He had one of

Lewis Jones' qualities, too. He could go from third gear to top and then into overdrive and he would surprise an opponent each time. He did it with much less use of energy than Lewis Jones, and he sensed the relative balance of an opponent like that of a dancing partner.

He sometimes did unexpected things in defence. He originated the gentle self-derision about his 'finger-tip tackling' and yet he once stopped Benoit Dauga, the great French lock, five yards from the line at the cost of a broken nose. This saved an international match for Wales against France. In the first test in New Zealand in 1971, he found himself confronted with Colin Meads snorting round the end of a lineout only twenty yards from the Lions' line. The Lions could not go to his assistance and all Barry John could do was get in Colin Meads' way, but he did that, inelegantly but effectively, until help arrived.

He was completely unaware of the organisational technique of Rugby football. He just was not interested. 'Just give me the ball,' he said. He would go to sleep in the team talks when Clive Rowlands was coach of Wales. He got on like a house on fire with the massive intellect of Ray McLoughlin, and every morning tried to remember whether McLoughlin was a loose head donkey or a tight head donkey, but when McLoughlin shared a room with him on tour, and asked him to specify what he would do in certain match situations so that the forwards would know in advance in which direction to run, Barry John asked, his eyes round with wonder, 'How can I tell you? I don't know myself until I get the ball'.

Barry John created his own private world in the dressing room before a match. He shut himself within himself. He did not want a build-up. He created a personal privacy which was so complete that no coach ever thought of intruding. Other players need attention, or reassurance, or motivation. Not Barry John. The only organisation that interested him was soccer. In many ways, he was a much greater student of soccer than Rugby. He knew the strengths of soccer players and could have been a professional himself. He would have enjoyed that. He would have taken to big time soccer like a duck to water.

And yet . . . he commanded a game from the kick-off. 'Let's see the numbers on their backs first,' he would say. 'Let's see them going backwards.' He could also destroy any opponent who was one-sided, as he did his rivals at outside-half in Wales, and he scored tries with such a complete lack of fuss that opponents rarely touched him. He was the first Rugby player in Britain to be crowned. The Lions called him 'The King'. In Wales, he was all but deified as well, but in the end, he gave it all away, and he did it almost off-handedly.

He played for one more season after the 1971 tour and then retired. He had been crowned the 'King' not only of Welsh Rugby but of British Rugby too, and it was probably the larger public which felt the keener disappointment at his departure. That public sensed, just as Gareth

Edwards sensed, that John and Edwards were on the threshold of a new dimension of half-back play. From Britain's point of view, even more than from the Welsh point of view, it would have been absorbing to see what more they could achieve.

Barry John left the game just as the All Blacks were about to arrive in Britain in the autumn of 1972 to begin what turned out to be such a sadly churlish tour that it was disastrous for the image of Rugby football in general and for New Zealand in particular. Keith Murdoch, one of the All Black props, was sent home in disgrace after a scuffle with a security guard in a Cardiff hotel had been seen by his management as the culmination of a series of unfortunate pieces of behaviour. Not all of them involved Murdoch, but rightly or wrongly, the public associated him more than anyone with the unacceptable face of Rugby touring.

Although Murdoch was sent home, it was many, many months before he arrived. He left the aircraft en route, and worked in the outback of Australia rather than face the opprobium that was waiting for him in New Zealand.

Barry John, with Gerald Davies in support sweeps through the midfield for Wales against Scotland.

The Murdoch episode proved how wrong the All Blacks were to dispense with Colin Meads as captain. Hamish Macdonald played in Meads' place in Britain, and with all due respect to Macdonald, Meads at any stage of his career would have been more effective. Carwyn James had learned that the success of a tour depends on the senior players. If they are all right, the tour is all right. If they are wrong, the tour has no chance, whatever the results on the field may show to the contrary.

The All Blacks discovered the truth of that in 1972–73. In their international games, they beat England, Scotland and Wales, drew with Ireland and lost only to France. That was a good record, but they lost to Llanelli, they lost to the North West Counties and the West Midland Counties of England, and they lost an epic match against the Barbarians. For that they were regarded as failures. Much of this judgment and most of their defeats stemmed from their failure as tourists rather than their failure as players.

Murdoch was sent home two days after the All Blacks had achieved the pinnacle of their tour by beating Wales at Cardiff Arms Park. New Zealand won 19–16 and there is not much doubt that the absence of Barry John was the deciding factor. John had a charisma which was unique in Rugby football at that time, and psychologically, his presence alone would have tipped the balance towards Wales.

Some of the uglier aspects of nationalism in sport had spread to Rugby football and nowhere was this unhealthy development more apparent than in the relations between New Zealand and Wales. Since 1953, the All Blacks had enjoyed an unbroken run of success in their matches against Wales, and it was a run which was to continue. Justifiably, the All Blacks will look back on their international victories in 1972–73 with pride. They were gained in the face of internal dissension and considerable local hostility, but ironically, their tour will be remembered for their match against the Barbarians at the end. It was a match which the All Blacks lost but as hundreds of millions of ecstatic television viewers will testify, it was a match which could lay fair claim to being the greatest ever played in the history of the game and it went a long way towards redeeming the less attractive features of the tour.

The only sadness was that Barry John was not a part of it, because the team chosen by the Barbarians was essentially the team that had represented the British Lions in New Zealand in 1971. John Dawes, captain of the Lions and the Barbarians, asked Carwyn James to coach the team in a training session on the Thursday before the match at Cardiff Arms Park. The Lions' coach said that he felt that it would not be appropriate for him to do so, but after discussing the matter with Geoff Windsor-Lewis, the secretary of the Barbarians, he agreed to give the team a talk on the morning of the match.

Apart from a game against Oxford University the previous autumn, the team had not played since it left New Zealand in 1971. A certain rustiness seemed inevitable, and perhaps a lack of familiarity, because Barry John's place at fly-half had been taken by Phil Bennett, and Bob Wilkinson and Tom David had been chosen as uncapped players in the pack. Gerald Davies had to withdraw, too, because of indisposition on the eve of the match so David Duckham switched to the right wing and John Bevan came in on the left.

Carwyn James reminded the players of what they had achieved, and what they could achieve. He told them not to be inhibited and to enjoy themselves. He turned on Phil Bennett, his club fly-half at Llanelli, whom he had known and nurtured since he was a schoolboy. 'Now what are you going to do, Phil?' he asked. 'You've got a great side-step, but I don't suppose you will use it. Yet these All Blacks are made to be side-stepped!'

It was not possible for Carwyn James to do more than encourage his players; to re-assure them; to stimulate them; even, in the case of one or two like Phil Bennett, to goad them a little. Even so, Carwyn James felt optimistic. Barry John, Gerald Davies, Mervyn Davies and Peter Dixon were missing from his team, but Phil Bennett had played for his own Llanelli club team that had staggered the All Blacks by beating them at the beginning of their tour, and so had Tom David. That was the day the pubs had run dry in Llanelli. It was a day immortalised in song by Max Boyce, who was becoming as much a part of Welsh Rugby as Grenville Jones who, under the name of Gren, had drawn an intensely amusing world of cartoon characters straight from the gut of Rugby humour. With their troubador to sing of their deeds, and their court painter to add to the legends, Bennett and David knew what it was like to beat the All Blacks, and they would not be afraid of doing so again.

Carwyn James tried to imbue his players with confidence. J. P. R. Williams said, 'When we went into the meeting, we were all a little bit hesitant, a bit uncertain. It had been a long time since we had played together. But as Carwyn spoke, suddenly it seemed all right. We knew we could do it.'

Indeed they could. They went out on to the Arms Park and played the game of their lives, and extraordinarily enough, they began with a breathtaking try scored from a sweeping counter-attack which had its origins in three staccato bursts of side-stepping by Phil Bennett from a position deep in defence.

From the moment that Bennett kicked off for the Barbarians, there was a feeling of tension and last-night drama in the air, probably because most people considered that it was the fifth test match between the All Blacks and the 1971 Lions. The first scrum went to the All Blacks; the first lineout to the Barbarians. There were a couple of exploratory kicks, and then Sid Going caught a high ball from J. P. R. Williams and went probing forward. Going linked with his forwards and Ian Kirkpatrick put Bryan Williams away on the right.

Williams cross-kicked when he was squeezed towards the touch-line and what happened thereafter must have stunned him as much as it delighted the crowd. Bennett had to chase the kick deep in his own 25 and looked over his shoulder to see Kirkpatrick and Scown bearing down on him. When he picked up the ball, though, he did not kick for touch. Instead, he turned sharply back and cut the first wave of All Blacks to pieces with his side-steps before passing to J. P. R. Williams. The Barbarians' full-back was almost garrotted by a high tackle but Pullin supported him and made room for Dawes near the left touch-line. Dawes sold the sweetest of little dummies before passing inside to David who gave a low, one-handed scoop of a pass which Quinnell somehow took from down round his knees. Quinnell recovered his balance and the Barbarians were in full cry near the half-way line. Quinnell went to pass to Bevan on the left wing but Edwards came snorting through to intercept the pass and beat the despairing New Zealand cover in a ferocious forty yard sprint to the line. It was one of the most exhilarating tries ever scored in top-class Rugby and the rhythm of the passing and the running was as definitive a statement of a theme as the opening of Beethoven's Fifth Symphony.

The build-up to the classic try at the beginning of the match between the Barbarians and New Zealand at Cardiff Arms Park in 1973. John Dawes continues the movement started by Phil Bennett.

What followed was every bit as majestic, because the players were inspired by that opening to sustain a level of attacking quality which was often quite incredible. New Zealand's achilles heel was Sid Going's injured ankle. Only a stoic such as he would have considered playing, but Bob Burgess, the All Blacks' fly half, must have questioned the wisdom of the decision as he groped and grovelled to try to pick up Going's erratic service. Burgess could not reach one ball from Going so Hurst, in the centre, tried to make the best of the situation by kicking ahead. The ball went straight to Duckham, veering infield from the Barbarians' right wing, and he took off with a series of graceful feints, half dummies, half side-steps, which were so typical of his attacking running. David, Slattery, McBride and Wilkinson stormed behind in support, and when the Barbarians won the loose ball at the point of check, they worked the ball out swiftly to Bevan on the left wing. Bevan had scored some memorable tries for the Lions in New Zealand, but for once his strength and determination were to no avail and he was cut down by a consuming cover tackle by Scown.

Bennett kicked a quick penalty goal, dead centre, for the Barbarians when Wyllie was penalised for infringing on the wrong side of a maul.

Tom David passes inside.

With barely ten minutes to go to half-time, the Barbarians thought they had scored another try when Going kicked to J. P. R. Williams and another ripple of side-steps by Duckham enabled Wilkinson, Quinnell, Edwards and Slattery to give Dawes an overlap. The French referee, Georges Domercq, said that the final pass was forward.

However, the scrummage position did produce a try. The All Blacks lost control of their scrum channel and Edwards harassed Going so much that Slattery was able to pick up the ball and hold off the tackles of Burgess, Williams and Karam to score a try which Bennett converted.

The Barbarians led 13–0 and yet still had time to deliver another crushing blow to the All Blacks before half-time. Again, a pass by Going from a lineout put Burgess under pressure and Slattery bustled him into error. Quinnell fed the loose ball to Dawes and he put Bevan away on the left. Remembering Scown's earlier tackle, Bevan gritted his teeth and braced his muscles, just as he had when smashing through the Canterbury defence to score a seemingly impossible try for the Lions in 1971.

David Duckham, whose counter-attacking for the Barbarians was brilliant.

Peter Whiting, a commanding New Zealand lineout forward.

Again the All Black cover reached him, but this time, it could not stop him and he fought his way over the line to score. The half-time score was Barbarians 17 pts, All Blacks 0. A lot of people felt like pinching themselves to make sure it was all true.

John Dawes sensibly addressed himself to the realities of the situation in his team-talk at half-time. 'If we can score 17 points in the first half, they can score 17 in the second,' he warned. And they very nearly did.

Peter Whiting took such complete control of the lineout in the next 25 minutes that the Barbarians' backs must have wondered where the next ball was coming from, and had the All Blacks taken their chances, they would have cut back most, if not all, of the Barbarians' lead. Kirkpatrick, for instance, dropped the ball as he was diving to score after J. P. R. Williams had lost his balance in going for a high kick by Burgess. Still, Edwards was penalised for a crooked feed in the scrum and Karam, the New Zealand full-back, kicked a penalty goal to bring his total of points for the tour to 125.

Tom David charges late into Grant Batty, long after the New Zealand wing has cross-kicked.

Bryan Williams then made a classic break, the first of three in the match. He came from the blind-side wing to the centre from a lineout in midfield, a move he frequently used with profit, and although Burgess had to stoop to pick Going's pass off his toes, Robertson made enough room for Williams to break through and he drew the last of the defence to put Grant Batty in for his sixteenth try of the tour. The Barbarians' lead shrank to ten points.

Going was limping so badly at that stage that he left the field and Lyn Colling came on as replacement. He settled down immediately, and his accurate passing must have brought joy to Burgess, who had had too many uncomfortable moments trying to pick up Going's erratic passes.

Burgess' joy was not shared by Batty, who was justifiably highly indignant when he was late tackled by David as he went to cross kick. Batty was always all ginger, and he went to take on David, who did not improve Batty's temper by patting him consolingly on the head, as if he was a child. Still, Batty had the last word. He had tried to beat J. P. R.

Justifiably, Batty is not amused.

Williams both on the inside and the outside and had been tackled unceremoniously both times, so when he picked up a kick ahead by Hurst, he decided to see if the Barbarians' full-back was a little more fallible on the turn. Indeed he was, and it was a lesson that so few international wingers learned. Batty ran up to Williams, chipped the ball past him, swerved round him in a flash, picked up the ball and made try-scoring look the easiest thing in the whole wide world. Unfortunately for the All Blacks, Karam was not in his best form as a goalkicker, and so they still had only eleven points to show for a long spell of almost total domination.

The match had been played at such a pace that the All Blacks were almost bound to make mistakes in their tiredness in the last quarter of an hour, as they strove to draw level, and so they did, but even then they were only buried by what many good judges believe was the finest try of the match. A few fleeting seconds are an eternity on an international Rugby field, but the Barbarians somehow sustained an attack for 91 seconds as they worked the ball from one touch-line to the other and back again, probing all the while for the opening to make the final thrust. Duckham gathered a wayward kick by Karam and inspired the whole orchestra around him to a tremendous crescendo which ended with J. P. R. Williams taking a return pass and side-stepping the last of the cover to score in the corner. Fittingly, triumphantly, as it was in the beginning, so it was in the end. Phil Bennett converted the try with a superlative kick from the right touch-line. The Barbarians had won 23–11 and every man, woman and child who were present at Cardiff Arms Park that day knew that they would never see a game like it in their lives again. Joe McPartlin summed it up beautifully when he told the story of the wife who watched the match on television with her husband, a humble and lowly player who never climbed higher than the third team of his local old boys' club. 'Is that the same game that you try to play every week?' she asked, in sheer and utterly awed disbelief.

14 England lose their way

The most important effect of the success of the 1971 Lions was the enthusiasm it generated among young players. That enthusiasm was shared by the men – and occasionally the women, too – who were devoting themselves in ever increasing numbers to the task of coaching. This enthusiasm in the schools and colleges covered the whole of Britain.

Sadly, there was only a marginal increase in enthusiasm at first-class club level, except in Wales and to a lesser extent, in Scotland. The leading clubs in England were not much interested in the idea of coaching. Most dabbled in it, but hardly any of them succeeded in establishing personalities as coaches who would contribute significantly to the game. Soon after the 1971 Lions returned, their coach was asked to address a coaching conference in Warwickshire. He accepted the invitation but asked if there was really any point in his coming, because Coventry, the leading club in the county and, arguably, in the whole of England, did not have a coach.

This attitude was to cost England dear. England had already gone eight years without winning the international championship and the establishment of a Lions back division containing five Welshmen meant that the domestic superiority of Wales in the British Isles was likely to be continued for a very long time unless the other countries, and especially England, made a big effort to re-structure their game with sufficient depth to provide an effective counter. That effort was not made, and Wales strode on through the 'seventies largely unchallenged by the one other country in Britain with enough playing resources to have mounted an effective challenge.

Unfortunately, too, much of the coaching effort that was made in England was made in the wrong direction. This was evident on England's tour of Japan and the Far East in 1971, a month after the British Lions tour of New Zealand ended. None of England's Lions who had toured New Zealand were chosen for the touring party, which was composed of what was to become a familiar mixture of experienced players, and others who were either proven failures at international level or nothing more than young hopefuls. It also contained one Welshman, Mike Hann, who, tragically was to die of cancer within three years.

The team was coached by John Burgess in a move to improve England's increasingly inept performances at international level, but unfortunately, his own success as a coach at county level in England had been based on a game deriving almost wholly from the play of the 1963 All Blacks. It was an anachronism to see an England coach busy at work trying to inculcate a style of play obsessed with second phase possession which the All Blacks themselves had just abandoned, and which had been rejected because of the advances made by a *British* team in another direction. When the irony of this was pointed out to Burgess, he just shrugged and said, 'I wasn't in New Zealand. In any case, what did England contribute to that victory? Just a couple of forwards and a left wing.'

Those who had seen the Lions play in New Zealand felt that this was missing the point, although it has to be said that at that time John Burgess was one of the very few men in English Rugby who were big enough to accept a difference of opinion without taking it personally. The play of the England team on tour was not a success, despite the indifference of much of the opposition, and Burgess was not asked to coach England in the international championship that followed.

As a consequence, the tour did not do England much good in the playing sense, but it did have a lasting value in that it created an awareness of Rugby in the Far East for the England players and for those who accompanied the touring party. It was a fascinating experience. From the moment that the Japanese Airlines flight carrying the England team touched down in Moscow on the newly opened direct route to Tokyo, it was very obvious that geographically, the tour would be rather different from the familiar club jaunts to the West Country or Wales at Easter.

At that time, Moscow Airport did not do much to soften the bleak image of Russia as a land of snows, empty of warmth and the good things of life. What with the armed guards and the hard lights and the bare walls and the spartan furniture and the leaflets extolling the virtues of Marx, it could have been converted into another Lubyanka prison in about five minutes. What is more, there were those accompanying the England team who thought there was a very fair chance that this might happen.

Rugby teams on tour invariably exhibit a zest for living and a capacity for enjoying themselves which is one of the great attractions of the game and which sets the world of Rugby apart from most other sports. However, one of the disadvantages of this is that Rugby players just will not approach Communism with the proper hushed reverence which is deemed essential to such religion-substitutes, and the sight and sound of Chris Wardlow and Nigel Starmer-Smith, two of the England team, playing a couple of raucous flutes and marching their men through the corridors of Mockba Aeroflot or whatever, as if they were *enjoying* themselves, sent shivers of apprehension through those who were just hoping to pick up a few thousand gallons of paraffin and clear off to Japan.

Those shivers were quickly magnified into a seismological disturbance deep into the red paint area of the Richter scale. One of the more determined of the deviationists seized a booklet of Lenin's choicer thoughts and hurled it to the ground with an imperial flourish. Then he jumped on it and shouted 'Feelth', in what he hoped was a heavy mid-European accent.

Fortunately, no armed guards happened to be watching, but the authentic icy sweat of apprehension was moistening a good few brows as the touring party and other passengers stepped briskly into the bus to take them back to the aircraft. The assembled company stayed in the bus for some time. The landing which had been so vigorously applauded by the newer aviators, and which had nearly displaced the vertebrae of the others, had also burst two tyres and the Russians thought that it would be suitably instructive if the passengers watched while the tyres were changed. Either that, or an aspiring Lenin was getting his own back on the determined deviationist.

Eventually, the bus moved on and the passengers were allowed back on the aircraft. Then the only difficulty which arose occurred when two of the intrepid voyagers insisted on taking photographs of all Russia's secret rocket sites out of the window of the aircraft. The fact that it was the middle of a pitch black night and they were using a box Brownie from 36,000 feet did not allay the alarm of the Japanese security man sitting discreetly at the back. He obviously knew his KGB.

After all that, it seemed as if Japan would be a rest cure, but the touring party did not know about the traffic and the heat and the humidity and the smog and the traffic. The England team spent nine days in Japan and the players all felt as if they had spent seven of them in a traffic jam. Not that this was in any way surprising. Streets have no names in Tokyo and the houses are numbered in the order in which they were built. Number 1, therefore, could be in the middle of a road three miles long, and number 2, could be at one end, or possibly even round the corner in a cul-de-sac. It simply was not possible to hail a taxi and shout '33, Riverview Road'. because the chances were that the taxi driver did not know which was Liverlew Load, and if he did, he would not know which was 33, even assuming he understood addresses in English in the first place. It was necessary to give the man directions by landmarks such as the Tokyo Tower and similar distinctive buildings. All that was necessary was fluent Japanese, both written and spoken, and several large note-books and a fresh stock of quills, ink and blotting paper. Even that might not have been sufficient, because very few of the taxi drivers understood any English, and most of them worked very hard to avoid picking up Europeans. It was hard to blame them, because for one thing, all Europeans look exactly alike, and half the taxi drivers were so new at the job that they did not know where they were or where they were going anyway. It was a miracle that the whole England team was not lost.

Apart from all that, the heat and the humidity were overpowering. It was fortunate indeed that the Rugby Union had had the foresight to appoint such an eminent physician as Dr T. A. Kemp as their President when they knew that England were about to tour the Far East. If ever a man earned his salt, he did. Indeed, he became such a master of the rates of athletic absorption and excretion of sodium chloride that he became known to everyone as 'Slow Sodium'. Morning, noon and night, Dr Kemp went through the exhausted ranks rattling his tins of slow-acting salt pills like a Latin American band leader and there is not much doubt that he and they alone enabled England to come back and win when they looked very much as if they were going to lose the first match against Japan at Osaka.

England went to Osaka on a 150 mph bullet train and any notion that British Rail or any similar body might have had that this was something unusual was quickly dispelled when the travellers learned that these trains left Tokyo for Osaka every quarter of an hour on the quarter of an hour and returned at similar intervals. The journey of 400 miles was accomplished in $2\frac{1}{2}$ hours, and various Madame Butterflies wafted to and fro the carriages en route dispensing drinks and sweeties and cooling the fevered brows with scented, moist cloths.

Osaka was unremarkable, except for the fact that the humidity was even worse than it had been in Tokyo, and it was even hotter. In addition, it looked as if the England team's hotel was being strangled by an encircling motorway, like some vast concrete python. Still, that particular pub did do a very nice line in bathrobes cum kimonos, though the stock situation must have slumped so disastrously after England left that it would be surprising if the facility was continued.

Both the temperature and the humidity were in the nineties in Osaka, but at least the industrial smog there was marginally thinner than it had been in Tokyo. No-one could have got sunburned in Tokyo. On what purported to be a clear day, the light reading for photographs in the Princess Chichibu Stadium was a third of what it should have been. Observers concluded that Japan was called the land of the rising sun because the poor thing never had the chance to break through. They also felt that it was no wonder the Japanese make the best cameras in the world. They have to.

The contrasts were astonishing. In the middle of a colossal industrial tangle at Yokohama, with steel works and car works stretching for miles, and oil tankers under construction stretching for even further, it was extraordinary to step through some trees and into the past; to discover a green and peaceful field with a Rugby club at the end of it that had celebrated its centenary five years before the Rugby Union itself.

The Rugby played in Japan was the same curious mixture of orthodox and totally Oriental. Oxford and Cambridge Universities had toured Japan, and Japan had toured New Zealand and Australia, but the

Japanese style of play was largely unknown, and for that reason, the Rugby Union had prudently equipped themselves with a first class referee, Major Chris Tyler, as part of the touring party. England's difficulties, however were of their own making. England were so committed to the artificial platform of second phase play that they did not discover that if they had concentrated solely on first phase play, on scrummaging and driving and mauling, and engaged the Japanese in a simple physical contest in which they could not compete, England would have won their matches without any trouble at all. That discovery was to be made and exploited in the next three years, when Japan toured both England and Wales, and later acted as hosts to Wales. In 1971, England's attempts to move the ball away from the scrummage and the lineout to create second phase possession was exactly what the Japanese wanted, because being such nimble men, they were quicker to the point of check and so were presented with some chance of recovering the ball. The Japanese moved to the loose ball like a swarm of mosquitoes and they were brilliantly quick to counter-attack. They also scrummaged with surprising ingenuity and used low throws to the front of the lineout or threw the ball over the top to minimise the effects of their lack of height.

Apart from the Rugby, England never really discovered whether the European image of Japan existed at all. No doubt it was there, locked away in the inaccessible mountains, away from the narrow strip of flat

The startling speed off the mark of the Japanese. Akira Yokoi, captain of Japan, eludes Gerald Davies in the match against Wales in 1973.

and therefore immensely precious coastal land. The England team did spend one authentically Oriental night in seclusion with the Japanese team in a monastery in Tenri, and two of the accompanying observers spent an even more authentically Oriental night in the best *geisha* house in Tokyo. Both experiences were not at all as anticipated, but were none the less remarkable and enjoyable for that.

England then went in and out of Hong Kong at almost the same rate as a typhoon which had left the place gurgling under torrential rain. The rain drops seemed as big as egg cups, which was a tragedy considering that scenically and commercially, Hong Kong is one of the most spectacular places in the world.

The Rugby in Hong Kong was that of expatriates in a colony which, like Singapore, was so ably governed that it was like a flashback to the days when Britain was Great. Already, it was beginning to feel its economic muscles and with an exchange rate which was still just about tolerable, touring there was a very agreeable experience indeed. It was not only the lovers of Chinese food and tape recorders who voted Hong Kong level with France and South Africa as among the best places in the world to tour with a Rugby team.

Singapore was not as wet as Hong Kong, except for the unwary who ventured too close to the hotel swimming pool, but it was even hotter. Because of the heat, training was called for eight o'clock one morning. England established several precedents on their tour of the Far East, and that was not one they hoped to repeat.

Having survived both that, and a midnight trip to Bugie Street, where they saw the origin of one of the more colourful lines of that epic poem, *Eskimo Nell*, England managed to win their match against a similar team of expatriates as easily as they had won in Hong Kong. They were also able to accept some equally lavish hospitality in the delightfully gracious colonial club, and some of them had enough sense to weep at the British abandonment of the naval base and the RAF base at Changi. Even then, though, it was evident that Mr Lee Kuan Yew would probably win the gold medal in the final of any world Prime Ministers' stakes because he had transformed his tiny country with a remarkable display of pragmatism and efficiency. Singapore undoubtedly lost something in the process, but it probably gained very much more. It was nostalgic to be entertained to dinner by the captain of a Royal Navy ship then in port, and to reflect that there might not be many more opportunities to indulge in such a pleasure.

Having survived the trauma of training at eight o'clock in the morning in Singapore, the mad dogs of Englishmen were faced with Oriental perils of a different kind in Ceylon, or Sri Lanka as it was then becoming known. The bus ride from the airport to the hotel on the far side of Colombo gave the passengers a feeling of the country which several times seemed as if it might become quite literal.

The two most common forms of transport in Ceylon were then the bullock-carts and the lurching red double-decker buses which had been the pride of London Transport in about 1936. After that, these buses had allegedly seen service in Ireland, Russia and India, and all three countries had written them off. A succession of these vehicles, keeling round corners to overtake double-span bullock-carts on narrrow roads and coming at you head-on, with all three parties either hooting or bellowing, induced a state of nervous paralysis which for a time rather dimmed the beauties of the rocky headland on which the hotel was so magnificently situated by the Indian Ocean.

There, the most delicious pineapples could be bought for 6d each, and characters straight out of It 'Ain't 'Arf 'Ot, Mum peddled sapphires of the most beautiful colour and the most excruciating cut. There, too, England went to sea on a couple of hollow tree-trunks lashed together with a wooden superstructure and it was there that they watched a snake charmer work with a king cobra. The Kon-Tiki expedition was bad enough, slewing in and out of the reefs with nothing more than a couple of poles to fend off shipwreck, but the sight of the England players watching the cobra with their knuckles showing white on the arms of their cane chairs, and with their leg muscles bunched in readiness beneath them, showed what a wonderful reaction exercise a hasty evacuation would have been. By then, Chris Wardlow had a wrecked cartilage and Geoff Evans had his foot in plaster, but both were clearly ready to shade evens in the 100 yard dash if the need arose.

Once again, the Rugby presented no problems to England. The Sri Lankans were too small to compete. The only difficulties were caused by the economic situation, which was so delicate that the Marxist govern-

England afloat on the Singhalese equivalent of Kon-Tiki.

ment had managed to dissipate the enormous credit balance left by the British in 1948 and had led the country unerringly to a point of such bankrupt chaos that a curfew was necessary. This was distinctly awkward for one of the visitors (not one of the players) who had accepted an invitation to look at a young lady's etchings, and found himself shortly after midnight faced with the alternative of penetrating a ring of tanks and barbed wire or staying where he was. It was an agonising decision, but he made it like a man.

England returned with their footballing aspirations in no way enhanced, but with their knowledge of the world of Rugby immeasurably widened. The secretary of Hong Kong was not just a Scottish name on a remote floor of the Jardine Matheson Company; he had a face and a nice pub situated just across the road (the Welsh president of the Mandarin Hotel would have forgiven the familiarity), and a thoroughly civilised bar at the cricket club on the way to the Rugby ground. There were also some extraordinarily hospitable members of the Hong Kong Rugby fraternity who all seemed to have quite beautiful houses, and there was at least one referee in the colony who, as a character, would rank with any in the splendidly diverse world of Rugby.

Shiggy Konno, too, was not just the emperor of Japanese rugby. He also had a face, and not only to the world of Rugby administrators. He became known as a friend to the England players. He had made himself known in the circles of Rugby administration the year before, at the world congress in Cambridge, but the game is not for administrators; it is for players. And suddenly, when the England players arrived in Japan, there was this impeccable, urbane man, speaking the most perfect Eng-

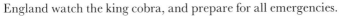

England watch the king cobra, and prepare for all emergencies.

lish. He had been to school in England before the war, and went back home to train as a *kamikaze* pilot. Happily, the war ended before Shiggy could fly his one and only mission, and as he said, the *kamikaze* pilots were then faced with the dilemma of what to do next. Their commanding officer decided that the only honourable thing to do was to commit *hari-kiri*, and disembowelled himself by subsiding on to his ceremonial sword. Shiggy confessed that he and several of his brethren thought that any extension of this practice would have been a terrible waste and did not follow the example. 'This is the origin of chicken chow mien,' grinned Shiggy cheerfully.

By making the tour, the England players knew what the Asian Rugby championship meant. Their only regret was that the Rugby Union had found it almost impossible to conduct a correspondence with Thailand, and so the planned visit to Bangkok had to be abandoned.

Ceylon also became a known Rugby quantity. Their lightly-built, wristy players were better equipped for hockey, but they looked as if they would make good opposition for schools and clubs rather than inter-national tours. Ceylon in turn wanted to learn and one distinguished referee even managed to drop in while passing by on his RAF duties. The world of minor Rugby was beginning a period of heady expansion.

Unfortunately, the world of major Rugby was doing just the reverse. South Africa's political difficulties on their tour of the United Kingdom and France in 1969–70 were aggravated by a thoroughly disagreeable tour of Australia in 1971. From the Rugby point of view, the Springboks could not have been more successful, but communist agitators made the tour a misery for the South African players. After that, only the French were prepared to invite the Springboks to tour their country. One by one, all the other major Rugby playing nations either postponed or cancelled incoming tours by South Africa. They just were not prepared to put up with the fuss.

For five more years, South Africa's traditional opponents continued to tour South Africa. England went in 1972, the British Lions went in 1974, France went in 1975 and New Zealand in 1976, but after that, Scotland excused themselves and so did Australia, and more and more Rugby administrators began to express doubts about the Lions tour of South Africa in 1980.

South Africans argued that their way of life and their laws were their own business. They pointed out that over the whole continent of Africa, the only two countries where there was any semblance of democracy were Rhodesia and South Africa. That being the case, South Africans and Rhodesians alike were dumbfounded that men of the same ancestry in other parts of the world should seriously suggest that they should allow their two countries to become another Uganda or Angola.

Ironically, Rhodesia plays as a province of South Africa in the world of Rugby, so their interests in that game are even more closely allied than their political interests, but when the world-wide agitation about apartheid began, the situation in the two countries was entirely different. There was no racial separation in sport in Rhodesia to speak of, which made the banning of their soccer team from the World Cup absolutely ludicrous. The team consisted of ten black men and one white man. In South Africa, the different races were not allowed to play against each other by law, and so the men running sport in that country began an energetic campaign to change their country's policies and ultimately, its laws. They did this even though, as Dr Danie Craven himself said, 'We know that whatever we do will not satisfy our enemies. The only thing that will satisfy them will be a communist take-over of our entire country. However, we are hoping that our efforts will satisfy our friends.'

Within six years, the efforts of men like Dr Craven resulted in perhaps the most dramatic change in the social fabric of any country anywhere in the world. The petty apartheid which Europeans always found so difficult to understand began to disappear like spring snow. Hotels and restaurants began accepting clients of all races, even while that was still officially against the country's laws, and the governing bodies of various sports again anticipated the future and began selecting multi-racial teams. Even the sports clubs within South Africa itself began accepting members of all races. The changes which took place in South Africa between the England tour of 1972 and the All Blacks' tour of 1976 were astonishing to those who knew the country. They were far, far greater than the changes which took place in Springbok Rugby, and they were profound indeed.

When England went to South Africa in 1972, they had already suffered their longest period of failure among the four home unions since the breakaway of the Northern clubs to form the Rugby League in 1892, and it had just culminated in the loss of all four matches in the international championship for the first time in their history. Almost their only comfort had been their defeat of South Africa at Twickenham in 1969, and prophetically, the words uttered by the Springbok coach, Avril Malan, after that tour began to come true in 1972.

England went with little hope of achieving glory. Their record at home had been so bad for so long that they had become something of a laughing stock, and some of the more irreverent Welsh, in what had become an annual exercise in exultation at both the Arms Park and Twickenham, were suggesting that perhaps Wales should either drop the fixture or let England play their second team!

Despite that, and despite the fact that they had to play three of South Africa's leading provinces on their three week tour, England went through unbeaten and ended by beating South Africa 18–9 at Ellis Park. They won their games more on South Africa's shortcomings than on their own merits, doggedly though they played, but to English ears, the gasps of astonishment and envy throughout the world of Rugby, and especially Wales, were the sweetest music. Wales have never beaten South Africa, and there was England, poor old hopeless England, beating the Springboks twice in three years.

That year, the international championship had been disrupted for the first time since the war. Terrorism in Northern Ireland, which was already manifesting itself during the Springbok tour of 1969–70, had long since involved bombings and murder, and it had spread to Dublin. As a result, Scotland and Wales declined to fulfil their fixtures against Ireland, and although the majority of England's players felt strongly that their match against Ireland should not be played either, the Rugby Union took it upon themselves to ignore the threats against the safety of the England team. They decided to go ahead with the match in Dublin. Two of the England players, Peter Larter and Sam Doble, decided not to make themselves available for the match. They were never chosen for England again. The whole episode was one of the least worthy in the Rugby Union's history and within a year, it was made even less agreeable by a decision which was precisely the reverse of that taken in 1972.

At the time of the Ireland game, however, the only thing the England players could do was grin and bear it. This was not made any easier by the fact that England were in the middle of a season in which they lost all four games in the international championship for the first time in their history. Still, John Pullin, the England captain, made a delightfully wry observation at the dinner after Ireland had beaten England in a match which required one of Eire's biggest security operations to allow it to proceed. 'We may not be much good,' said Pullin, 'but at least we turn up'.

Pullin had a farmer's facility for saying something sensible, pointed and amusing in a very few words, and he showed it again in South Africa. After England had defeated Natal comprehensively in Durban, he said that before the tour he had gone to night school to learn to make speeches. 'But it didn't do me any good,' he said sadly. 'When they heard I was the captain of England, they only taught me how to make losing speeches!'

England capped that remarkable achievement by touring New Zealand the following year and beating the All Blacks. It was an unusual tour in more ways than one, because it was only put together at the last minute when England decided that the risk of insurrection in Argentina was too great for them to tour that country. Not surprisingly, the Argentines were more than unhappy about that decision especially in view of what had happened in Dublin the year before, and they were even more put out when, within a matter of weeks, the Rugby Union announced that they had arranged an alternative tour to Fiji and New Zealand.

Before they went, England won a world sevens tournament held at Murrayfield as part of Scotland's centenary celebrations, but on tour in the fifteen-a-side game, they only scraped home by the narrowest of margins against Fiji in the first match, and then suffered all manner of indignities against the provinces of New Zealand. The contrast with

England's provincial record in South Africa the year before could not have been more marked, but against all expectations, England succeeded in beating New Zealand almost as decisively as they had beaten South Africa. Again, the world of Rugby goggled.

England did beat Wales the following season, for the first time since 1963, but success in the international championship was as elusive as ever, and more and more of the men at the heart of Rugby football in England began to accept that it was not likely to be otherwise until the game in that country was re-structured into bigger and more powerful units than the counties of which the Rugby Football Union itself was composed.

This had been obvious to some people for a long time, and it was a view which was supported by a committee, under the chairmanship of Sir George Mallaby, which had been appointed by the Rugby Union to examine the state of the game in England at the end of its first 100 years and to make recommendations about its future. The findings of the Mallaby committee were something of a compromise, but the broad direction of the recommendations was essentially sound.

One of the central recommendations of the Mallaby committee was that the county championship in England should be abolished in its current form and that an area championship should be inaugurated in its place. This went to the root of the problems of the game in England where the majority of county Rugby was of a significantly lower standard than that played by the major clubs and therefore provided no intermediate proving ground between club and international Rugby. There was also far too much county Rugby, which added to the pressure on the country's leading players without requiring them to improve their standards of play. As a result, England's best players were not having to play their best Rugby often enough. In this respect, Wales were much better served by the accident of geography which had compressed so many good clubs into such a small area.

From Newport in the east to Llanelli in the west, Wales had at least one first-class club every ten miles and often more than one. The competition between these clubs and the playing opportunities they provided meant that Wales suffered much less wastage of schoolboy talent than England, who simply did not have enough first-class clubs in enough parts of the country to develop the abundant talent which was emerging in schools.

England's county championship structure was at least 40 years out of date, and it did nothing whatever to repair the deficiencies in English Rugby. If anything, it aggravated them. However, the representation on the Rugby Union itself was based on the counties, and as very few men are ever inclined to vote themselves out of an agreeable job, their instinct was to reject almost everything in the Mallaby report except some minor recommendations about the reorganisation of the permanent staff and its offices. It would have been far better to have received the report and to have allowed sufficient time for everyone to digest its implications. In any case, within three years, the Rugby Union had accepted a system of area trials which was not far removed from the area championship that the Mallaby committee had suggested and there was not much doubt that sooner or later an area championship would replace the county championship. This would have several advantages. It would take pressure off the leading players, which ought to be a prime consideration in the administration of a decreasingly amateur game. It would provide England with a viable base from which to play provincial fixtures against touring sides. It would provide far and away the best trials system England have ever had. It would give England's best players the chance to sharpen their skills in company with players of similar calibre, and such a championship would be especially valuable if it was played in the month of December, before the international championship. It would also clear the first three months of the season for the clubs, who would be able to enjoy the services of their best players without interruption.

It would even be of benefit to minor clubs, and to the great majority of players who do not play first-class Rugby, because the county championship could then be restricted to the minor clubs and as such would be of great value. One of the greatest weaknesses of English Rugby has always been that the first-class players have far too much to play for and the rest far too little. A county championship restricted to players not involved in major club Rugby would be a thoroughly rewarding incentive.

What is more, such a reorganisation would even be of benefit to the Rugby Union. All that would be necessary would be for the present counties to be grouped into eight areas, and if the area system was found to work, administratively the change in the system of representation could be introduced in phases, rather than with one stroke of the axe. Sadly, the quality of Rugby Union representation no longer matches that of its early years and fully substantiates the fears of the late Sir William Ramsay that the declining quality of representation among Rugby Union members was its chief concern for the future. To date, the Rugby Union have rejected such reforms, because not only do they want to retain the outdated county structure, but they are also frightened of creating an elite. Apparently, this fear is why they have persisted in rejecting the major clubs' perfectly reasonable wish to organise themselves into area leagues for about one third of their total fixtures. The irony of this is that it would be difficult to imagine any body of fifty men whose whole lives are governed more completely by the principle of an elite than the members of the Rugby Union. Socially, educationally, domestically, commercially, professionally – even militarily – they live their lives not only enjoying, but defending to the last cross of the ballot box, the benefits of the elitist principle, and yet when they are asked to extend the same advantages of Rugby football, they react as if they are all among the wetter modern disciples of Karl Marx.

15 World revolution

Nineteen seventy four was a year as significant in the World of Rugby football as 1984 was to George Orwell and his uncomfortably perceptive fantasy of a world revolution. In Rugby football the revolution arrived. In South Africa, Springbok Rugby was destroyed by a British Lions team playing a game of scrummaging and kicking which embraced organised violence and which was totally alien to the British heritage of back play. In New Zealand, the men in the corridors of Rugby power deliberately turned their faces in precisely the opposite direction from that taken by Britain in South Africa in an attempt to improve the increasingly un-savoury image of the game in their country and to expand the style of the All Blacks' play to involve the backs as well as the forwards. In Australia, they digested the need for improvements in the technique of their forward play, demonstrated so clearly on short tours of Britain, and marvelled at the power and physique of an England schools' team that toured their country unbeaten. In France, the burgeoning power of the Béziers club, and the success of the American football techniques adopted by its coach, Raoul Barriere, persuaded the national selectors that it was time to re-examine the fundamentals of the approach of the French national team. In England, the trauma of the Mallaby report and its recommendations stampeded the Rugby Union back towards the proven failures of the past. In Ireland, the Irish Rugby Union celebrated the centenary of the Irish Football Union. In Tonga, they celebrated the individual brilliance shown by their captain, Sioni Mafi, on their short tour of England and Wales. In Japan, they mourned the fact that their team had lost its capacity to surprise the major countries.

It was the year in which seven of the major Rugby playing countries in the world forsook their traditional style of playing the game, either by accident or design, and chose to move in another direction. It was also the year in which the country which had ruled the world of Rugby for so long, South Africa, finished in ruins at the bottom of the heap. The British Lions beat South Africa 3–0 in the test series, with one match drawn.

Many factors had contributed to the collapse of South Africa, not least the loss of continuity in team-building which had always given New Zealand and South African Rugby such an advantage over the rest of the world. For the better part of seventy years, the national teams of New Zealand and South Africa had been constantly evolving, with often only a matter of months between different series of matches against different countries. The result had been that South Africa and New Zealand had always known their strengths and had always known just who were their international players. From one series to the next, there would rarely be a turnover of more than two or three players, whereas British teams, which had played irregularly in the early years and then in 1950, 1955, 1959, 1962, 1966, 1968 and 1971, had to build a fresh team every time they went on tour, and consequently, made a far higher number of mistakes in selection. They did this partly because the men picking the teams had lost touch with the playing of the game and partly because different selectors never had the advantage of learning from their mistakes and so made them over and over again with different players.

By 1974, South Africa had lost that advantage. In the previous four years, they had played only a short tour of Australia and one match against England. For the first time since the turn of the century, they did not know who their international players were and, as Avril Malan predicted, they had been overtaken in the techniques of teaching and playing the game. The uncertainty of the Springbok selectors in the test

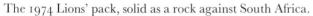

The 1974 Lions' pack, solid as a rock against South Africa.

series was painful to behold. In the first three matches alone, they used 32 players. They used six different half-backs in three of the four matches and tried a different style of play in every one of the four games. They bounded this way and that like the springbok that is about to provide the lion with its midday meal and in the words of Gordon Brown, the Lions' best forward, 'they got minced'.

Syd Millar, the Lions' coach, and Bill McBride, the captain, concentrated on dominating the game in the scrummage, traditionally the area of South Africa's greatest strength, and Gareth Edwards used the possession to kick for position, developing a heavily topped kick to drive the ball to the corners. These tactics succeeded beyond the wildest dreams of the Lions' which perhaps was just as well because the rest of their game was so limited that they left themselves with few other options.

Before the tour was a month old, some of the Lions' backs were writing home to their clubs to say how disappointed they were with the way the team was playing the game, and small wonder. For years, British Rugby had worked to improve its forward organisation so that it could release the skills of its backs. The pot of gold at the end of the rainbow was always 50 per cent of the ball. In South Africa in 1974, the British Lions won more than 70 per cent of the ball, and yet they played the ten-man Rugby that the British themselves had always derided when it was played by New Zealand.

The sad thing was that it was all so unnecessary. It was argued in the first place that the Lions had to play as they did because their leading backs, like Gerald Davies and David Duckham, were not available to tour, but the backs who went in their place were all very much better than any of those in South Africa. Had the Lions played South Africa on their merits, the Springboks would have suffered at least two defeats even greater than the 44–0 thrashing South Africa gave Scotland in 1951.

Quite apart from all this, the most disturbing feature of the tour was the Lions' use of organised violence. They resolved, as a matter of playing policy, that if there was any fighting on the field, they would use the code-word 'ninety-nine' as a signal for all the players to join in the brawl, arguing that the referee was much less likely to send off the whole team than one man. The theory worked. The Lions went through South Africa like latter-day Genghis Khans, and some of the teams, like Orange Free State, they left behind looked as if they had been in a road accident.

To some people, the end justified the means. They did not care how the Lions won, just as long as they *did* win. They did not stop to think of the implications for the future of Rugby football contained in the way the Lions played the game. They shut their minds to the fact that British back play would have no future if that style of play was adopted. They excused the violence. They were not remotely concerned about the battle for the hearts and minds of the young, and of the enthusiasm of all those selfless people who teach the young how to play. Winning was all that mattered.

The poverty of this philosophy was soon exposed. Within three months, British back play was being shown the way ahead by a New Zealand team, of all people, and four months later, the International Board felt constrained to introduce legislation requiring team captains to be sent off the field if a referee was confronted with organised violence such as that used by the 1974 Lions. It was not a pretty epitaph.

Ironically, while the Lions were turning away from 15 man Rugby, the men responsible for choosing the New Zealand All Blacks were doing exactly the opposite. They had recognised that John Dawes, the captain of the British Lions in New Zealand in 1971, was speaking nothing but the uncomfortable truth when he drew attention to the decline in interest in the game in New Zealand, even between the Welsh tour of 1969 and the Lions tour of 1971. Dawes said that more and more people in New Zealand were turning away from Rugby, more and more parents were encouraging their children to take up some other sporting activity. Dawes said unequivocally that this was because the game in New Zealand was too intense, too dour, too brutal and too restricted in its scope. For too many years, New Zealand's style of play had been confined to the forwards and the half-backs, and the consequence was that it just was not fun to play. Dawes pointed out that enjoyment of the game by the player is the one criterion that decides the survival of any game. Judged by that, he said, the state of Rugby football in New Zealand ought to give the New Zealand Rugby Union cause for concern.

It did, and when the unfortunate events of the All Blacks tour of Britain and France in 1972–73 were digested, the New Zealand Rugby Union decided to so something about it. New Zealanders are a practical people, because they live much closer to the earth than most of the Rugby playing communities in Europe, and they are very much quicker to absorb lessons and to profit from them. They did not need a Mallaby report to state the obvious, and even more to the point, they did not shrink from grasping the nettle.

They appointed John Stewart as the convener of their selectors, and within three years he had changed New Zealand's whole approach to the game. He deliberately threw away the trappings of autocracy which had always been associated with coaching in New Zealand, and he involved the players in decision-making. He asked them what they thought, and encouraged them to make constructive suggestions as to how the team effort might be improved. Instead of looking like ceremonial drill practices under Regimental Sergeant Major Brittain, on the main barrack square at Aldershot, All Black practices suddenly resembled debating societies. Some of the senior All Blacks scoffed, though they did not do it to Stewart's face. The younger ones enjoyed the experience, and all of them were given to understand very clearly that New Zealand Rugby in future would be for the enjoyment of all 15 players in the team, and not just for the forwards and the half-backs.

Fred Allen had inculcated the same expansion in the range of the All Blacks' play, but his approach was as hard as John Stewart's was soft. Fred Allen even dressed down Colin Meads, and did it in public.

John Stewart was involved in teaching as his profession, and he was constantly in contact with the young. He believed passionately that the rising generation had to be persuaded to participate, rather than commanded to do so. He did not think that Rugby football had a divine right to dominate their lives. If it did so, then he thought it ought to be on their terms, and because they wanted it so. In New Zealand, this was nothing short of a revolution.

Whether by accident or design, the personnel of the All Black squad changed significantly, too. The Mafia of the 1972–73 tour disappeared. Some very good players went with them, but there is no doubt that the entire image of New Zealand Rugby was changed. It was a brave act, by a brave man, and he had his reward much quicker than he could have imagined. The All Blacks toured Ireland in 1974 as part of the celebrations when the Irish Rugby Union celebrated the centenary of the first football Union formed in Ireland and played what was effectively Ireland, Wales and the 1974 British Lions within the space of eight days at the end of the tour. The All Blacks beat Ireland and Wales, and the Lions, playing in the colours of the Barbarians, were only saved by the referee,

John Stewart, former coach of New Zealand.

Georges Domercq. He put his whistle in his mouth and took it out again when the Lions won the ball from a palpably crooked throw into a lineout at the end of the match, and allowed Mervyn Davies to go on and score a try which enabled the Lions to escape with a draw. They did not deserve it. They knew they had been outplayed by a team playing with a much broader vision of the game. One of the Lions tight forwards tried to shrug it away. 'Ah well,' he said, 'It was only a one-off game'.

So was the match played by the 1971 Lions, also in the colours of the Barbarians, against the All Blacks the year before in Cardiff. There could have been no greater contrast in the philosophies of the game.

While South Africans surveyed the wreckage of their Rugby, and New Zealand stepped forward eagerly along the road to total Rugby from which Britain had turned away, France took advantage of an opportunity to re-examine the fundamentals established by Lucien Mias 16 years before. The French had developed almost a special relationship with South Africa, for which the Springboks were immensely grateful, because it enabled them to tour France late in 1974 and restore some of their self-esteem after the disasters of the series against the Lions. The Springboks won both the international matches played against France and in the international championship that followed France were beaten both by Wales and Ireland. That in itself might not have persuaded the French to make a fundamental change in the structure and approach of their national team but when, at the end of the season, some of the senior French players decided that they were not available for a return tour of South Africa, the selectors had no alternative but to introduce some new players. The most significant of these were two new props, Robert Paparemborde and Gerard Cholley, and two new locks, Jean-Francois Imbernon and Michel Palmie. Imbernon contracted appendicitis after the team was chosen, and was not able to tour, but these four tight forwards represented a startling change of type. All four were scrummagers, really hard men. Neither of the locks had any pretensions as jumpers in the lineout. Neither had any pretensions as loose forwards. Their strength was their mauling and scrummaging. All four were ferocious close quarter specialists and only one, Paparemborde, had the facility in the loose which the French traditionally required from all their forwards. Alan Ashcroft would have happily accepted them all as donkeys. He may have looked a bit askance at Paparemborde, but then, Paperemborde was something special. He scored tries in both the internationals against South Africa, and gave notice that he could scrummage against anyone.

Paparemborde was an extraordinary shape. His bull neck seemed to run straight into his hips without going through the formality of shoulders. This made him very difficult to scrummage against, because opponents kept slipping off him. Above all, he had that iron strength so essential to the few props that history has set apart from the others.

Cholley was altogether different. He was tall for a loose head prop, which was hardly surprising, because he had been one of the best amateur heavyweights in France and he had also played much of his Rugby as a lock. What was surprising was the fact that he became so successful as a loose head prop at such a late stage in his career. His height was against him and so was his lack of experience. It did not seem to inconvenience him in the least.

When they went to South Africa in 1975, France were beginning to discover some of the constituent parts of one of the best packs produced anywhere in the history of the game, but although they lost both the internationals played against the Springboks, they were not deterred. When they got back home, they simply fitted the other pieces of the jigsaw together.

England's experience in 1975 was rather different. They went to Australia with yet another band of young hopefuls, and once again, left seven or eight of their most experienced international players at home. Once again, they paid the price. They lost both the internationals against Australia, discovered that most of their young hopefuls were not good enough and sadly, so disenchanted two of them that they dropped out of the game. Meanwhile, the England players who should have been in Australia were left a little more disenchanted with a selection process that had been so consistently unsuccessful for twelve years that it could no longer be excused as a quirk of fate. John Burgess, who coached England in Australia, was aware of this. With typical honesty, he accepted that England's record of twelve wins in forty-seven matches spoke for itself. Almost throughout their history, England had been winning an average of more than thirty matches out of any span of forty-seven. Since 1963, their record had been calamitous.

In Australia in 1975, it became even worse. This was predictable, because however great the inroads by Rugby League, Australian Rugby Union, in Australia, can never be taken lightly. There are many reasons for this. The Australians are a competitive race, and until comparatively recently, they were of a physique superior to European Rugby players. Their grounds are hard and fast, and those surfaces encourage the development of a different type of game. Australian Rugby players have never been short of the ability to look after themselves in any episodes of violence, either, and in addition to all that, Australian referees have always constituted a factor which has to be taken into account by any team touring their country. As the 1971 Lions found, and countless New Zealand teams have found before and since, Australian referees have a facility for producing rulings which infuriate visiting players. More than one All Black captain has been so incensed by Australian referees that he has been on the point of taking his team off the field in protest. Almost every team which has visited Australia has gone back home and told the same story. Therefore it was absolutely pointless for England in 1975 or

Wales in 1977 to go there thinking that it would be any different for them. The home town bias of Australian Rugby referees is as much as part of Australia as Sydney Harbour Bridge. It is part of the deal which you have to accept when you agree to tour Australia, just like the sun and the hard grounds and the hard fists of Australian forwards. It is no good complaining about them. As Harry Truman once said, 'If you don't like the heat, keep out of the kitchen'.

This was why England were so mistaken to take so many inexperienced players in 1975, and why Wales, when they went to Australia two years later, were so mistaken to start tilting at every windmill in sight except the one exclusively related to the job in hand. Both in 1975 and in 1977, Australia were eminently beatable, but their visitors almost went out of their way to beat themselves. England perhaps had less excuse than Wales, because at least Wales took as many as they could of their best players, whereas England, yet again, succumbed to the English disease of thinking that the grass on the other side of the fence was greener.

They discovered, yet again, that indeed it was green, but in entirely the wrong sense of the word. England went to Australia to play eight matches, and they lost four of them, including both internationals. They learned then that the notion of filling half the team with young uncapped players may look all very well in theory on a Sunday morning in March, but it does not work out too well in practice on a Saturday afternoon in Sydney in May.

To add to England's problems, they had an appalling run of injuries. Fran Cotton, who was the key to their scrummage, injured a sciatic nerve in the second match and had to drop out of the tour. Keith Smith, one of the backs, aggravated a knee injury and also had to be replaced.

Other injuries followed, but the one to Cotton was crucial, because he was one of the few really experienced players chosen for the tour. The others sat round his bed, as he lay on a board, and contemplated the task ahead. Players like John Pullin, Roger Uttley and Dave Rollitt had never had any illusions about the dangers of touring without locks like Chris Ralston and Nigel Horton and without a scrum-half like Jan Webster or Steve Smith to make use of the ball they won. Fifteen of the players who had represented England in the international championship just ended, including five British Lions, were not selected. Garrick Fay, the leading Australian lock, did not stop laughing for five minutes when he telephoned London and learned of the selection.

After the defeat by Sydney in the second game, all the England players in Australia knew that there was no way that a young flanker like Steve Callum, who the year before had been in the England schools team, could get enough experience in two matches to make anything like as effective a contribution as loose forwards like Peter Dixon or John Watkins, who had played so well for England in South Africa in 1972, or Tony Bucknall or 'Budge' Rogers.

A short tour is not the occasion when a player can easily gain experience. At best, a player will have only five matches, and the ones who really need the experience will have only two or three. Alec Lewis, the England manager, admitted 'If winning the matches on this tour had been the only consideration, we would have chosen a team very different from the one we have here. We are not thinking so much on a short term basis. We are looking more to the medium and long term.'

But as England discovered, international Rugby is not about the medium and long term. It is only ever about winning the next match, and producing the team with the best chance of doing so. To work on any other assumption is to devalue the whole process of winning an international cap, and regrettably, players were capped on that England tour who never should have been asked to represent their country.

The Australian team planners were far more realistic. They had worked hard on basic forward techniques since an unsuccessful short tour of England and Wales in 1973, and, as always, Australian Rugby Union had shown itself to be marvellously resilient to the pressures it has always faced. There have been years when the lure of the professional code has decimated the Australian team, but as Russell Fairfax has said, the experience of playing Rugby football for Australia and touring with them is so enjoyable that the game in that country always seems to recover.

Co-ordinating an amateur game like Rugby football in such a vast and disparate and mercenary place as Australia is a task to daunt even Hercules, but in the two years before England arrived in 1975, a group of enthusiasts had banded together, just as they had in Britain eight years earlier, determined to bring the game into the second half of the twentieth century; determined to understand coaching and playing techniques; determined to improve their country's forward play by improving its organisation; determined, above all, to be a competitive force in the playing sense.

Nothing is more fun than an adventure such as that. Four years earlier, British Rugby had surprised itself by its discovery of how quickly forward organisation could be mastered, and it had shaken its head in despair that no-one in the previous forty years had bothered to do the same and therefore had conceded half the Rugby battle to the South Africans and New Zealanders before the game had even started. The Australians had to work from a much more limited base in terms of playing population and involvement, but the progress they made delighted themselves as much as it surprised their opponents. At that time, this progress was more evident in the matches they played in Australia than those played on tour abroad, but it was an essential beginning.

Even when playing at home, Australian teams have a manager and a coach, just as New Zealand and South African teams do. In 1975, Australia were managed by the genial Ross Turnbull, himself a former

Australian prop, and coached by David Brockhoff, who played for Australia as a flanker. Brockhoff was an articulate man, with a gift for metaphor couched in language so dramatic as to be quite startling. This worried some of the more conservative members of the Australian Rugby Union, but it was meat and drink to the Australian journalists who needed all the colour they could find to sell the game as much to their own sports editors as to the public.

Not that Australia's newspapermen and broadcasters were short of human interest material on England's tour. From the moment that the England team arrived in Sydney, after running up 64 points against Western Australia in Perth, they began to hit the headlines in a way which always makes Rugby Union committee men blanch. To start with, they lost to Sydney at Rugby football, which would not have occasioned much comment, and they also lost to Sydney at the noble art of self-defence, which occasioned a thundering great splash of two inch head-lines. A young Sydney prop named Steve Finnane took it upon himself to straighten up three of the England pack, and as Finnane was a quite exceptional puncher, the results were nothing short of spectacular.

Finnane even floored Mike Burton, the England prop, as they were running across field to a lineout. After years of experience in the West country, Burton was thoroughly well versed in these matters himself, but he did not see the punch coming. He held this to be a serious oversight, but the blow was so beautifully delivered that afterwards he shook his head admiringly about it. 'We may lose a few matches at Gloucester,' he said, 'but we don't lose many fights'.

This gave the Sydney scribes the chance to recount the story, probably apocryphal, of the occasion Finnane had gone into one of the city's night clubs with a girl friend, and had walked by a couple of men standing near others seated at a table. One of the men passed an offensive remark within the hearing of the girl. Finnane, with sleepy eyes and gaucho moustaches, had something of the appearance of the fastest gun in the West, and even Billy the Kid could not have beaten the speed with which he went into action. Within about three seconds, the man who had passed the remark was stretched on the floor. Finnane turned to see one of the men seated at the table pointing a revolver at him. 'OK sonny,' he said. 'You've made your point. Now get lost.'

Finnane rapidly obliged.

The man with the gun was apparently one of the heaviest mobsters in Sydney, and a few days later, Finnane had only just finished counting his blessings when he received a note which said, 'I liked the way you handled yourself the other night. If ever you want a job, just ring this number . . .'

By that time, Sydney sports editors knew all about Rugby Union football, because the week before England arrived, Rugby League had been knocked off its complacent perch astride threequarters of the column inches in the newspapers by a delightful happening in a match between Sydney and a New South Wales Country team captained by scrum-half John Hipwell.

This unpretentious country team had come to the big city and had conned the slickers there with a Rugby move which was so colourful that it had the newspapers buzzing for days. What is more, it won the match. The Australians were the first to appreciate that anyone who can con another Australian in Sydney has to be taken very seriously indeed, because as a nation, they reckon to have set all the world and Olympic records in that particular sport.

What happened was this. The Country team were narrowly losing the match when, just before the end, they were awarded a penalty kick near the halfway line. The whole team then lined up with their backs to the opposition, shoulder to shoulder in a shallow crescent. It was a bit like the reverse of the Zulus' famous buffalo horn fighting formation.

The man in the middle of the crescent then took a tapped penalty kick,

John Hipwell has the ball in the centre, and all the Australians are pretending to hide it up their jumper as part of a move performed by NSW Country against England. Barry Nelmes and Roger Uttley peer, as curious as English giraffes, to try to see what is going on.

still with his back to the opposition, and made as if to pass the ball both ways. The Sydney players, of course, could not see which way round the crescent the ball had gone, or even if it had gone at all because the Country team were lined up shoulder to shoulder. What was more, the players on both sides of the man who had taken the kick moved their arms and shoulders as if they were passing the ball. Then, at a given signal, they all broke away and turned and ran in different directions towards Sydney's line.

The idea was that the player who did have the ball should have it hidden up his shirt, and that he would therefore reach the line, or get very near to it, before he was detected in the confusion. In the event, the man with the ball could not quite stuff the ball up his jumper because by that stage of the proceedings his jumper was sticky with sweat, but even so he did get a very long way before Sydney realised where the ball was and Country scored a try to win the match.

The move delighted the Australian sporting public and it gave Rugby Union football in Australia a surge of marvellous publicity. In fact the move was not new, because something very like it had been tried at least 50 years earlier, but at least it showed initiative, and when England arrived in Canberra to play N.S.W. Country themselves, they found that the locals had a lot more tricks like that, if not up their jumpers, at least up their sleeves. What is more, one of these trick moves produced a try, and that enabled N.S.W. Country to beat England by a single point.

By the end of the tour, though, the fisticuffs had taken over again, and the Rugby Union officials accompanying the England touring party were shaking their heads in public about the incidence of violence. They also warned the Australian Rugby Union that if there was any repetition of that violence, the Australian touring team would not be welcome for the English section of their major tour of Britain and Ireland later in the year.

The cause of this concern was a brawl at the beginning of the second test between Australia and England at Brisbane. Barry Nelmes, who had been flown out to Australia as a replacement prop when Fran Cotton was injured, caught the ball from Australia's kick-off at the beginning of the match and was kicked quite deliberately by one of the Australian forwards as he was swept off his feet in the first rush to the ball. This later prompted John Thornett, one of Australia's most respected former captains, to write a letter publicly deploring what had happened and to say that England had suffered most unjustly as a consequence.

The kicking of Nelmes created an explosive situation and in the lineout which followed, there was a fight involving almost all the forwards of both teams. The referee, however, made the mistake of singling out one player and warning him. That player was Mike Burton, the other England prop.

Within a minute, England took a drop-out from their 25 and Burton followed up to try to charge down a kick by Doug Osborne, one of the Australian wings. Inevitably, the adrenalin was flowing much too vigorously in Burton's veins, and as he leapt to try to block the ball, he followed through with his charge and bowled Osborne over. The referee sent Burton off the field. Despite that, the depleted England team led 15–9 at half-time, and did enough to show that at full strength, the chances were they would have won, but in the end, their two man back row ran out of cover and Australia overhauled their opponents to win.

That weekend, the president of the Rugby Union, Ken Chapman, had a meeting with his senior vice-president, Tarn Bainbridge, and with the England tour management. At the end of the meeting, Mr Chapman told the Australian Rugby Union in no uncertain terms that England would not tolerate such violence on Australia's forthcoming tour of Britain.

Mr Chapman said: 'We informed the Australian authorities that if their players' illegally aggressive approach was maintained in England, we should not want them there. We told them that there would be sendings-off and all sorts of other trouble which we were not prepared to tolerate. Fortunately, the Australian authorities seemed as disturbed as we were, and they assured us that they would take steps to put their house in order. They have a meeting shortly and we hope that their decision will mean that the violence we saw will be eradicated. However, until we can be assured that we will not be confronted by the same over-aggressive approach as England experienced in Australia, the English section of the full tour remains in jeopardy.'

John Burgess, the England coach, was just as forthright. 'In their last two tours of Britain, the Australians reckon that they have been trampled on, and they have decided that they have had enough of it. They have gone out to play a physical game in an attempt to soften people up, and if necessary to get someone sent off the park. It makes you wonder where international Rugby is going to. If they play like that in Britain next season, they are going to run out of players after about eight games.'

As it turned out, the President of the Australian Rugby Union, Bill McLaughlin, warned both the Australian tour management and the Australian players that his Union would not tolerate rough play. Then Tarn Bainbridge, elected to the presidency of the Rugby Union after England had returned from Australia, said, 'Let's start again and wipe the slate clean'. That is what happened, and Australia's tour of Britain in 1975 and 1976 passed off without any untoward incident, but unquestionably, the image of Rugby football had been damaged and that damage was to be increased in the years ahead.

As England came to the end of their tour of Australia, Scotland were halfway through a similar short tour of New Zealand. News of Scotland's tour had been readily available across the Tasman Sea, and the Scots had run into trouble in their second match, just as England had. The Scots, anxious to make a good impression, had picked too many of their best players in their first match, and had won it very easily, but instead of keeping the bulk of the team together for the second match against

Otago, they brought in most of the reserves, and lost. They lost the next match against the formidable Canterbury team, too. This was hardly surprising, because the Scots, like Ireland, pick from such a small base of players that in most years they struggle to find twelve of international standard and never in their recent history have they had fifteen all at one time. Indeed, it has often been said that Ireland and Scotland would win the Triple Crown every year with England's rejects because these players would have the chance to establish themselves that they are never given with England. It is also said, with some truth, that if Ireland have ten international players, they win one match. If they have eleven international players, they win two matches. If they have twelve in-ternational players, they win the international championship, the Triple Crown, the Grand Slam and the Inter-Services championship as well!

Something of the same is true of Scotland, though they were handi-capped badly in New Zealand by the absence of Gordon Brown, their best lock. Scottish Rugby simply does not have the depth to withstand the loss of so important a player, and to those arriving in New Zealand halfway through the Scottish tour, the sound of scraping barrels filled the land. At least, though, the Scots chose the best team they thought they had, which England patently had not done, and at least the Scots were playing far more difficult opposition than England had in Australia.

Some of the senior Scottish players envied England their prodigality. Both Peter Brown, Scotland's captain in their centenary season, and his younger brother Gordon had never been able to understand why Nigel Horton was not a fixture in the England second row. Horton had first been capped for England in 1969, and Gordon Brown said bluntly, 'If he had been a Scotsman, he would have won forty caps by now, and he would have been looking forward to his next forty'.

Still, whatever depth Scotland may have lacked in their playing resources was more than made up by the weight of water that fell on Auckland in the 12 hours before their test match against New Zealand at the end of the tour. What the local meteorologists described as a tornado centred on Auckland and deposited six inches of rain on the pitch at Eden Park and its surrounds. The ground was flooded to a depth of nine inches in places and the local pumping appliances were completely over-whelmed. Half of one in-goal area and part of the field in front of it was covered by a lake so deep that the ball could be submerged. More than 150 yards of the pitch markings were under water and smaller lakes puddled the rest of the playing area. To say that the pitch was unplayable was possibly the biggest understatement in the entire history of Rugby football, but rather than return the money which had been taken in advance ticket sales, the New Zealand Rugby Union proposed that some sort of contest should take place, and to their eternal shame, the manage-ment of the Scottish team agreed.

Rugby football is supposed to be an amateur game, and when it is suggested or demonstrated that the game is fighting a losing battle against professionalism, no one bemoans the fact louder than the national unions. However, when presented with a situation which left them with no choice but to rise above the sordid dictates of commercialism, the representatives of both New Zealand and Scotland shifted uneasily from one foot to the other, looked the other way, and declined.

The match should have been postponed for 24 or 48 hours, or even abandoned completely. The tour had already made a profit. The trouble was, it had not made *enough* of a profit, and so a game of wading water-polo was instigated, and New Zealand won it very comfortably indeed.

The technique, which the All Blacks immediately discerned, was to kick the ball as high as possible into the biggest of the lakes near the opposing goal-line. It was not necessary to be concerned about the bounce of the ball, or its run, because it did neither. It just came down with the most enormous splash and floated. Sometimes, it even floated backwards.

This required two things. First, it required persistence in following up (though the boys at Rugby School would have needed bathing hats and goggles rather than caps), and above all, it needed to be done in the opposing half. Somehow, anyhow, the ball had to be transported out of defence, where mistakes were irretrievable, and then it had to be kept either in the air or in the water. It was of course impossible to ground the ball to score a try, because the referee was not equipped with aqua-lung and goggles and therefore could not see whether the ball had touched the bottom when it was submerged.

For some unaccountable reason, Scotland persisted in trying to play Rugby football, which was much the same as trying to play tennis in a swimming pool. The All Blacks took to the new game like ducks to water, if you will pardon the expression, though it must be acknowledged that they were helped significantly by a macabre shift of wind direction which meant that they had threequarters of a gale behind them in both halves. The importance of this to the kicking was immeasurable, and with a kicker as accurate and as powerful as Sid Going, and a wader as fast and as well camouflaged by spray as Grant Batty, New Zealand, again if you will pardon the expression, were home and dry. They won by four goals to nil.

The Scots were captained on tour by Ian McLauchlan, the sturdy and spirited prop who had served the Lions so well in 1971 and 1974, and who clearly regarded it as mildly seditious to admit that his name was really John. 'The Mouse,' as he was known, thought that Scotland's defensive limitations were responsible for most of his country's difficulties against New Zealand, but the problems went much deeper than that. The Scottish tight forwards had done well enough in the international championship over the previous five years to have much the better of their annual encounters with England, and this persuaded some people that

Scotland might emulate England's achievement of 1973 in actually beating New Zealand in Auckland. As soon as Scotland lost to Otago and Canterbury, however, a sense of realism set in and those few players with enough experience of Lions tours to form a judgment knew that the cause was lost. Perhaps this could be called defeatism, but it was obvious that the Scottish team would be happy to keep their heads above water in the remaining provincial games and to go down fighting to the somewhat restricted limits of their capability in the test. That is what happened.

The portents of England's tour of Australia and Scotland's tour of New Zealand were borne out almost exactly. John Burgess, the England coach, resigned within a matter of weeks. He was a member of the Rugby Union himself but he sensed at once the lack of support from the men around him. 'O ye men of little faith,' he said. He was replaced by Peter Colston, of Bristol, whose low profile approach to coaching was that beloved by the Scots, that of adviser to the captain. By then, however, the England selection process was so unrealistic that even a combination of Vic Cavanagh and Fred Allen would have been exercised to refloat the ship and the following season, England went down with all hands, losing all four matches in the championship for the second time in their history.

Scotland's fall from grace was rather slower but it was just as inevitable. In 1976, they won two matches, and finished in the middle of the table, below Wales, who won all four of their games, and France who won three. In 1977, Scotland won one game and finished fourth. In 1978, they lost all their games and finished last, and stayed there in 1979.

Australia also came down to earth with a bump after their two victories over England in Australia. When they toured Britain themselves, they were far from impregnable, and lost to England, Wales and Scotland before beating Ireland in the last of their international matches. They lost to Cardiff in the second match of their tour and drew with Llanelli in the third, which persuaded them that it would be unwise for an Australian team to accept such hard matches so early in their itinerary in future. For all that, David Brockhoff felt that in the course of the tour the Australian forwards succeeded in almost closing the gap in forward techniques which had existed between them and the best British packs, and this view was borne out by subsequent events.

Ross Turnbull, the Australians' manager, said that in his opinion, a tour of Britain and Ireland had become totally different from what it was ten years earlier. 'In those days, the minor matches we played were a cakewalk,' he said. 'They are not now. There are no easy games. All the provincial teams now go on the field with the serious intention of beating a touring side. That happens nowhere else in the world, not even in New Zealand.'

Mr Turnbull did express reservations about the development of the game in Britain. He felt that British Rugby was becoming over-concerned with what he called 'the set-piece syndrome'.

'I think you place a lot of emphasis on what happens in the scrum and the lineout and the maul, and not enough on what happens in between,' he said.

As evidence of their new surge of enthusiasm for the game, the Australians had produced a 100 page booklet on what they could expect in the way of playing opposition, refereeing interpretations and match conditions on tour, and when they returned to their own country, they had what Ross Turnbull called 'a comprehensive debriefing exercise' to identify the lessons that had been learned and to profit from them. To some observers in Britain, the zeal of the Australians was reminiscent of Japanese car manufacturers, and was likely to earn the same rewards. Despite their poor international results there was a feeling that Australia would earn a far greater return from their Rugby resources in future than Britain. It was a feeling which was to prove thoroughly justified.

6 Changing national styles

Ever since the British Lions tour of South Africa in 1968, suggestions have been advanced that referees from neutral countries should be appointed for the series of test matches played whenever South Africa, New Zealand or Australia are hosts to a visiting team. Players visiting those countries have always felt themselves to be handicapped by home town refereeing, and on more than one occasion, have exploded in exasperation in the course of an international match and called the referee a cheat.

This situation is unnecessary, because Rugby tours make so much profit for the host country that it could well afford the expense of inviting a referee from a neutral country to handle all, or a part, of a series. When South Africa, Australia, and New Zealand play in Britain, Ireland and France, they always have the services of a neutral referee, and if the principle was extended, it would be of value in unifying the interpretation of the game throughout the world. It would also provide referees from the Southern hemisphere with opportunities to referee in other countries and pass on the knowledge gained from their experience. In any case, the remarkable progress made in the television coverage of Rugby football, both in the quality of the comment and camera work, and in the new use of satellite transmission to bounce top quality pictures of matches all over the world, means that the game simply cannot afford to appear to be partial, because the demonstration of that partiality is becoming so very, very public.

Typically, Dr Danie Craven, the president of the South African Rugby Board, was the first man in the International Board countries of the Southern Hemisphere to accept that neutral referees should be introduced, and he invited Norman Sanson, the outstanding Scottish international referee based in London, to take control of the two test matches played between South Africa and France in 1975. It was an historic development, and South Africa immediately extended it by offering the same facility to the New Zealand Rugby Union in the discussions preceding the All Blacks' tour of South Africa in 1976.

The New Zealand Rugby Council declined the offer, seeing in it, apparently, a precedent which would make it difficult for them not to follow the same example. If they accepted South Africa's offer, New

Zealand felt that they would have no alternative but to offer the Four Home Unions the services of neutral referees for the British Lions' tour of New Zealand in 1977. They also felt, according to some of their members, that by accepting the offer, there would be a chance that an Australian referee would be appointed for the series, and New Zealand viewed that possibility with such horror that they instinctively shied away from it.

The interpretation placed on New Zealand's decision in other parts of the world, however, was much more sceptical. It was held that the All Blacks had always owed part of their success in their own country to the partiality of their referees, and by showing their determination to preserve that state of affairs, the New Zealand Rugby Council had acknowledged, by implication, that they shared the same view. The fears of the depredations which might be wrought by inexperienced Australian referees rampaging all over South Africa were dismissed as an unconvincing red herring, because the chances were that at least one of the neutral referees would have come from Europe anyway, and that New Zealand would obviously have had some say in their appointment.

Three years later, in 1979, New Zealand did appoint a neutral referee for two home test matches they played in a shared series against France, but it was understood at the time that the French would have refused to tour if that concession had not been made. Even a neutral referee was preferable to no tour.

Whatever the real reason for New Zealand's refusal to accept the appointment of neutral referees in South Africa in 1976, it cost them the series, and at the end of the day, no one knew that better than the management of the All Blacks who toured South Africa, Noel Stanley and J. J. Stewart. By the end of the tour, they were saying categorically that if the decision had been theirs, or if they had been consulted, they would have accepted neutral referees without hesitation.

One other factor had a decisive influence on the series, and that was goalkicking. Nearly six hours of test Rugby was played in the four match series, and out of the whole of that time, the Springboks dominated only thirty minutes of the third test, and yet they won because of the superior goalkicking of Gerald Bosch. This was an inevitable consequence of the way Rugby football was developing in the major countries of the world, and in the long term, it was of even greater concern than a hiccough on the road to acceptance of the appointment of neutral referees in all matches involving International Board countries. Dr Craven saw this at once, and immediately began to explore the possibilities of reform of the law to reduce the injustice whereby a team, for instance, could lose a test series by putting the ball crooked into a scrum, but would only concede possession to the other team if they put the ball crooked into a lineout.

Because of this, the tour was undoubtedly a set-back to J. J. Stewart's great work of restoring the game to the players in his own country, and involving them all in total Rugby. He knew that the All Blacks' defeat in

South Africa would cost him his appointment as coach. He shrugged his shoulders and grinned, 'Ah well. It's a goalkicking game. Let's all go surfing.'

South Africa's victory was greeted in some quarters of the Republic as clear evidence that the Springboks were world champions again! This claim was advanced because the 1974 Lions had only drawn with the All Blacks, and were lucky to do even that, whereas South Africa had beaten the same All Blacks 3–1. Hence the Springboks were champions again!

It was a ludicrous claim, because apart from the goalkicking of Gerald Bosch, South Africa had only one advantage over the team crushed by the British Lions in 1974. That was the Springboks' traditional advantage of knowing just who their test players were. They had been identified in the holocaust of 1974 and preserved in the matches against France the following year. It is true that this was an important advance, but it did not sustain the claims for a leap from the bottom of the first division to the top. The truth was that the game in all the International Board countries, except perhaps France, was beginning to be played so indifferently that there was some justification for thinking that perhaps the whole of the world's traditional first division ought to be relegated.

This uncomfortable suspicion was strengthened when Argentina, one of the smallest and most truly amateur Rugby countries of the world, toured England and Wales later in 1976 and all but beat the Welsh in a full scale international played at the Arms Park. Only with the last kick of the match, which was advanced a few vital yards by a regrettable piece of sharp practice undetected by the referee, did Wales scrape a penalty goal over the bar from long range to win the match.

The Welsh suffered all sorts of indignities in that game. Argentina scrummaged well, as they had in all their matches in Wales, but above all, they showed British Rugby a glimpse of its own past through the high level of the Argentine's individual skills. Hugo Porta looked as if he was probably the best fly-half in the world, a status he subsequently confirmed. Alejandro Travaglini, although nearing the end of his career, showed what a tremendous centre-threequarter he must have been, a fierce-moustached hammer of a player, standing 6 ft 4 ins and nearly 15 stones, and yet possessed of all the skills. Gauweloose, on the wing, once ran round J. P. R. Williams as if he did not exist, and earned immortality for that alone, and Martin Sansot, still a boy, looked the best attacking runner at full-back in the whole wide world. Argentina did not have the reserve strength of the International Board countries, because they had to choose their team from a much smaller base of players, but it was a salutary experience to be reminded that high individual skills could still be produced, and they were by no means the preserve of the established giants of the game.

The quality of Rugby football has always ebbed and flowed in the major countries of the world, but for at least four years in some of those

Hugo Porta, lately possibly the best fly-half in the world.

countries, and for much longer in Britain, no young stars had emerged to grace the game as they always had in the past.

It remained a fact that not since 1969, when J. P. R. Williams and David Duckham first played international Rugby, had a really outstanding back emerged. Wales had based their domination of the Four Home Unions on a group of talented backs who had all emerged before nationally organised coaching had had any influence on the development of the game. Gerald Davies, Barry John, Phil Bennett, Gareth Edwards and J. P. R. Williams had all established themselves by the traditional method of learning the game by themselves at school but by 1976, it was beginning to look increasingly as if they were going to be the last of the succession of really exceptional backs who had been produced by all four of the home countries for more than seventy years. The dawning realisation of this came as even more of a shock because the production of star quality backs had always been taken for granted in Britain. The Four Home Unions had always had them, especially England and Wales, and Britain's whole approach to the game since the technical revolution following the 1966 Lions tour of New Zealand had been based on the assumption that forward organisation was the only development needed to release the brimming talent eternally available behind the scrum and that this would put Britain and Ireland on top of the Rugby world for ever.

Sadly, it soon became clear that this assumption was no longer valid, and although Wales and France began to alternate as the champion countries, the thoroughly absorbing drama of their battles did not disguise the fact that the crust of international excellence, at least in Britain, was becoming thinner and thinner. The same applied to South Africa and New Zealand. This alarming decline was borne out when the British Lions toured New Zealand in 1977.

It was a series which stood history on its head, because for the first time, the Lions went to New Zealand with a selection of forwards capable of beating the All Blacks both physically and technically. It took the Lions far too long to establish their test pack and the result of that failure was that New Zealand were presented with the first test – the match which a touring side always ought to find the easiest to win in any series because if they have been doing their job properly, they ought to have acquired a state of fitness and organisation far beyond the reach of their hosts. Psychologically, this defeat was a crushing blow, particularly as it was so unnecessary, but from that point the Lions forwards went from strength to strength, and finished by completely dominating their opponents. However, that domination did not extend to the backs. The further the tour went, the more disorganised and lacking in confidence their performance became so that in the end, New Zealand won the series 3–1 because they were able to beat the Lions behind the scrum.

It was not a distinguished series, and no one was more aware of that than J. J. Stewart, who, as he had ruefully predicted, had lost his position as coach of New Zealand after the All Blacks' defeat in South Africa the previous year. Nevertheless, the All Blacks' defeat of the Lions in 1977 thoroughly vindicated Stewart's decision to take New Zealand Rugby away from a game obsessed with forward power, with kicking and with a running scrum-half playing the ball back to his loose forwards amid an atmosphere of dictatorial coaching, and instead to move it towards a more fluent, open game, in which the players participated in the decision making. The wheel had come full circle, because the All Blacks, under the shrewd guidance of Jack Gleeson, made better use of their more limited resources and won the series from a position of weakness.

The Lions, for their part, paid the price for the fatally wrong turning taken by their predecessors in South Africa in 1974. In 1977, the Lions were based on the successful Welsh team, and it was coached by John Dawes, the Welsh national coach, but without Gerald Davies, J. P. R. Williams and Gareth Edwards, who were not available for the tour, it failed because it was not good enough behind the scrum to beat an All Black team which itself was fairly modest in its pretensions, at least when compared with the great players of the past.

Phil Bennett, a reluctant hero.

From the British point of view, one of the greatest sadnesses of the tour was the lack of fulfilment and the unhappiness of the Lion's captain, Phil Bennett. He undoubtedly felt the absence of Gareth Edwards very keenly, just as Edwards had felt the retirement of Barry John. Part of this was due to a fundamental change in the psychological emphasis. Barry John had been the dominant half of the partnership with Gareth Edwards, and Edwards, in turn, had taken on more of the directional responsibility in his partnership with Phil Bennett.

Phil Bennett was an entirely different character from Barry John. Bennett was a diffident, quiet, shy man; truly a reluctant hero. He never enjoyed the spotlight in the way that Barry John did. Barry John would have always wanted the lead part. Phil Bennett would have taken most pleasure from winning his Academy Award for a supporting role. When Phil Bennett was a boy, Carwyn James arranged for him to be given a scholarship to Llandovery College. Everyone thought it was a marvellous idea, except Phil Bennett. He preferred to stay in his village at Felinfoel.

Bennett was a typical Iberian, of Mediterranean stock, a small, quick-silver, side-stepper, straight from the Welsh fly-half factory. He learned about life in the school of Rugby football, and overcame his natural diffidence through the people that he met. Carwyn James always felt that Bennett would have been an even better fly-half in his own era because he was not in essence the organisation player best suited to the era of team coaching. Instead he was a touch player, an instinctive player, who would have relished the latitude given to fly-halves in the 1950s.

Because of the reticence of his nature, he never really expressed himself fully at international level, despite his record number of points for Wales. His value to his club at Llanelli, and to the whole of football in West Wales, was immense. The next generation of side-steppers from the fly-half factory is assured because of the example he set, and men will carry to their graves the memory of that beautiful screw kick, made under pressure near his own line, which took play back to the half-way line right at the end of the match and made sure that Llanelli would beat the All Blacks in 1972. The memories of that kick and that match were so much more worthy of Phil Bennett's ability as a player than the memory of the deeply unhappy man who returned to his home after the decline and fall of the 1977 Lions.

Much of this decline was due to the profound social changes taking place in the countries traditionally in the van of the development of Rugby football. In all these countries, more and more children were developing the habit of watching television, rather than involving themselves in the playing of games, and the range of leisure activities was increasing to such an extent that inevitably there was less of a concentration on the staple games of football and cricket. In Britain, too, a fundamental change was taking place in the system of state education which was having a crippling effect on Rugby football.

Schools which, for something like seventy years, had always had attendance registers of between two and four hundred pupils, began to be combined into giant comprehensive groups of 2,000 pupils. When this happened, it may have done wonders for the salary structure of the headmasters, who regrettably are paid on a bob a nob basis, but it largely destroyed the organisation of games. The units of scholastic population had become too big to handle.

All of Britain's traditional sports suffered, with the possible exception of athletics, but none of the team games suffered more than Rugby football. Not only was the link with the traditional elementary and secondary schools severed, but above all, the grammar schools, which had been at the very heart of the development of Rugby football in Britain, were almost wiped out. Harold Wilson, a grammar school boy himself, said when he was Prime Minister that the grammar schools would be closed over his dead body. Well, the grammar schools have been closed and he is still alive, and Rugby football is the poorer for it.

Both the authors of this book were grammar school boys and they have watched in despair as the iron curtain of educational dogma has clanged down and shut off a huge section of the potential Rugby playing population from contact with the game at the most important time of its life. Scores of old boys' clubs throughout the country have lost their feeder schools and when even a great Rugby school like the Queen Elizabeth Grammar School, Carmarthen, is forced to go comprehensive, everyone who has the good of the game at heart must feel concern.

Recognising this fact, the coaching committee of the Welsh Rugby Union were moved to form a sub-committee (a national pastime in Wales) to report on the decline of the game. This suggests that there were many factors involved.

1 Two or even three schools have been merged into one big comprehensive. One school XV has taken the place of three.
2 In some instances the large comprehensive initially found it difficult to field even one school XV.
3 The loss of tradition.
4 The loss of a family atmosphere and therefore a lack of identity.
5 A diversification in the number of games and recreational activities offered – e.g. even Llanelli Grammar School (killed in 1978) had a soccer team!
6 The 'special responsibility allowances' offered to teachers responsible for running a particular discipline had led to the 'let him do it, he's being paid for it' attitude.
7 Gone, therefore, in many instances is the amateur Rugby coach in the schools, the enthusiasm of the man who taught geography or, dare we say it, classics. He has been replaced by the professional, the P.E. man who has coaching certificates.

8 The professional finds it difficult to get assistance in the running of the under 11, under 13, the junior and senior Colts and the 2nd XV for the reasons already noted.

9 There is more glamour in taking the children on a free Continental skiing holiday than there is in running a Rugby team after school hours.

10 Boys often prefer to work after school on Saturday mornings to earn pocket money so that they can pursue other interests.

These are some of the reasons for the decline of the game in the schools. Fortunately, there are glowing exceptions where the old amateur traditions are being maintained.

Of the many disquieting features, one of the most worrying was the uncomfortable feeling that the spread of qualified physical education instruction had not been of undiluted benefit to Rugby football. In the past, the game had always been taught by schoolmasters who had no qualifications to teach Rugby football other than their love of it or the fact that they had once played it, and understandably, their reaction was to take a step back in deference to the young men in their track suits who had been turned out by the colleges specialising in physical education and who had been added to the staffs of schools throughout the country. This was a comparatively new development, and on the face of it, it should have improved the quality of the product, in this case, the schoolboy player. In practice, it did no such thing. Indeed, it often had quite the reverse effect, so it was only natural that doubts should be entertained about the value of the exercise. The individual skills, in particular, were being much less widely taught than in the days before British Rugby understood very much about forward organisation.

Unfortunately, the public schools did not fill the gaps as they might have been expected to, either. They had all the facilities they needed – an intelligent and enthusiastic playing population, superb facilities, equipment, time – and above all, the essential discipline which is built into the public school system. As the output from the grammar schools dried up, and the playing population in the state schools fell, the public schools had an unrivalled opportunity to lift their representation in the national teams of England and Scotland to the level they had enjoyed fifty years earlier. But that did not happen, and although a welcome revision in the admissions policy at Cambridge University enabled games players to broaden the life of the undergraduate community once more, Oxford continued to concentrate on academics and neither the public schools nor the two senior universities recovered their erstwhile Rugby playing prestige.

In the wake of the turmoil of educational change, which is still with us, the mini-Rugby game was invented. Inspired by a similar kind of game in France and Izaak van Heerden's *Simplified Game for Beginners*, another sub-committee thrashed out the possibilities of inventing a simple game involving the basics for under 11's and under 13's.

It was a successful innovation and throughout the world there is evidence of the amateur enthusiast and the keen father, spending his Sunday mornings teaching the young ones. Already there are reservations about the over-enthusiasm of the parents, but it could be argued that mini-Rugby is a positive example where Rugby is club rather than school centred. It also prompts us to consider, although in many ways it might be a retrograde step, whether much of our Rugby in the future will become club centred.

The game is in a far healthier condition in Australia where the number of schoolboys playing has increased considerably during the last decade. If a national team mirrors the level of coaching then the Australian Schools team which toured the UK in the winter of '77 and '78 revealed that they are many kangaroo leaps ahead of us. Their performance against the Welsh Schools at the Arms Park was the only entirely pleasing and rounded one of the whole season and revealed that Rugby football can still be enjoyed. They won easily and with a flourish. There was the joy of Barry John and Jo Maso in the play of a colourful team which included three Aborigine brothers. According to Russell Fairax the increase in the popularity of the game in Australian schools is considerable.

Unfortunately, some of these promising players are likely to swell the ranks of the professional game. It is difficult to imagine that a 70-year old habit is about to be broken particularly at a time when the senior players have lost the flair, the passing, attacking flair of their predecessors and when too many of their leading players, too often, have resorted to excessive physical and violent methods. Australia needs to recover the style of the 1966 team and their approach, too.

Regretfully, this is unlikely to happen until there is a major revision of the laws of the game. It is now clear that the major changes in the lineout laws, which were introduced in 1973 without a period of experiment, have had almost exactly the opposite of the effect intended. The mandatory spacing of a yard between the forwards standing in the lineout has not significantly improved the quality of the lineout possession, because it has made support for the jumper more difficult, and it has impaired the ability of the team winning the ball to make effective use of it because it has perforated the screen of forwards standing in front of the scrum-half and thus has removed much of his protection. The one yard spacing also means that the lineout is much looser than it was before and it means that the forwards standing at the back of the lineout are at least six yards nearer to the open side wing than they were in all those years when the lineout was compressed. Gerald Davies himself has said that the effect of this was to halve his chances of scoring a try from a lineout.

It is equally clear that the creation of a 20 yard no-man's land between the backs at the lineout has also had almost exactly the opposite of the effect intended. For a time, the backs who had learned their skills under the physical pressure of intensive close marking did indeed flourish in the new space with which they had been provided. However, within four years, it became obvious that this 20 yard gap had destroyed the essential environment which had required those skills to be developed. If a fly-half or a centre has a flanker as awe-inspiring as Don White, formerly of Northampton and England, or Kel Tremain, of New Zealand, bearing down on him, as well as his immediate opponent, he has no alternative but to develop either a side-step, or a change of pace, or breath-taking speed off the mark, or a dummy, or a jink, or a hand-off, or a beautiful pass made quickly and accurately no matter what the pressure. If the back in question cannot perform any or all of those skills, he faces physical obliteration, and as the human race exists because it has developed the capacity to survive from within its environment, those skills were acquired by the very best players as a matter of course.

The 20 yard gap, however, immediately created a fundamentally different requirement. It eliminated the hand to hand combat which required such high individual skills and substituted a yawning space in which backs could only really charge at each other, like knights in the lists. That in turn shifted the emphasis away from nimble players of high skills to those who simply had the physical presence to crash through the opposition. The light-footed fencers were replaced not so much by the broadsword as by great hulking men weighed down by armour sitting on carthorses. Another consequence of this was that it cut deeply into one of the most precious assets of Rugby football, and that was its unique capacity to provide a team game to be enjoyed by players of all physical shapes and sizes. The 20 yard gap put the Rugby deities unmistakably on the side of the bigger battalions and more and more coaches of all levels of the game right down to the schools saw that their teams would win more matches if they picked strapping loose forwards in the centre simply to charge at the opposition and tackle them. To that extent, the game took another step towards American football, while denying the players the body armour used in that sport.

The team which unquestionably took the playing of the game under the new laws to its logical conclusion was Béziers, in France. Under the guidance of Raoul Barriere, their shrewd coach, they had dominated the French club championship since 1971 and had produced a fascinatingly successful concept of the game.

This concept was based on commitment through physical power. In essence, Barriere made his players – all his players – run into the opposition until one of the defenders missed a tackle. Then Béziers scored. This required all but one or two of the players in his team to have the attributes of a forward. They had to have the strength not only to take a tackle but to dominate the tackler, and to retain possession of the ball while doing so. All the Béziers team, backs as well as forwards, had to challenge for possession of the ball and contest for it when the opposition had it. They all had to be able to maul, particularly the midfield backs, but even the wings had to commit themselves to win the loose ball at the point of breakdown rather than retire into the customary defensive formation. As Barriere said, 'While preparing my team, I have always tried not to separate the backs from the forwards from the point of view of playing two separate games. I strive to encourage each player to develop similar skills, whether he is a back or a forward, and he should have the same technique. And I want them to have the same approach to the game, too.

'By that I mean that a forward should be capable of running, passing, using his timing instincts, and in the same way, a threequarter must know how to take physical knocks, how to mask the ball, how to set up a maul, and at the same time, he should have all the skills one expects from a back.

'In recent years, we can justifiably accuse Wales and South Africa, and above all, New Zealand, of setting a poor example in this respect, and it is an example which we have tended to copy. I have always been struck by the way the forwards and backs in these countries play almost in a separate game, and so until quite recently, we have gone for the big, heavy forward, who worked to get the ball for the virtuosos behind the scrum for them to use until the next breakdown. I think you can have some virtuosos, but they must put their skills to use for the general benefit of everyone in the team. There is nothing quite so heartbreaking for a forward to see a threequarter throw the ball away and have a try scored because of it. This is inadmissible. And it is this consideration for each

Raoul Barriere, coach of Béziers, directing the early season training of his team while being filmed for *The World of Rugby* Television series.

other in the team that is important. Forwards and backs must understand each other, and so I look for a tight collaboration. Once you have established that, you can start to do something in an orderly fashion.

'People say that we play only with our pack in Béziers. But that is not true. In France we have a competition that rewards the club who scores the most tries, and we have won this trophy a record number of times. How could we have scored all those tries if we had played, as we are accused, of playing only eight or ten-man Rugby? I make the claim that we use everybody, both forwards and backs, but perhaps we do not use them like other people. We do not use them in a fashionable way.

'It is true that we have a formidable squad of players and it is also true that we are very competitive. The same basic principles of the game are taught at every level of the club, and these fundamentals are based on realities – winning the ball, keeping possession of it, pushing in the scrums, defence, tackling, gaining ground, the principle of going forward. Once we have established these basic principles, we do give some players liberties if they have the class to expand their games, but if a player does not have that talent, he is not given the same freedom of expression.

'In our system, we insist on training with opposition, and so we are always as near as possible to the real thing. Even in the close season, when we are doing mostly fitness work, we train with a ball and we train with opposition. All the moves we practise are done against opposition so as to make it as lifelike and as close to the game as we can. You cannot learn to swim without water; you need a ball and you need opposition. That is a basic rule at Béziers. All our training is centred round that. There is also, of course, the search for fitness. We also try to prepare for physical contact and we try to inculcate into all our players the spirit of physical contact. Obviously, we seek to stay within the limits of the Rugby law, and to respect the opposition, but still, we concentrate on the physical requirements of getting there first and getting there in greater numbers. With those bases, everything is possible.'

The style of play evolved at Béziers was absolutely foreign to French temperament and tradition because it was not in the least flamboyant or romantic. It eschewed risks. Every ball won had to be won well. The scrum-half, Richard Astre, threw the ball into the lineout and left the forwards to make sure that they had it properly under control while he took up his position for the pass. There was no tapping back. It was entirely calculated. Even the moments of extempore brilliance by a running full-back like Jack Cantoni had been allowed for, even planned, as an essential diversion to the repeated smashing thrusts of the forwards and the sheer physical presence of an exceptionally well-fleshed midfield. Some Frenchmen hailed it. Others hated it. But none could deny its effectiveness and it culminated in one of the greatest displays of Rugby ever seen when, in 1978, Béziers beat Montferrand at Parc des Princes to win the championship of France for the sixth time in eight years.

251

Béziers scored tries that day which were such classics either of controlled forward technique, or back-play, or counter-attack, or individual genius, or of all of them put together, that they should be produced as instruction films on cassettes and sent all over the world. It was the triumphant culmination of all Raoul Barriere's work, and it was marvellously appropriate that it should be so because, within a matter of months, a sad and shabby little squabble within the club led to Barriere being deposed as chief coach.

Looking back on the game, Barriere said, 'I will tell you one thing that will surprise a lot of people. It was a final we could easily have lost. We were leading 13–9 and Montferrand nearly scored a try. They had gathered themselves for a great effort and they were about to score when one of their most important forwards lost the ball. That is another fundamental mistake, giving the ball to an opponent.

'The psychological effect of that was incalculable, because we counter-attacked immediately and made another score. So instead of drawing level, and possibly taking the lead, Montferrand were two scores down. That enabled us to open up a gap, a mental gap. At that moment, Montferrand sagged and we suddenly knew that we could go on.

'This showed the prime importance of the psychological aspect of all sport, and particularly in Rugby. I have made a study of psychological preparation, because it is important that that aspect of the game should

The Béziers players watching their colleagues in early season training.

be handled very carefully, especially with reference to rough play and violence. I believe that very often, the foundations of violence are laid in the dressing room. The way I approach my psychological preparation of the team is to try to get the player balanced mentally. He must be stable. He must be emotionally balanced. It is vitally important that the player is calm when he goes on to the field. He must be self-controlled enough to feel that he is capable of coping with everything, so he must not be inhibited in any way at all when dealing with an opponent or with any other contingency, whether it is crowd behaviour or anything else. He must be able to express himself and take advantage of available chances between 80 and 90 per cent of the time. That requires enormous concentration, but that is what I aim for in my preparation.

'It is quite clear in my mind that the most important thing a coach must have is control over his players. He must be able to communicate as though a current flows between the two, so that there is enthusiasm in both directions. Enthusiasm is important because it is born of enjoyment. It so happens that I am a schoolmaster, a physical education instructor, and so it was quite straightforward for me to progress from player to coach. Perhaps some of the success of Béziers has been due to the fact that I have been able to establish this communication with the players; we can share ideas or attitudes that relate to Rugby football. A coach can succeed as long as that relationship exists.'

When Raoul Barriere spoke those words, in the summer sun at Béziers in the weeks before the beginning of the 1978–79 season, he spoke his own epitaph, although he did not know it at the time. Two months later, increasing difficulties between Barriere and Alain Esteve, one of Béziers senior forwards, came to a head. Barriere said to the players, 'It's either Esteve or me'. The players voted for Esteve.

Perhaps this was not surprising. When the BBC cameramen were filming the Béziers team in practice, the referee wore a T-shirt proclaiming, in English: My God is Esteve. The vote was terribly democratic. When the result became known, Barriere went. One of the players, Louis Martin took over as coach, and Béziers settled down to wait for the day which would assuredly come when they would regret their decision.

Within four months, Esteve had been banned from all Rugby for a year by the French Federation because of 'repeated brutalities'. This effectively meant the end of Esteve's career, and the playing community who had voted to reject Barriere had cause to reflect even more deeply on their folly when Michel Palmie, another of Béziers' international forwards, was successfully sued by a player of another club for compensation for an injury which was inflicted deliberately. When Palmie lost his appeal in the courts, the French Federation banned him from international Rugby for life.

There has always been a Jekyll and Hyde quality about the game in France. At best, the French game has no parallel in the world for its inventiveness. Like the Harlem Globetrotters, they are superb handlers of the ball, they are masters of the short and the flick pass and like the better soccer players they are excellent runners off the ball which allows the blinkered ball carrier to pop the ball into the two points at the base of the imaginary triangle behind him.

At worst the game in France is motivated by the championship and its win-at-all-costs attitude can be brutal and violent, the kind of stuff which one has seen played in Southern Italy, the kind of stuff as Terry McLean put it, 'could only be played by the Mafia'. It is little wonder that France led the world in taking players like Palmie to court for vicious play. There

The French referee at Béziers' training. His T-shirt carried a symbolic message, in English, for the future.

have been similar instances in New Zealand and Wales, but not because of the intensity of the club championship.

When Raoul Barriere suffered the equivalent of being elevated to the peerage, it was thought across the channel that Béziers' loss might be France's gain, because France, as a team, had never approached the disciplines or the organisation or the quality of selection that Barriere brought to Béziers. Barriere was asked if he would like to be coach of France. He said, 'I think I'm too old now. In sport, as in education, it is all to do with young people. That is not to say that you lose qualities as you grow older, because I think I still have the same driving force, but I believe that communication is easier between generations who are closer to each other. I think that in future, France should have a younger coach.'

Perhaps, but there was no doubt that there was no one in France who matched Raoul Barriere's qualifications for the job, and there was equally no doubt that he was just the man who could have taken France through to the realisation of their unmatched playing potential for the first time in their history.

It took four years for the example set by Béziers to find some expression in the French national team, and even then, that expression was a compromise. This was understandable, because although Béziers reached the final of the French championship seven times in eight years, and won the title on no fewer than six occasions, some of their Rugby had not matched the breadth and the quality it achieved on that astonishing day in May, 1978. By 1975, the French national selectors had accepted the need for tighter forward disciplines, but in view of the controversy within France itself about the style of Rugby Béziers had developed, they stopped short of going all the way and choosing a team to drive and maul and play the physical commitment game that Béziers did. Worthily, they aspired to what they held to be a grander vision of the game. The problem was none of them seemed to know quite what that vision entailed, and as a consequence, France were never as good as they should have been.

France have not been helped by their reluctance to embrace the principle of squad training, adopted so enthusiastically by all the other major countries in the last ten years. Initially, the French felt that they would be accused of professionalism if they sought the national team organisation achieved most notably by Wales. The reluctance of the powerful French clubs to release their players has been another factor. In all those years, France have had only one squad practice. The gap in their team preparation has cost them dear.

17 The coaching crisis and the second big bang

Raoul Barriere's achievements as a club coach ran counter to much of the experience in Britain and Ireland, where the state of the game is now much less satisfactory. The reasons are many and varied. Perhaps the most potent is the fact that we have not lived long enough with the professional approach to understand it fully.

It is less than a dozen years since Wales, the first in the field, appointed a full time professional coach to direct and organise the game in the Principality. There were many raised eyebrows and dark mutterings at the time about producing unthinking, unsmiling robots who would play the game by numbers in the fashion of American football. However true those mutterings may have been, the wind of change blew fast and far and clubs and countries were soon appointing their coaches until, by now, it is commonplace to see a small club advertising in the local and the national press for a coach. The practice has even spread world wide.

The Rugby coach is with us to stay – accepted and approved with the stamp, albeit varied, of authority. In some clubs he is the equivalent of a Soccer manager; in others he is merely an adviser to the captain and to a host of selectors. These days he will have learned his trade on a coaching course which, if run by the national coaching system, will have given him some title or another and eventually a pretentious one such as 'staff coach', the elite of the game.

The nettle has been grasped but, too often, it has been grasped tentatively and to such an extent in some cases that it stings and hurts. At club level the committed, unpaid, amateur coach who spends many of his evenings in dreadful, wintry conditions teaching and directing his players is expected to be highly professional in his approach and he is expected not only to seek but achieve the ultimate and only reward of the professional game, that of winning.

This is true even in those clubs which only pay lip service to the ethos of coaching. Like Soccer managers the only security of tenure for the poor coach is a winning team. There have been sackings. Other coaches have found the pressures too intense. Swansea do not play Llanelli any more: the banner headline reads, 'Evans versus James'. The willing amateur has already taken over the daily pressure of a Clough or a Docherty.

Even at national level the coaches have come and have gone with an amazing rapidity within a brief decade. England have had White, Burgess, Elders, Burgess, Colston and Davis; Wales, Nash, Rowlands and Dawes; Ireland, Dawson, Millar, Meates and Murphy; and Scotland, the last country to accept the concept that a captain needs an adviser, have had Dickinson and MacEwan.

In Ireland, the pioneering efforts of Judge J. C. Conroy, Des Scaife and Ronnie Dawson for Leinster inspired the other provinces to follow suit. At national level, Ray McLoughlin's intellectual approach to the game as captain was of significant importance. He was a man ahead of his time, and like all visionaries, he paid the penalty, but much of the credit for the Lions' successes in the early 'seventies must go to McLoughlin.

In Wales, Cadfan Davies of the Central Council of Physical Recreation held coaching courses as early as the 'fifties and early 'sixties and leading clubs like Bridgend and Newbridge appreciated the need to appoint club coaches. Alun Thomas, assistant to D. J. Phillips in Wales' unsuccessful tour of South Africa in 1964 preached the coaching gospel on his return and the Welsh Rugby Union were persuaded to appoint Ray Williams, already doing excellent work on the Rugby Union coaching panel and in the Midlands, as director of coaching in Wales. Both he and subsequently Don Rutherford in England have worked with the zeal of missionaries to further the cause of coaching.

The four nations have always held on firmly to the idea of national selectors despite appointing coaches. In some instances the coach has not even been allowed to be a member of the selection panel. This is probably the most outrageous example of our theory that certain members of the Rugby Unions who make the appointments have not understood the meaning of the professional approach. On the other hand perhaps they understand the concept but are afraid of its implications. Having national selectors certainly places less pressure on the coach and, of course, it may be argued that the term 'national coach' is a misnomer. Because of the laws of amateurism, international players in Europe may only assemble a couple of days before the match and during this short period of time even a deity would not pretend that he was actually coaching. The coach, in fact, is some kind of a manager to his team.

It has to be admitted, however, that some unrealistic claims have been made with regard to the results achieved at national level by coaching. Ray Williams, who is the director of coaching in Wales, says in his book *Skilful Rugby*: 'Many people have asked me, "What kind of Rugby do you advocate?" My answer is always the same. "Go and watch our national team play." One of the most remarkable features of Welsh Rugby over the past nine years has been the way in which the WRU selection committee and the national team coach have aligned themselves totally with the concepts which have been projected by the coaching committee.'

However, the point has to be made that the coaching concept in Wales

Don Rutherford and Ray Williams, coaching organisers of England and Wales.

during those nine years might not have been nearly so successful without such high class players as Gerald Davies, Barry John, J. P. R. Williams, Gareth Edwards, Phil Bennett, J. J. Williams, Mervyn Davies and latterly, Terry Cobner. There were others, too, almost in the same golden bracket, players of natural flair. All of them learned the game before coaching could have had any influence on the development of their individual skills which were so high that the wonder is that as players they did not achieve more, not perhaps in terms of results, but in the way they played the game. It is argued, for instance, that despite the individual talents available to them, Wales, in the last five years, have presided over the demise of the centre-threequarter, and there is enough force in the argument to make it uncomfortable.

In the hands of the players available to Wales in the period in question, the possibilities ought to have been unlimited, yet rarely have we seen them play Rugby as it was played by the Barbarians against the All Blacks in 1973, and we have never seen them beat the All Blacks. It would not be fair to counter with the argument that other members of the Five Nations tournament played negative Rugby. Certainly such an argument would not help the course of coaching since all five countries have almost totally embraced the coaching philosophy and there is no reason to believe that the coaching in one country is better than in the others.

What then has been the contribution of coaching? The outstanding contribution in Britain has been a significant improvement in forward organisation. In the last decade, at all levels, every forward has learned his function in life, his own personal skills and his particular contribution to the forward unit in all phases of play. The modern forward is a bigger and faster specimen who has to learn the disciplines of his trade.

In jest the forwards are often referred to as donkeys, and the backs as *prima donnas*. Unfortunately, somewhere along the line, we seem to have lost the art of nurturing our backs. Law changes, in particular those relating to the off-side line, have given the mid-field players more time to think and for the natural genius the thought process is less potent than the sudden instinctive impulse. The Bennetts of this world play far better in the open field from second phase possession or even from the non-quality ball which has 'hospital' written all over it than they do from the quality possession, from the first phase set-piece.

In the modern game, probably because of the time and space factor, there are far too many pre-conceived ploys called by the pivot even before the ball has emerged from the set-piece. The crash-ball ploys have become compulsive; the most pronounced, repetitive drill of the centre-cum-flanker type which we are breeding by the score. The variation has become the rule and the rule, which has stood the test of time, the variation.

Of greater significance in the theory of the professional approach has been the acceptance of the squad training idea at national level. Since matches are played on a Saturday the weary players after, say, a hard slog between Gloucester and Bristol or Cardiff and Newport are asked to present themselves at a suitable centre for squad training on the Sunday. Will the day come when the squad training takes place in mid-week? After all, players in the past have been away from their work for three or four months on Lions' tours. Kindly, philanthropic employers have given those players leave of absence with pay while the host Rugby Union has made a profit of at least a million dollars.

Wilfred Wooller is of the opinion that the ten match tour made by Wales to Australia in the summer of '78 was undertaken only because Wales, very attentive to the needs of completing the National Stadium or, more accurately, the Arms Park, need a reciprocal tour. This view is not shared by Ken Harris, the treasurer of the Welsh Union. Still, so far, players and their families and their employers are making sacrifices to play Rugby Union. How long will the Unions, all over the world, accept the generosity of employers? And if they do not, will they be compromising themselves in relation to the laws appertaining to amateurism?

Phil Bennett, the captain of the 1977 Lions, maintains that the pressures have grown considerably since he first started playing for Llanelli ten years ago: 'I think there has got to be a halt or a slowing down period soon, otherwise the top players will be burnt out before they are thirty years of age.'

Bennett did not go on the Welsh tour to Australia in 1978 for two reasons: 'One was my new business, and secondly and perhaps most

259

importantly, I felt that I couldn't have given my best to Wales and to myself. I was just in the wrong state of mind. After a long tour to New Zealand then coming back and going through the Grand Slam season with Wales, after the French match I just sort of collapsed in the dressing room and said that that was enough for me for a while. I think that had I gone to Australia I wouldn't have wanted to play any Rugby at all.'

Paradoxically, the playing quality of the game in both Australia and France, where professionalism of one sort or another is never far away, looks in better condition than it does in Britain, where the piecemeal evolution of Rugby football and the decline of the game in the schools has left England and Wales without an effective structure above club level and has left all of the Four Home Unions with a dwindling supply of talent. It is significant that only once in a hundred years has a club anywhere in Britain and Ireland matched the prestige and the playing success of that achieved by Béziers in France, and that was the Cardiff team in the years immediately after 1945.

Ireland have an effective club and provincial structure and Scotland have instituted a league structure which will make better use of their resources, but both countries lack the great town and city teams necessary to concentrate the available talent and in any case, both countries have to operate from a much smaller base of players.

Wales have shown by their domination of the international championship in the last decade that their club structure is easily the most effective in Britain and Ireland, because of its geographical intensity, and although reservations are beginning to be felt about the future of the game in Wales, the situation in that country is still vastly more encouraging than it is anywhere else in Britain and Ireland.

The chief culprit in the British failure, which was expressed so starkly by the Lions' unhappy performance in New Zealand in 1977, has unquestionably been England. It has not punched its weight in British Rugby for 15 years and despite the agitation of the major clubs, many of whom realised the shortcomings, it is crippled by a constitution which almost precludes effectiveness.

Only one man succeeded in disturbing the inherent inertia of the Rugby Football Union, and that was its President in 1976–77, R. E. G. Jeeps. Dickie Jeeps had been one of England's most successful and determined scrum-halves and captains. He was a patriot through and through who cared immensely for the prestige of English Rugby and who was sick of the years of failure which had culminated in 1976 in England losing all four matches in the international championship for the second time in four years, the only occasions this had happened throughout history. Jeeps accepted that the failure had gone on too long to be explained away by bad selection and his opinion gained significantly in strength when England went to Paris in 1976 and were beaten so overwhelmingly by a developing French pack that it was no exaggeration to say that they could have lost by 50 points if the French backs had taken their chances. That game was played four months before Dickie Jeeps succeeded to the presidency of the Rugby Union and it left the many entrenched opponents of reform with very little ground on which to stand when Jeeps sought to instigate changes.

His first attempts were rebuffed but that only increased his determination. He undertook a remarkable whistle-stop tour of England, similar in many ways to a presidential campaign in America, and succeeded in persuading the clubs and the counties to accept a regional and divisional competition for the following season to take the place of the preliminary England trials in December. It was a remarkable breakthrough, because for the first time, England was to have a domestic competition featuring the eight areas into which it was logical to divide the country. What is more, they were to play their competition in the logical month of December, leaving the clubs free in September, October and November and providing a more comprehensive system of trials than England have ever had before.

These days, it is so rare for anyone to succeed in making fundamentally effective reforms at any level of government, whether it be of a nation or a sport, that the value of Jeeps' achievement cannot be overstated. Normally, incoming officials, whether they be government ministers or presidents of governing bodies, find themselves so overwhelmed by bureaucracy that most of them are content just to get through the literal and the metaphorical paperwork before handing the job on to the next

Dickie Jeeps, ex-President of the Rugby Union, and an advocate of reform.

man. Jeeps did much more than that. He not only acted as chairman at committees and spoke at dinners, demanding though that work is. He actually did something which resulted in progress in his term of office.

Unfortunately, that term of office was too brief for it to be carried through to a successful conclusion. The major clubs wanted Jeeps to stay on as President of the Rugby Union for at least one more year, but successful men are rarely appreciated by men who have been much less successful, and the earlier president of the Rugby Union who said that Jeeps would be re-appointed 'over my dead body' was enunciating an opinion which carried the day.

The regional and divisional matches instituted by Dickie Jeeps were played in December 1977, and despite some inevitable mutterings, they clearly represented the basis on which the Rugby Union should approach the future, but at the very time they were being played, the Four Home Unions decided that the political climate was not right for South Africa to be invited on their scheduled tour of Great Britain in 1978, and a sixteen match tour by New Zealand was substituted. As this was to take place before Christmas, 1978, the Rugby Union decided that the pressure of fixtures would be too great to leave room for the regional championship, and so for 1978, at any rate, it was left in abeyance.

By that time, Dickie Jeeps had stepped down from the presidency of the Rugby Union and had withdrawn from his position as one of England's representatives on the International Board. He accepted the prestigious appointment as chairman of the Sports Council, a demanding national post, but one which gave him a sense of perspective both about his year of office as President of the Rugby Union and what he had tried to achieve.

Looking back, he said, 'I think the county system is outdated in England. I believe that we need either to restructure it, or do away with it completely. I always put England at the top of my own pinnacle. I want to see England playing well, and doing well in the international championship, because I believe that if England is doing well, the game will be attractive to youngsters who want to identify with that success. Unfortunately, in lots of our thinking on the Rugby Union, we never put the England team and its well-being first and foremost. Members of the Rugby Union tend to represent their counties to the good or evil of all else, and I think that is sad for the game. England is not the force in the game that it was for the simple reason that we, as members of the Rugby Union, will not sit down and sort ourselves out, major clubs, constituent bodies, and all the rest. We dodge the issue.

'I think we should disband the present county structure of the Rugby Union completely and have a divisional structure instead. The country should be divided into four divisions, each with two playing areas, so that we have eight established regional teams to play matches against touring sides visiting this country. Those eight regions should then elect representatives to the Rugby Union, with provision made for the major clubs, for the referees, for the schools, for the universities and for the services. If we did that, England would soon start to come back as a force in world Rugby.'

Jeeps accepts that as far as the opponents of reform are concerned, the key to the whole argument is the future of the county championship. 'The best solution would probably be to make the county championship a junior club competition. That would take a lot of pressure off our leading players, who have too much on their plates at the moment, and it would give the opportunity for advancement to junior players who at the moment have no chance of being seen in a prestige competition, and who have no chance of raising the standard of their game.

'As things are, we are absolutely destroying the major clubs by taking away their players for such a large part of the season. I would not say that major club Rugby has improved but it has become much more competitive and those clubs need the services of their best players. Unfortunately, we just will not face the issue.'

The traditionally more conservative Scots surprised the Rugby fraternity in the United Kingdom by being the first to introduce a championship and league structure. It should work well for the positive reason that Scotland has always maintained the strictest possible code on the laws relating to amateurism.

Ireland seem happy with their regional structure whose cup competitions at the senior and schoolboy levels have nurtured a keen interest and support for an enthusiastic minority. Both Scotland and Ireland hitherto, however, have suffered from a lack of depth in playing quality. Quick to realise that their base was not sufficiently broad, Ireland were holding coaching courses in the early 'Sixties and their very first was directed by Jean Prat.

Despite the recent successes of the national team, the structure of the Welsh Rugby Union is in just as urgent need of revision as England's. The success of Wales in the international championship means that there is not as much pressure on the Welsh Rugby Union to institute reform as there is on the Rugby Football Union in England, but representation on the Welsh Rugby Union contains so many anomalies and militates so strongly against the recruitment of men of stature that ultimately, it is bound to be unhealthy. This was recognised by some of the men within the Welsh Rugby Union and indeed Hermas Evans even went as far as preparing a draft rewrite of the constitution, but because it threatened to reduce the self-perpetuating element of the present Welsh Rugby Union, it was given only the most cursory consideration.

One of the biggest weaknesses of the Welsh Rugby Union – like the Rugby Football Union in England – is that it glorifies the lowest common denominator. It does not make room for men of stature who have something to offer Rugby football even though they have achieved their eminence in some other part of the community. Above all, it has not come to terms with the need to recognise the major clubs in Wales and to give them direct representation on the Union. The result is that the district representatives are drawn from too narrow a section of the game in Wales and more often than not, that section is so far down the scale in playing terms that it is fair to say that the tail is wagging the dog. Every dog has to have a tail, of course, and it should be represented, but not at the expense of everything else. It would be healthier, too, if there was a bigger turnover in the representation. Continuity is important, particularly among the officers, but it should not be extended to the point of fossilisation. Members of the Welsh Rugby Union wear a little badge identifying their membership. The words at the bottom of the badge say, 'Ich dien'. Twenty-five years is a long time to serve for life membership. Too long, alas, for too many.

It is not surprising that the Rugby administrations of England and Wales are finding it so hard to adjust to the changed world around them, because that world is developing at a pace which even the International Rugby Football Board clearly finds bewildering. By 1976, the parade of countries touring Britain and acting as hosts to British teams began to resemble the march-past at the Olympic Games. Japan, Fiji, Australia, the Argentine and Tonga were followed by Canada, the United States of America (whose game is so widely spread that their coach, Dennis Storer,

Mike Halliday, the brilliant centre-threequarter who played for the USA against England in 1978.

had to train his players by post), Italy, Rumania and even Russia. The Penguins, an unusual British touring club capable of spanning the entire range of playing standards from happy-go-lucky coarse Rugby right the way up to the level of the Barbarians, had been breaking new ground all over the world for years. They had toured Belgium, Germany, Denmark, Sweden, Holland, France, Switzerland, Portugal, Malta, Zambia, Rhodesia, South Africa, Bermuda, California and even the Channel Islands and ended up in 1977 by representing the West in an eyeball to eyeball confrontation with Communist Eastern Europe. They played in a tournament in Tbilisi, not far from Stalin's birthplace in Georgia, and beat Czechoslovakia 44–13, Poland 16–12, Rumania 20–9, Russia 'B' 50–15 and Russia 25–13. They thus won the tournament with five straight victories, and within less than a year, this looked as if it would be an achievement which might well remain unique.

In that time, an England 'B' team visited Rumania and found the game not only ready to flex its muscles at full international level, but also to some extent indignant that Rumania's excellent results against France were not being acknowledged with an immediate invitation to play in the international championship in Europe!

Russia, too, went back home and did some work. They found one lock 6 ft 10 in tall and another 6 ft 7 in. They worked on their scrummaging. They found a couple of really fast wingers. They worked on their defence. They found some footballers to play number eight, half-back and full-back. They worked on their kicking. Within fourteen months, they had improved to such an extent that they were able to arrange an international against the full might of France and hold them to 13–6 before conceding three late tries in injury time. More than one England team would have settled for that in the previous fifteen years.

The advances made by the Russians and the Rumanians were no surprise to Carwyn James. He had played in both countries himself twenty years earlier, and had been left in no doubt that they meant business. Their pursuit of physical fitness was absolute anathema to a Welsh fly-half of that generation, whose idea of training was to jog for a couple of laps round the pitch and then to retire for a restorative cigarette! Even then, the Russians and Rumanians warmed up for twenty minutes before a match, and did it so vigorously that they dripped sweat. This was something that Llanelli's fly-half of the time always tried to avoid, even in a game, and even though he had studied Russian in the Navy!

Llanelli had played against Rumania, Czechoslovakia and West Germany in Moscow in 1957, and would have played against France too, but the French under the captaincy of Jean Prat, chose to withdraw from the competition because Llanelli were not a national team. After a fortnight in which the Russians made copious notes about everything that Llanelli did, their parting words were, 'You come back in twenty years' time, and we'll play you'.

The World of Rugby

Whether the Four Home Unions will want to extend their playing contracts with Eastern Europe much beyond the present spasmodic level is another matter. Neither the Penguins players nor those of the England B team enjoyed playing in Russia and Rumania. It is just not possible for totalitarian states to produce the fun and carefree pleasures of the Rugby community in the rest of the world, though in the case of Rumania, with its historical associations with France, this is a pity because if ever there was a Latin Rugby community bursting to break free of its political chains, it is theirs.

Russia, like Canada and the United States, have to play split seasons because of the severity of their winters but like Rumania, and other Eastern bloc countries, their government has now taken a political decision to encourage Rugby football because of its character-building qualities. When they played France in 1978, they chose their team from a base of no more than 15,000 players but they felt that if Rugby football could be incorporated in the Olympic Games, as it was in 1920 and 1924, the number of Russians playing Rugby football would increase tenfold.

Similar advances are being made in Italy. In 1975, Italy played an England Under 23 team at Gosforth, and were beaten quite easily. This was not surprising, because the Italians have always been apologetic about their Rugby. Their temperament is not really suited to the game and they use it as an excuse or a well-rehearsed confession of their sins of omission. These include their reluctance to train hard. Italians regard the pain barrier with about as much enthusiasm as a bullet through the head. They also indulge in over-eating, often before a game. Their approach is quite different from that of the French. The basic indiscipline of the Latin temperament often expresses itself in an eruption of violence, or the unnecessary late tackle; questioning the decisions of referees is commonplace and so is criticism of a team-mate's mistakes. The crowds, too, are over-emotional. Playing is not enough. They want to win at all costs. It is the mentality of Soccer and the professional game.

As in Russia, Rugby football has had only a comparatively brief history in Italy, where the primary sport is Soccer. The high standards achieved in Soccer have been analysed and attempts have been made to transplant the same techniques into other sports. In all Italian team games, the coach is a dictator. His word is law. Without complete acceptance of his authority, the game would never thrive. Unfortunately, their coaches have assumed such an exaggerated concept of their importance that they are unwilling to concede that their players can think for themselves. Like small-minded schoolmasters in Britain who parade the touch-line, the coach in Italy shouts instructions from the bench or touch-line. Soccer managers do this the world over.

Fortunately, Italian Rugby brought in coaches from Britain and players from the International Board countries. Their advice and example quickly had a beneficial effect, because within three years of their defeat by England Under 23, Italy had beaten Argentina 19–6, shortly after that same Argentine side had drawn 13–13 with England at Twickenham. In 1977, too, the All Blacks were startled to be hunted all the way in a game they played against Italy before the start of their tour of France. The All Blacks were particularly impressed by a centre named Rino Francescato and when he produced the same dazzling form against

Rino Francescato, of Italy, possibly the best centre in Europe.

Argentina the following year, British coaches in Italy thought that he was probably the best centre in Europe.

By that time, thanks to strong urgings from its overseas advisers, the Italian Rugby Federation had decreed that coaches must watch games from the stand, and not from benches on the touch-line. This was greeted with profound relief by Italian referees, whose greatest problem is that of most countries learning the game – they do not understand *why* a law has been introduced because the game has not been a part of their heritage. Even so, no one should under-estimate their desire to learn.

No one should under-estimate the determination of the Italian authorities to stamp out foul play, either. As well as the referee, the Federation appoints an observer to watch each match from the stands. If he sees any foul play, he will make a report, and on his recommendation a player can be suspended. That player has no defence. A telegram arrives decreeing how many matches the player will miss. Unfortunately, the playing misdemeanours are often the result of inadequate refereeing. At the moment, it is a vicious circle. Unfortunately, too, referees and coaches are often poles apart in their thinking in Italian Rugby.

Rugby has to be club-centred in Italy, because it is not taught in the schools, and to that extent, it may well have lessons to teach British Rugby, where the collapse of the teaching of the game in the state sector of education means that more and more clubs will have to go to the schools to introduce boys to the game. Mini-Rugby is now being taught in Italy and throughout the whole structure of the game, the standard of coaching is quite high.

The players of all ages are well looked after. It is a middle class game, as it is in England, but all players in Italy are given their playing kit. This equipment is provided by commercial sponsors who also under-write the finances of many of the clubs. Sponsorship therefore is a prominent feature of Italian Rugby, as it is in France, and in many other ways, the games in the two countries are similar. For instance, the game in Italy is based entirely on a club championship. Winning, and the two points that go with it, matter. There are 14 clubs in the first division, and they all play each other home and away in a 26 match season. Winning the championship matters more than the quality of the Rugby. Staying in the first division means more than playing brilliantly in the second division.

Italian Rugby has been too dependent on France for too long, and in 1978, it appointed Pierre Villepreux, the former French international full-back, as coach of the Italian national team. Gradually, though, the Italian Federation is becoming aware that it needs to broaden its playing contacts. This process has been accelerated by the arrival of so many leading Australian, New Zealand and South African players. Each club is allowed two 'strangers'. It is a thriving market, and it contributes to the great sense of adventure which is always attendant upon a game growing up in a new country.

This sense of adventure is now world wide. A new national flag seems to be unfurled in the game of Rugby football every year and sooner rather than later, the International Board will have to take the lead in instigating some kind of world federation. At the moment, the International Board is unquestionably ducking the issue, and if it goes on doing so, it will soon be overtaken by events.

Asked whether he thought the developing countries could look forward to some representation at international level, Mickey Steele-Bodger, one of England's representatives on the International Board, offered as a personal view his opinion that, 'It would not be for the good of the game to greatly enlarge the supreme authoritative body at this stage'.

This may well be true, but now that the younger countries of Europe, in particular, have lost France as their natural leader, because of France's accession to full membership of the International Board, it is only a question of time before they tire of seeking recognition and claim it for themselves. What is needed is a grouping of countries subsidiary to the International Board, possibly along the lines of the original spheres of influence designated for the major countries, but based on Britain and France, and possibly New Zealand. This suggests itself as the most workable arrangement, because it is usually much easier to communicate

Dirk Naude, the mighty man of the Rovigo pack coached in Italy by Carwyn James and winners of the Italian First Division. Naude is the brother of the former Springbok 'Tiny' Naude.

with London, either by air travel or mail, than it is with anywhere else. When this world organisation is instituted, we make only one plea, and that is that Russia is included in the committee of nations which has Scotland as its chairman! The Scottish Rugby Union versus the Kremlin would be compulsive viewing.

The only country excluded from this bustle of national activity is South Africa and in 1977, the feeling that this exclusion might last at least until such time as a Conservative Government was re-elected in Britain gathered enough strength to persuade Dr Danie Craven to fly to London to put his country's case. Dr Craven wanted the Four Home Unions to accept the planned tour of Britain by the Springboks in 1978 but as early as 1976, he sensed that the chances of the tour taking place were diminishing, and so he launched himself into a typically vigorous public relations exercise to try to save the day.

No sport anywhere in the world has produced a leader more dynamic than Danie Craven, or one capable of arguing his country's case with more passionate conviction. He called a Press conference in London and detailed the remarkable progress that had been made towards multi-racial Rugby in South Africa in less than five years. He said club Rugby in South Africa was already multi-racial, and that the government of the country had just made an announcement approving multi-racial sport. 'We will select a multi-racial team to tour Britain,' said Dr Craven. 'At the moment, there are probably not more than two or three Africans or Coloureds who would be worth a place on merit in a South African touring party, but we must give them as much assistance and encouragement as possible. After all, in every touring party that was ever chosen – whether it be Lions, or All Blacks or Springboks – there have always been five or six players who have turned out to be not really worth their places. What we hope to do, therefore, is to give those marginal places to African and Coloured players who we think will gain most benefit and develop most through the experience of a major overseas tour.'

The Lions in South Africa in 1974 had played against a loose forward named Morgan Cushe who was outstanding in the match between the Lions and the African Rugby Board team known as the Leopards at Mdantsane, just outside Port Elizabeth. Dr Craven also admitted that he had been bitterly disappointed when Green Vigo, a highly talented Cape Coloured threequarter, had accepted an offer to turn professional and play Rugby League. 'That boy would have been worth his place in any Springbok team,' said Dr Craven.

Even at the time of Dr Craven's visit to London, one sensed that he knew that he was fighting a losing battle and so it proved. Ironically, the great majority of the community of Rugby Union football in Britain, players, ex-players, club committees and supporters, have always felt that South African Rugby players are just as entitled to tour Britain as Russian gymnasts, and that as they are legally entitled to do so, it is nothing short of a cowardly abdication of responsibility on the part of the Four Home Unions, both individually and collectively, to accept a denial of their rights by giving in to political pressure.

However, within a matter of months, the Scottish Rugby Union, rarely the most crusading of bodies, had meekly announced that, far from supporting a South African Rugby tour of the British Isles, it had also decided to 'postpone' Scotland's short tour of South Africa, planned for 1978. This decision certainly did not represent the wishes of the Scottish players, most of whom would have been only too delighted to tour South Africa. What is more, the decision was never satisfactorily explained. It was conjectured that the Scottish Rugby Union had declined the tour because of fears that militant political pressures would have prevented the Scottish soccer team from playing in the World Cup in Argentina. As it happened, it transpired that positively the kindest thing that could have happened to Mr Ally McLeod's ill-fated Scottish soccer team would have been exclusion from the World Cup. Then the whole Scottish nation, and the rest of the world, would have been spared one of the most humiliating experiences in modern sport.

At the same time, it was announced that Australia would not be going ahead with their planned tour of South Africa either, and it was not long before the Four Home Unions also announced, rather sheepishly, that they did not consider that a tour of Britain by South Africa was appropriate at the time. They accepted that South Africa had achieved a multi-racial sporting society, not only in Rugby football and therefore, by implication, they accepted that the original objections to South Africa's participation in the world of Rugby had been removed, but they did not carry that acceptance to its logical conclusion.

This lack of leadership was both abject and demoralising and it came at a time when a development in cricket was demonstrating to governing bodies of sports everywhere that they did not have a divine right to shape the destinies of players, even professional players, against their wishes. Mr Kerry Packer, who had substantial interests in commercial television in Australia, gave lucrative contracts to a group of the world's leading cricketers when his attempt to break the monopoly of televised cricket coverage in Australia failed. The governing bodies of cricket rallied against him, and the latter day derivatives of the MCC in London even went to the High Court in an attempt to prevent him doing what, after all, had been common practice two hundred years earlier when the leading cricketers of England grouped together and toured the country for monetary reward. Predictably, Mr Packer won the action in the High Court, just as George Eastham, some years before, had won an action which gave professional footballers in England freedom from the principle of a maximum wage and restrictive contracts.

Mr Packer thus established a precedent which could clearly be followed in other sports, and not least Rugby football. When Scotland,

Australia and the Four Home Unions decided to leave South Africa isolated from the rest of the world of Rugby for at least three more years, they merely hastened the day when South Africans turned round and asked themselves what benefit they were deriving from their membership of the International Rugby Football Board, and further asked themselves whether they might not be better off if they accepted international tours organised by a Rugby football equivalent of Kerry Packer.

Mickey Steele-Bodger, one of England's representatives on the International Board at the time, accepted this as a possibility, and so did Hermas Evans, who represented Wales. When Hermas Evans said, 'The International Board must retain its influence throughout the Rugby playing world. . . . one can almost feel that if we, as a Board do not do something, it is quite feasible that they [the emerging Rugby countries] could form another organisation similar to the Board' he was not only voicing fears about the threat to the governing authority of the International Board, he was also envisaging the emergence of a Kerry Packer in Rugby football.

Mickey Steele-Bodger was even more specific. 'We are all sympathetic to South Africa's problems,' he said, 'and we all want to re-establish normal touring relations with South Africa, but I admit that they are entitled to ask if they are getting a fair deal'.

Mickey Steele-Bodger, one of England's representatives on the International Board.

And in reply to a direct question about the possibility of a Kerry Packer, he asked, 'Are there any potential Kerry Packers in Rugby football?'

At the time Mr Steele-Bodger asked that question, a positive queue of Kerry Packers was waiting to move into Rugby football touring, and some of them were unashamedly motivated by nothing more altruistic than sheer commercialism. The welfare of Rugby football was not a concern of theirs. They knew that South Africa badly needed Rugby tours, they knew that practically every international player in Britain and Ireland wanted to tour South Africa, and they knew that a great deal of money could be made for everyone by satisfying those two needs. After all, there was nothing new in the commercial sponsorship of sporting tours. The first major cricket tour of Australia from a British team was sponsored by Messrs Spiers and Pond, the Fortnum and Mason of their day. And since then, any number of thoroughly attractive touring packages have been put together at all levels of practically every sport. It could even be argued that a commercial organiser would do the job very much better than the Four Home Unions, because he could hardly fail to be in closer touch with the current thinking of the players than that august body, which perpetually seems to be at least ten years late with its reforms, and he would also be far less penny-pinching in his attitude to the treatment of Rugby footballers who are undoubtedly star players. Unless the Four Home Unions and the International Rugby Football Board make a fundamental change in their attitude to South Africa, there is not much doubt that the South Africans themselves will soon have to make a choice between oblivion and Packerism.

The one country with the size and the quality of life and the depth of playing resources to replace South Africa in the touring itineraries of the members of the International Rugby Football Board is France. There would be difficulties, of course, because of the difference of hemispheres and the reversal between summer and winter, but there is not much doubt that French Rugby is strong enough to receive major tours both by the British Lions and by New Zealand. What is more, there is no doubt at all that from the point of view of weather, playing facilities, geographical size, gate-taking capacity, the quality of their hotels and the sheer delight of touring the country, France could rival even a country as immensely varied and as hospitable as South Africa. International Board members admit that this possibility has been considered, and it may have had something to do with the decision, in 1978, to invite France at long, long last to become full members of the International Rugby Football Board. It was no less than they deserved.

18 The Union game stumbling into its second century

The dilemma facing both South Africa and the International Rugby Football Board is only one of many facing the world of Rugby Union Football as it approaches the last twenty years of the twentieth century. That world finds itself confronted by changes as profound and as perplexing as those taking place in society itself. The very amateurism on which the game was founded and which cost England, especially, such a fearful price to preserve is being eroded in an increasingly materialistic society. The quality of back play has declined alarmingly because of changes in the laws made without a proper period of informed discussion, without a proper period of experiment and without a proper appreciation of their repercussions. Other well-intentioned, but misguided, law changes devalued the low tackle round the legs, one of the classic fundamentals of the game, to the point where its very existence was threatened. The same thing happened to the ruck or running scrum, which has been the one classic development of the game in modern times and which therefore should be treasured and preserved. Because of social and educational changes, the game itself is in retreat in all the member countries of the International Rugby Football Board, except perhaps France and Australia. The authority of the governing bodies is being challenged, and so is the supremacy of the International Board itself. The incidence of violence in the game appears to be increasing, which again is a mirror of society.

While this process of erosion and contraction is so evident in those countries where Rugby football had its origins and its first surge of growth, the game throughout the rest of the world is developing and expanding at an astonishing rate. The day may well be approaching when the players representing countries less privileged in the traditions of the game become more skilful than those in the more advanced and sophisticated societies where the game had its roots. The same thing happened long ago in the game of Association Football, that vigorous offshoot of the true football game which was preserved by such a marvellous accident of history at Rugby School.

Perhaps the most significant change in this welter of contradiction is that of the players' attitude to professionalism. Players today feel no sense of dishonour or impropriety at receiving the many perquisites which are now regarded as a part of the game. They see nothing wrong in playing as semi-professionals in France and Italy or of being paid inflated expenses to play the game in Wales. In this regard, the governing bodies of the game are performing successfully that most difficult of athletic contortions, which is to sit on the fence while sticking their heads firmly into the sand at the same time. As Wilf Wooller, one of the game's great players and now a forthright critic, has said, 'There is no doubt that by the standards of even ten years ago, most of the leading players are now professionals.'

The International Board cannot have it both ways. They cannot define, as they do, that the very first object of their existence is, 'Determining and safeguarding the principles relating to amateurism in Rugby Football,' while presiding over a headlong retreat from those principles. The point is: What is professionalism? Is it any breach whatever of the rather Victorian rules drawn up by the International Rugby Football Board? Or is it something less? Or is it, indeed, something that is changing all the time, like the game itself and the society within which it has its existence?

Wilf Wooller, forthright former Welsh international. 'By the standards of even ten years ago, most of the top players today are professionals.'

An interesting answer to the question was given by an official of the Béziers club, when some of the material for the television series of *The World of Rugby* was being gathered. A jocular reference was made to the fact that the Béziers players are required to train on Tuesday and Thursday *mornings*. There is no question of the Béziers players fitting in their training as they can, after they have completed their daily toil, which is what all British clubs have always supposed to be an inevitable consequence of true amateurism.

The Béziers official saw nothing odd in compulsory morning training. 'We regard professionalism as consisting of actually paying players to play the game,' he said. 'Now according to our information, every first-class club in Wales, with the exception of Newport and Cardiff, actually pay their players to play. The money that is given to them in their weekly packets may be described as expenses, or something similar, but it is in fact payment to play.

'We do not do that. We have wealthy patrons of the club who make available jobs and business opportunities for players. It is a practice common throughout France. At Béziers, those jobs and business opportunities are so arranged as to make time available for players to train in the mornings.

'We believe that what we do is no different in principle from what happens in many clubs in Britain. In the Harlequins, for instance, which is probably as powerful and as influential as any in England, there are committee men and former players who have become extremely successful in the business world. They make available jobs and business opportunities for other members of the Harlequins club, just as we do. I am sure that the Harlequins would be very hurt if it was suggested that this commercial freemasonry amounted to a form of professionalism, and quite rightly so too, because obviously, such an assertion would be ridiculous in the society in which we live.'

There is no doubt that there is a lot of truth in this point of view. There is equally no doubt that professionalism does exist in France, as it does in Wales. Human nature being what it is, professionalism exists in every sport which is sufficiently popular as a spectacle to provide substantial gate receipts from a paying public. It does not only exist among players, either. In England and Wales it exists among club officials. Obviously, very few clubs in England attract the popular support that makes cash available in the same way that it is in France and Wales, but there is one famous English club which has a whole row of stand seats which does not appear on the club's seating plan and the receipts from which are never put through the books. Where does that money go? The players of that club believe that it goes into the pockets of one or two club officials.

There is nothing new in this, of course. Turnstiles have worked for something or someone other than the club or the relevant ground authority for as long as people have paid to watch Rugby football. The point is that it is not only the players who are involved in considerations of professionalism.

A few years ago, Chris Laidlaw, the former All Black, wrote a cheerfully ribald book called *Mud in your Eye* in which he itemised instances of professionalism in France. He had played the game there himself, and so he was in a position to know what went on. Laidlaw named names, including several players who were to become British Lions, and he suggested that they were not going through the slog of travelling to play in France each weekend exclusively for their love of the game or the local wines. The International Board in conjunction with France and the Four Home Unions, stopped this cross-Channel traffic, but they were not in a position to prove that any professionalism had taken place.

This question of proof, of course, was the crux of the matter. Here the International Board are making things more difficult for themselves than need be if, at the end of the day, they feel not only that they can contain the advancing tide of professionalism, but also that they really want to do so. In all the Board's regulations about amateurism, actions which result in monetary gain are proscribed. This places the onus of proof on the Board, and that proof is almost always impossible to obtain. The governing authorities of the game would be far more successful in containing professionalism if they simply banned those activities which they know lead to payment rather than ban the payment itself.

A good example of this has been provided recently in the exclusive news made available to one newspaper or another, rather than all of them, about the retirement of certain leading players. Those players were paid for those exclusive stories, but neither their parent Union nor the International Board had any prospect of *proving* that they were paid.

However, these instances indicate quite clearly that the tide of professionalism *is* advancing. Cheque book journalism, as it is called, has existed in soccer and cricket for many years, but it did not exist in Rugby Union football before 1978. Now it does.

The same thing has happened in relation to players writing books. We have no doubt that the intention of those who framed the laws of the game relating to amateurism was to proscribe amateur players receiving financial benefit of any kind from the game, and yet Colin Meads was the first of several New Zealand players who was allowed to keep a large sum of money deriving from a biography and put it into a family trust while retaining his own status as an amateur. Since then the publishers have employed lawyers to find loopholes in the letter of the law in order to frustrate the spirit of the law. The situation has become quite absurd.

One of the greatest difficulties facing the International Board in their progressively more fruitless attempts to control professionalism is that the situation is constantly changing. As fast as they draw lines in one position, the tide moves somewhere else, and at the back of it all they are nervous of attempting to enforce a set of laws so strict as to interfere with what is apparently called 'natural justice'. Indeed, the edges of amateurism and professionalism have now become so blurred that it is impossible to discern where one ends and the other begins.

The position is made even more complicated by the fact that the problem differs completely in different parts of the world. More than one Australian Rugby Union touring team, for instance, would have been decimated if the International Board regulations decreeing 'thou shalt not play Rugby League, even as an amateur' had been strictly enforced. This particular regulation is probably unenforceable in law anyway. Dickie Jeeps thinks so, and so do we.

It is very apparent, too, that on the question of club championships, the French have never wavered from the position which contributed to their exclusion from the international Rugby fraternity fifty years ago. All the changes have taken place in the Four Home Unions and they, not France, are the ones who have changed their position. The same is true of the provision of job opportunities for players and even accommodation. The French are still pursuing exactly the same practical path of meeting the laws of supply and demand as they were fifty years ago.

By the standards which applied then, or even of those which applied after the 1939–45 war, the countries of Eastern Europe who are now developing both their Rugby football and their international aspirations so rapidly, are professional. So are countries like Italy, who are outside the Eastern bloc. Yet the Four Home Unions are extending their playing contacts with those countries and are doing it despite the fact that playing against professionals is automatically an act of professionalism in itself.

Sponsorship is perhaps the most significant development in this area of overt professionalism, and it is essential to control it. Something which began quietly in Britain in 1959 when the Scottish Rugby Union, of all organisations, accepted the gift of an under-soil heating system at the national stadium at Murrayfield from the late Dr Charles Hepburn, a whisky distiller, began to escalate rapidly ten years later. Continental firms manufacturing playing equipment – all of them carrying identifiable markings – began to give boots and track suits to leading players. Those firms then expanded that to the point where they were equipping whole clubs and even national sides. Sponsored national club competitions were introduced, and were immediately highly successful; sponsored coaching films were produced; even the University Match between Oxford and Cambridge found an enterprising sponsor from the City of London. Now sponsorship has reached the point where it is underwriting the finances of entire clubs.

Nothing could be more innocent and honourable than the provision of money by the great clearing banks to finance coaching films. Nothing could be more worth-while vehicles for sponsorship than the national cup competitions in England and Wales or a regional championship in England. Equally, nothing will destroy the traditional basis of amateurism more quickly than the wholesale sponsorship of clubs. On the continent, clubs rely heavily on sponsorship from wealthy companies who are looking for success. Jerseys bear the name of the sponsors, but although the sponsors do not interfere in any way with the running of the club they can easily withdraw if they are not happy with the playing record. Sports firms compete in earnest to give a free supply of kit which bears their name.

It is amazing how quickly we in the UK have moved along the very same road as the Continentals. Little did Scotland realise at the time, when they accepted the gift of an electric blanket for Murrayfield that they were the forerunners of the kind of sponsorship which is bound to have a profound influence on the game in the future.

In Italy, the names of the clubs even change from year to year, depending on whether they are sponsored by a firm of ice cream manufacturers or one manufacturing electrical equipment. The money which has been made available by these firms has enabled the clubs to recruit Rugby players from all over the world. They are rationed to two per club but this has developed to such a point that there is now an international community of club Rugby players who travel the world playing for sponsored clubs in the different seasons of the different hemispheres. In Italy, you can meet South African, Australian, New Zealand and British Rugby players. They provide the essential technical and temperamental stiffening to the local players. They discuss the going rates of jobs and perks just like any other business community. Yet they play as amateurs in their own countries, and even, as in the case of Andy Haden, of New Zealand, as internationals. The International Rugby Football Board must know that horses and carts are being driven through their regulations regarding amateurism all over the world. The Board must either re-write those regulations to make them workable or accept that in the end, the game will become wholly professional, and it will do it very quickly.

The dilemma is that most professional Rugby players look back on their amateur days with affection for the fun and the friendships which they derived from Rugby Union. Russell Fairfax the former Australian full-back, made the point most felicitously. When he was asked if he ever regretted leaving the Union game, he said, 'Oh, do I ever! Yes, I regret it very much. I would love to put on a shirt and play a fifteen man game but . . . the offer they put to me was more or less my future.'

The point was made in another way by Tony O'Reilly, who is enjoying such a spectacularly successful career in the world of commerce and who is now based in America as one of the senior executives of Heinz foods. He said, 'Experience of living in America has taught me a great deal of how creeping professionalism can destroy a team sport. It is an interesting fact that in the United States, unless you become professional, there are no team sports available to anyone after they leave college. Football goes, basketball goes, baseball goes, and out of the cream of college football players, only one per cent can make it to the pro's. The increased professionalism of sport in the United States has produced a very selective gladiatorial type of infra-structure. Sport has much more to offer than that. The danger is that the criteria that are being applied to professional sport will begin to be applied to Rugby Football. This increased professionalism is tending to take the game towards the model of France, where the game is somewhat more professional than you and I would accept as being the contemporary definition of an amateur sport. I would be a determined opponent of that. I believe that Rugby football is an afternoon's enjoyment. I like to win. I don't mind to lose. I don't think that the nation's honour is that important. Rugby football should be a small component of what life hopefully allows you. If it becomes part of the national prestige and if forces within the game are prepared to underwrite it with money, the spirit of the game will suffer.'

These sentiments are both admirable and understandable. But are they valid? Are they realistic? Are the underlying suppositions true? Is the game less enjoyable to play in France than it is in England? Do the players get more fun out of playing for Ponsonby, in New Zealand, than they do for Bagnères, in France? Is it not true, in any case, that the horse at the centre of the discussion has already gone, so there is no point in shutting the stable door?

The situation is immensely difficult for the International Board and they must realise that it is now out of control. In a recent statement, they admitted themselves that their regulations concerning amateurism were written for a different age. They cannot be surprised, therefore, if the players share that opinion, and act accordingly.

However, the difficulties inherent in the control of professionalism do not extend to the laws of the game. Those laws should be framed to preserve the fundamentals of the game, and to reward skill, athleticism, organisation and initiative. In recent years, those objectives have not been achieved. The International Board has introduced a lot of bad, ill-written law which has contributed significantly to an obvious decline in handling and running skills and which devalued both the tackle and the ruck to the point of absurdity. These ill-advised law changes not only damaged some of the finest elements of Rugby football but they also institutionalised something called the pile-up. This is the collapsed heap of bodies burying the ball. As its name implies, the pile-up is the least attractive and most physically dangerous development in the game in recent years, but unless it is eliminated at source, by re-establishing the proper rewards for a tackle and re-establishing the environment which gave birth to the ruck, it will soon be necessary to add another law to the game, Law 29, devoted exclusively to The Pile-up. It would not look well alongside The Scrummage, The Tackle and The Lineout.

Most of this bad law has been adopted because the International Board have sought to achieve various objects without knowing how to go about it. This was most apparent in the major revision of the law which was made in relation to the lineout, a revision which undoubtedly was precipitated more by the calculated mockery of the existing lineout laws by the coach of the 1971 British Lions than by anything else. Unfortunately, the International Board which then sought to make the changes did not have the services of a practical legal authority of the eminence of Cyril Gadney, who had been one of England's representatives in previous years, and the consequence was that possible adverse repercussions were not anticipated.

This weakness has been acknowledged by Air Vice Marshal 'Larry' Lamb, chairman of the Rugby Union's laws committee, and until comparatively recently, himself a former distinguished international referee. He said, 'I think it was David Lloyd George who said that war was far too serious a business to be left solely to the generals, and with respect to the

Air Vice Marshal 'Larry' Lamb, member of the Rugby Union and former international referee.

International Board, I would say that law making is really far too serious a business to be left entirely to the International Board. The structure behind the law-making arrangements really has not kept pace with the modern game. Proposals for changes in the law have to be with the International Board by November 1 and as the season doesn't really get under way until the middle of September, the resultant time schedule is much too tight.

'I would like the International Board to recognise that there is a great deal of expertise outside their own ranks and to form a drafting sub-committee on the lines of the parliamentary drafting sub-committees. This would examine any worthwhile proposals to change the laws, kick them around among the experts from all parts of the game, make definite recommendations and leave the International Board solely with the job of endorsing or rejecting the proposals. Experienced referees like Kevin Kelleher of Ireland, Gwynne Walters of Wales, and Bob Burrell of Scotland, could provide an invaluable panel of assessors.

'One of the great criticisms I have of the laws at the moment is that they do not really pay due attention to the playing of the game. The laws are treated as an end in themselves rather than as a means to an end. Take the present tackle law as an example. It was decreed in 1977 that the maul would end a tackle, but nobody gave any thought to this so-called pile-up situation which we now have. As a result, everyone is getting very concerned about it, and I am quite sure that there will be proposals to change the tackle laws. The implications of many other law changes, too, have never really been thought out. We have got to come round to thinking that changes must not be made without an experimental period for a start. There is no point in putting a thing into law and then finding it is not what you intended or what you wanted.

'This is what happened in the lineout. I do not believe that the law-makers gave due thought to the implications of the changes they made in the law relating to the lineout. It is alleged that many referees do not referee the lineout properly because they have too many things to look out for. If that is indeed the problem, then surely the solution must be to simplify the lineout and to reduce the number of things a referee has to concern himself with. But what did the International Board do in 1978? They actually *increased* the number of things that referees have to concern themselves with.

'This is not a matter solely for referees. It concerns the playing side of the game as well. It concerns coaches and players and indeed anyone who has anything constructive to say. The game is played best when it provides quality possession for skilful players and when it gives those players and their teams the opportunity to profit from those skills. What we have to do is work out how this can best be done, and then we have to enshrine it in law which has been well written and which has been carefully thought out as to all its possible consequences.'

These evident truths have been amply borne out in recent seasons. Smashing tackles, absolutely thrilling examples of the art, have gone unrewarded because the player being tackled *managed to keep the ball off the ground* and therefore, by interpretation of the law, he had not been tackled. This apparently innocuous change was made to speed up the game; it was an attempt to sustain the attacking flow of a movement. Whether it achieved its original object is arguable, but there is no doubt that that change in the tackle law is threatening to destroy not only the tackle itself, but also the ruck, which had its derivation in the loose ball which was made available when the tackled player had to release the ball.

In 1978, for instance, in the match between Wales and France at Cardiff, Ray Gravell passed the ball off the ground, as he was perfectly entitled to do under the new law, after he had been brought down by what would previously have been recognised as one of the finest tackles anyone is ever likely to see. Phil Bennett backed up and took the pass and scored a try.

Now if the tackler, in this case, Christian Belascain, is not rewarded with at least an interruption in the attacking side's control of the ball, he will soon come to the conclusion that there is no point in him making the classic side-on or head-on tackle at all. He will, instead, stand up and maul for the ball, as they do in Rugby League. Is that really what the International Board wants from Rugby Union football?

Similarly, in the match between Wales and Scotland, Steve Fenwick was allowed to go on and score after Jim Renwick had arrested the progress of J. J. Williams (he had not tackled him within the definition of the word) and Williams had managed to release the ball in a conveniently forward direction. It looked awful and it was awful. It also happened to be against the law. But is that really what we want from Rugby Union football, with its traditional rejection of both the knock-on and the forward pass?

The changes in the tackle law were made to speed up the play. They have not succeeded. Instead, they have introduced the pile-up, as players seek to keep the ball off the ground and opponents seek to smother it. They have devalued the tackle and they have almost eliminated the ruck.

The solution is obvious. There must be a return to the old law which required a player immediately to release the ball once he had been brought to the ground. This would give the successful tackler a fair reward but it would still provide the attacking team with the possibility of recovering possession by a ruck, or a running scrum. The beauty of the ruck is that it is dynamic, rather than static, like the maul, and therefore it provides much better quality possession. By all means retain the maul, but the International Board should legislate to preserve the ruck.

The Board must also accept that its re-write of the lineout laws has turned out to be an almost total failure in practice. Possession has deteriorated in quality, and there is much less space for wing-threequarter play than there was under the old law. As Norman Mair says, 'I think the International Board have wrecked the lineout. The finest Rugby played was around about the time of the 1971 Lions tour, when Wales were so good, and a tremendous amount of that quality play derived from the lineout. When the lineout was very tight and com-pressed, the backs had more room than they had had in many decades. They were really only concerned with their opposite numbers, rather than with all the cover as well. The lineout ball at that time was the most useable ball there had been in generations. It was also the most illegal ball there had ever been in the history of the game. The object surely should have been to produce the same quality of possession, and to retain the same space for the backs, but to make it all legal. The artificial spacing between the forwards was a mistake. By all means keep the two foot gap between the lines of forwards. But close the one yard gap be-tween the forwards in those lines. We must get back to a compressed lineout.'

This view is undoubtedly right. It is shared by Colin Meads, by Wilson Whineray and by Lucien Mias among many others. The International Board are planning a major re-write of the laws for 1980 and no doubt the lineout will be re-shaped but the danger is that the revisions will be introduced as substantive law, rather than for an experimental period. There is also a danger that these revisions will be the familiar jumble of half-baked and well-intentioned irrelevancies. Apparently, these re-visions are to be based partly on a series of playing experiments conducted at Stellenbosch University in South Africa. Well, with all due respect, that forum is nothing like wide enough. South Africa is now largely cut off from international playing exchanges. Their game and their players have lost contact with the real world of Rugby. The focal point of that world is still Europe, still Britain, and it is there that the great debate should be held. And there *should* be a debate. With the greatest of respect to the International Rugby Football Board, there is far more expertise and knowledge both about the game and the best way it might achieve its objects outside the Board than there is within it.

'Larry' Lamb sent out 1,000 questionnaires seeking opinion from all sections of the game about the revision of the lineout laws. Some of the replies were highly original. All of them should be taken into account in the consideration of framing a law to enable the lineout to take its proper place in the game while rewarding the athleticism of jumpers and the skill of throwers and catchers.

Apart from possession of the ball, and control of it, one of the prime objects of the game of Rugby football is to reach and cross what used to be known as the advantage line, and is now known as the gain line. This is the imaginary line across the field at the point at which the ball is won initially. If the team in possession of the ball succeeds in advancing across that line, the defending players have to run back, often in a loop to remain onside, while the attacking side simply moves forward. The advantages are obvious. It might be worth experimenting, therefore, with a system which vastly improves the chances of the team throwing the ball into the lineout of crossing the gain line in both attack and defence. This could be done by requiring the backs of the defending team to stand back ten yards from the lineout, as they do now, while allowing the backs of the team throwing in the ball simply to observe the requirements of offside in relation either to their scrum-half or the lineout. If the side throwing the ball into the lineout won possession and if they made their passes quickly and accurately, they would be across the gain line before the defence could reach them. Similarly, if the side throwing in the ball lost possession, they would still be able to cross the gain line in defence. It may be that such a provision would even do away with the necessity for the restrictions on kicking directly into touch outside the 25, but it is a system which would at least discourage kicking for touch, and above all, it would reward the side throwing in the ball. As things are, that team is at something of a disadvantage, because the act of throwing in the ball temporarily deprives it of one of its players.

Successive attempts to encourage two-handed catching in the lineout have also failed. Again, this failure derives from the fact that the player who can jump above his rivals and who can catch the ball has not been rewarded for his skill. He has not been protected, either. Again, it might be worth experimenting with a system in which no player of either side could interfere with a player who has jumped for the ball and caught it until he has returned to earth. That ought to ensure quality possession.

The point is, though, that no one would know for certain whether it would work until it had been tried, along with other suggestions. This is why experimental periods are essential. Everyone agrees that the lineout as such should be preserved, because it is a fundamental element of the game. Most people also agree that the lineout at the moment is providing neither quality possession, nor a proper reward for skill and endeavour, nor the environment to allow backs to flourish. The lineout has been the problem child of the game for far too long. It is time it grew up.

It is also time that the International Board banned most of the boot studs at present being manufactured for use in Rugby football. Some of these studs now so closely resemble mediaeval instruments of torture that it is no wonder they cause such appalling injuries. The incidence of serious flesh wounds has increased to the point where it is no longer acceptable.

Rugby football is, by definition, a violent game. It is a physical contact game in which the scrummage, the maul, the lineout, the tackle and the ruck create situations of violent physical confrontation. Human nature being what it is, there will always be moments when players lose their temper and strike each other. They always have. They always will.

As Judge Rowe Harding says, we now live in a world without discipline, but the game is probably not much more violent now than it has ever been, despite the increasingly hysterical publicity. The game is harder, in that it involves more running than it did, particularly for the forwards, and it is played by much bigger men. For instance, it is not generally realised that the England back division of the early 1970s was physically bigger than Wavell Wakefield's England pack of the 1920s. This remarkable increase in the average height and weight of Rugby players, particularly in Europe, means that the impact is obviously bigger at moments of physical collision and therefore more damage is done. It is also true that at about the time coaching began to have an influence in Europe, players stopped smiling. The game became much too deadly serious and few of them looked as if they were really enjoying themselves.

That said, it is hard to escape the conclusion that the real difference between now and then as far as this endlessly debated question of violence is concerned is that the public now is so much better informed on the subject than it was. This stems from the fact that the game is reported and photographed in infinitely greater detail than it was. Cameras and lenses have been improved out of all recognition and motors have been incorporated in cameras to take high speed sequences of film in minute detail. There are far more photographers, too. Until comparatively recently, the Rugby Union restricted entry at Twickenham to one photographic agency. They now admit ten or a dozen photographers. In France, international matches are attended by literally scores of cameramen, all of them impressively professional at their craft.

The athletic beauties of Rugby football, and its dramas, have thus been exposed as never before, but so have the warts, and the same thing applies to an even greater extent with regard to television. The improvement in cameras and lenses and in directing technique, the use of the slow motion replay, and the use of technical comment as informed as that of Bill McLaren of the BBC, has meant that the viewing and reading public have been able to see, as never before, the good and the bad and the ugly aspects of Rugby football. This was very evident in South Africa in 1976, when 'Moaner' van Heerden stood on Peter Whiting's ear in the third test against New Zealand at Cape Town. Before the days of television zoom lenses and incredibly efficient Japanese cameras, only two or three people would have known what had happened – just as many, indeed, as knew what Kevin Skinner did to Chris Koch and Jaap Bekker when the All Blacks beat the Springboks in New Zealand in 1956. Ignorance of what had happened to Koch and Bekker enabled the New Zealand public to accept the All Blacks victory in 1955 as the righteous outcome of a holy war. Knowledge of what happened to Whiting in 1976 caused a large section of the New Zealand public to rise up in indignation, clap their hands on their breast and sob, 'Bring back our boys from this heathen land'. Television, therefore, has given us a microscope through which we can look at the game as never before, but we should beware of losing our sense of proportion about the warts and the pimples that are revealed. Cheese is delicious, but it looks horrible under a microscope.

What *is* clear, however, is that the plastic and aluminium studs and the plastic soles from which football boots are now made are causing injuries of a nature unknown when boots were made of traditional materials like leather and canvas. In dry weather and on hard grounds, plastic soles and studs can develop edges like a razor and the appalling flesh wounds that are being inflicted on players are clear proof that this is so. Similarly, aluminium studs can be made so pointed as to be dangerous even when undamaged, and the simple act of walking across a concrete path to the playing field, or across a gravel path, can knock up a burr on an aluminium stud which turns that stud into a scalpel.

Inspection of boots is totally inadequate to guard against these dangers. It is a common practice for players deliberately to change their boots after a stud inspection. The only effective control would be to ban all forms of plastic and metal as materials used in the manufacture of soles and studs and to substitute either a composition or rubber sole. It may be argued that rubber studs are, in some conditions, marginally less effective than aluminium, but that is a small price to pay to avoid injuries such as those which are now disfiguring the game as much as the players. This is not an issue which can be dodged by the governing bodies, either. It is *their* responsibility. They cannot hide behind the excuse that players are entitled to freedom of choice, on economic grounds, and that manufacturers are too heavily committed to plastic and aluminium. The International Rugby Football Board lays down precise regulations about the manufacture of footballs, the dimensions of the posts and playing area. It has a duty to be just as precise about the manufacture of football boots.

There is not much doubt, either, that in consideration of the wider issue of foul play, the International Board will soon have to make a decision about the introduction of a penalty kick from a spot in front of the posts, just as they have in Association Football. The differential penalty, recently introduced, is manifestly a step in the right direction, because it reduces the number of opportunities to kick penalty goals, and therefore score three points, from technical infringements, but equally clearly, it does not go far enough.

Nothing would reduce foul play quicker than the knowledge that a penalty kick for such an offence would be automatically awarded to the opposition in front of the posts of the offending team. There is even a case for making the value of a penalty goal kicked from such an award six points, the same as a try and a conversion.

The objection to this has always been aesthetic, in that more often than not, the foul play being penalised would take place in parts of the field far removed from the penalty spot, and that therefore the whole assembly of referee, players and touch judges would have to troop back to the penalty spot so that the kick could be taken. But surely that would add to the drama of the occasion? It would bring home to everyone playing and watching the gravity of the offence and the severity of the punishment. It would be like a funeral procession and the player who had committed the offence would be in no doubt as to whose body was in the coffin. It is hard to think of anything which would have a more salutary effect on those contemplating an act of foul play.

Such a penalty would be wholly consistent with the principle of rewarding skill and initiative and penalising misdemeanours in proportion to their importance, which ought to be the basis of all the thinking behind the laws of the game. These laws are in the process of a major revision, so now is the time to shape them to the likely demands, not only of the game itself, but of the society within which that game will exist in the next twenty years.

For these changes to be made wisely, or even for them to be made at all, Rugby Union football needs leadership, and here the game is missing the natural assumption of authority which, in the first 75 years of the game, always came from England. No one has fought for the cause of his country with more determination than Dr Danie Craven of South Africa, but he is the first to acknowledge the debt the administration of the game owes to England. He also laments the abdication of the Rugby Union from its position as the game's supreme power. 'England had the wisdom and the confidence and the experience and the knowledge to suggest the right thing much more often than the rest of us,' he has said. 'The International Board worked much better then. Now, England seem to feel diffident about fulfilling their traditional function, perhaps because for so long their results in international matches have not been as good as they should be. Perhaps it is a question of personalities. Whatever it is, the gap England has left in the administration of the game has never been filled.'

Unhappily, the whole world is short of great men, not just English Rugby, but it is immensely sad to see the fears of Sir William Ramsay being realised as small men fight to preserve a playing and administrative structure which has been a positive disadvantage to English Rugby for at least thirty years. Sir George Mallaby and Dickie Jeeps have shown English Rugby where it must go. Both have pointed in substantially the same direction. There is no doubt that they are right. English Rugby must be reorganised. A regional championship must be introduced to challenge the club championship of France, the provincial structures of New Zealand and South Africa, the happy geographical accident of South Wales and the flourishing leagues in Scotland. Until England undertake such a re-organisation they will never achieve consistent international results and they will never take their proper place in the world of Rugby. One hundred and fifty years ago, the boys of Rugby School had a far surer grasp of the practicalities and the essentials.